Congress in Black and White

The symbolic importance of Barack Obama's election is without question. However, beyond symbolism, does the election of African-American politicians matter? Christian R. Grose argues that it does and presents a unified theory of representation. Electing African-American legislators yields more federal dollars and congressional attention directed toward African-American voters. However, race and affirmative action gerrymandering have no impact on public policy passed in Congress. Grose is the first to examine a natural experiment and exceptional moment in history in which black legislators – especially in the U.S. South – represented districts with a majority of white constituents. This is the first systematic examination of the effect of a legislator's race above and beyond the effect of constituency racial characteristics. Grose offers policy prescriptions, including the suggestion that voting rights advocates, the courts, and redistricters draw "black-decisive districts," electorally competitive districts that are likely to elect African Americans.

Christian R. Grose is assistant professor at the University of Southern California in Los Angeles. He has previously taught at Vanderbilt University and Lawrence University. He holds a PhD from the University of Rochester and a BA from Duke University. He has received grants from the National Science Foundation and the Everett Dirksen Congressional Center, and his work has appeared in numerous journals, including the *Journal of Politics*, the *British Journal of Political Science*, and *Legislative Studies Quarterly*.

To Robert and Jacqueline Grose

Congress in Black and White

Race and Representation in Washington and at Home

CHRISTIAN R. GROSE
University of Southern California

CAMBRIDGE
UNIVERSITY PRESS

CAMBRIDGE UNIVERSITY PRESS
Cambridge, New York, Melbourne, Madrid, Cape Town, Singapore,
São Paulo, Delhi, Dubai, Tokyo, Mexico City

Cambridge University Press
32 Avenue of the Americas, New York, NY 10013-2473, USA

www.cambridge.org
Information on this title: www.cambridge.org/9780521177016

First published 2011

Printed in the United States of America

A catalog record for this publication is available from the British Library.

Library of Congress Cataloging in Publication data
Grose, Christian R.
    Congress in black and white : race and representation in Washington
and at home / Christian R. Grose.
        p.   cm.
    Includes bibliographical references and index.
    ISBN 978-1-107-00351-4 (hardback)
    1. United States. Congress – Membership.   2. African American legislators.
    3. Gerrymandering – United States.   4. African Americans – Government
    policy.   5. Civil rights – Government policy – United States.   6. Representative
    government and representation – United States.   I. Title.
    JK1021.G76   2011
    328.730089'96073–dc22   2010035788

ISBN 978-1-107-00351-4 Hardback
ISBN 978-0-521-17701-6 Paperback

Contents

List of Figures and Tables		*page* viii
Acknowledgments		xi
1	African-American Legislators, African-American Districts, or Democrats?	1
	Summary of Book's Argument and Findings	8
	The Book's Roadmap	11
2	A Unified Theory of African-American Representation in Congress	14
	The Unified Theory of African-American Representation in Congress	17
	Three Competing Theories of Racial Representation in Congress	18
	Racial Trust between Black Voters and Black Legislators	21
	Congressional Decision Making, Political Parties, and Race	24
	Electoral Coalitions, Turnout, and Substantive Representation	29
	Black Faces, White Districts: The Supreme Court and Racial Redistricting	37
	White Legislators and Black-Influence Districts	48
	Why No One Has Examined Both a Legislator's Race and a District's Black Population	49
3	The "Hollow Hope" of Civil Rights Change in the U.S. House	54
	Perverse Effects, Beneficial Effects, or Minimal Effects? Does Racial Gerrymandering Affect Median Civil Rights Policy Outcomes in the U.S. House?	58
	What Are Black Interests on Roll Calls?	62

How Can We Determine Legislators' Preferences
  on Civil Rights?   64
Has the Civil Rights Policy Space in Congress Changed
  Over Time?   66
The Relative Unimportance of the South for Civil
  Rights Floor Outcomes in the House   68
Civil Rights Ideological Shifts in State Delegations
  Due to Racial Redistricting   71
Political Parties, Agenda Setting, and Civil Rights
  Voting Records in Congress   74
Counterfactual Analysis   76
Did the Creation of Black-Majority Districts in 1992
  Give the House to Republicans?   78
Summary: Racial Redistricting in 1992 and Aggregate
  Policy Outcomes in the U.S. House   81
What About at the District Level? Does Party or
  Race Matter More?   82
Implications for the Future of Majority-Minority Districts   84

4   Location, Location, Location: Delivering Constituency
     Service to African Americans   87
     Constituency Service as Substantive Representation   89
     The Importance of Race: Helping Constituents in the District 90
     Talking with Congressional Staff to Assess Constituency
       Service to African Americans   91
     Reaching Voters with Service: Race Trumps Geography
       and Party   96
     Randy Forbes: "Big Shoes to Fill"   97
     Earl Hilliard: "He Was Elected to Represent the People Here" 100
     Congressional Offices in Black Neighborhoods?   104

5   Constituency Service in the District: Connecting
     Black Legislators, Black Staff, and Black Voters   110
     African-American Staff and Substantive Congressional
       Representation   111
     White Staff and Substantive Representation via
       Constituency Service   115
     The Racial Backgrounds of Congressional District
       Staff Across the United States   119
     Which Members of Congress Disproportionately
       Hire African-American Staff?   122
     Commonality versus Difference: No Difference   127
     Conclusion: Race and the Quality of Constituency
       Service to Black Constituents   131

6   Bringing Home the Bacon: Delivering Federal
    "Pork" to African Americans   134
    Pork Is Substantive Representation   138
    Bringing Home the Bacon to Predominately Black
        Counties and Historically Black Colleges and Universities 139
    Black Legislators Deliver More Projects to African Americans   150
    The Effect of a Legislator's Race on Project Allocations   151
    The Effect of Party on Project Allocation to Black Constituents 153
    Racial Trust: The Interactive Effect of District Black
        Population and a Legislator's Race   155
    Pork Delivery, Electoral Coalitions, and Racial Representation 159
    Conclusion and Discussion   165
7   The Future of Racial Redistricting: Black-Decisive Districts   167
    Race, Legislative Representation, and the Importance
        of Elections   168
    The Need for Black-Decisive Districts: Policy Implications
        for the Future of Majority-Minority Districts
        and Representation   172
    Criteria for Drawing Districting Plans Maximizing
        Black-Decisive Districts   178
    Conclusion and Closing Thoughts   183

Appendix 1: Methods Used to Measure the Civil
Rights Issue Space   187
Appendix 2: Methods for Qualitative Research   193
Appendix 3: Data, Methods, and Models for Project
Allocations to African Americans   197
References   215
Index   231

Figures and Tables

Figures

2.1 Georgia's 1992 and 1996 congressional
district maps   *page* 40

2.2 North Carolina's twelfth district in 1992, 1998,
and 2000   41

3.1 Shifts in civil rights policy preferences in selected
state delegations   72

3.2 Increasing civil rights conservatism across all regions 73

3.3 What if no black-majority districts were drawn
in the South in 1992?   78

3.4 The small effect of black-majority districting on
the Republican takeover in 1994   80

5.1 Black Democrats, white Democrats, and white
Republicans: Hiring patterns of African-American
staff in congressional district offices   130

6.1 The number of projects allocated to predominantly
black counties: The interactive effect of a legislator's
race and district black population   156

6.2 The number of projects allocated to historically
black colleges and universities: The interactive effect
of a legislator's race and district black population   157

Tables

2.1 The Substantive Representation of African-American
Constituents   19

2.2 Selected List of Individual Federal Projects Requested
by Congressman Harold Ford, Jr. (D-TN), 109th
Congress (2005–06)   26

2.3 Congressional Parties and Legislative Behavior   27

2.4 Electoral Coalitions and Turnout Differentials   33

2.5 The Courts and Congressional Districts, 1993–2001   42

2.6 African-American House Members Representing
Districts that Changed Due to Court-Ordered Redistricting,
104th to 107th Congresses (1995–2002)   45

2.7 Legislator's Race or Legislator's Black District Population?
Selected Previous Analyses of Substantive Representation
in Congress   51

3.1 Hypothetical Legislature with Seven Legislators   60

3.2 Position of the Decisive Legislator (the Median Legislator)
on Civil Rights Roll-Call Votes in Congress, 91st to 108th
Congresses (1969–2004)   67

3.3 Position of the Decisive Legislator within the Majority
Party Caucus (the Democratic Median Legislator from
91st to 103rd Congresses and the Republican Median
Legislator from 104th to 107th Congresses)   75

3.4 The Effect of Both Race and Party on Individual Civil
Rights Voting Records   83

4.1 Districts/Legislators Visited   94

4.2 Congressional District Office Locations in Virginia's
Fourth District: Sisisky versus Forbes   99

4.3 District Office Locations and Predominant Racial
Composition of Neighborhood of Office   106

5.1 Party, Race, and the Hiring of Black Staff in District Offices   123

5.2 Comparing the Hiring of Black Staff in District Offices
to the District's Black Population   124

5.3 Commonality versus Difference: No Difference?   129

6.1 John Spratt News Release   142

6.2 Bringing Home the Bacon: Black Democrats, White
Democrats, and White Republicans and Projects
Allocated to Heavily Black Counties   152

6.3 Bringing Home the Bacon to Colleges: Black Democrats,
White Democrats, and White Republicans and Projects
Allocated to Historically Black Colleges and Universities   152

6.4 Shifts in Roll-Call Voting Among African-American
     House Democrats   161
7.1 Black Electoral Success in General Elections for the
     U.S. House, Incumbents in 2000, 2004, and 2008   176
7.2 Black Electoral Success in General Elections for the
     U.S. House, Challengers Running Against Nonblack
     Incumbents and Open Seats in 2000, 2004, and 2008   177
7.3 Summary of Findings   184

Acknowledgments

This book is about the role of race in an American political institution. Scholars of American political institutions often ignore race, while scholars of race and ethnicity infrequently tread into the realm of political institutions. While these scholarly streams of research may not always cross, many of those working within both traditions have been instrumental to this book.

Many read this manuscript or earlier portions of it, gave feedback informally or formally as conference discussants, suggested avenues for new inquiry as I revised, provided support and encouragement as I wrote and finished the manuscript, or provided assistance in some other way. I thank Ted Anagnoson, Stephen Ansolabehere, David Becker, Ken Bickers, Glen Browder, John Clark, Kevin Clarke, Christopher Edley, Jeremiah Garretson, Stephen Gent, Suzanne Globetti, Lani Guinier, Ana Henderson, Bill Hixon, Jason Husser, Cindy Kam, Poonam Kumar, Frances Lee, David Lublin, Michaela Mattes, Seth McKee, Michael Minta, Larry Rothenberg, Mitch Sanders, Curt Signorino, Valeria Sinclair-Chapman, Dena Skran, Katherine Tate, Neal Tate, Shawn Treier, Jennifer Vagle, Kenny Whitby, and Sonya Winton. I would also like to thank those who provided feedback at talks that I gave at the University of Wisconsin Law School and the Carl Albert Center at the University of Oklahoma, and at conferences sponsored by the University of California, Berkeley, and the University of Rochester.

There are a few people that deserve more specific mention for their help and assistance. From idea to manuscript, and then to revisions and completion, I have them to thank in particular. Mentors and colleagues I first met in graduate school provided me with guidance, criticism, support, and advice beyond what is normally expected. Harold Stanley introduced me to the fields of voting rights and southern politics. He also provided many incisive comments on this book, helping me craft it into a more precise piece of social science research. Dick Niemi also deserves substantial credit for improvements to this book. His suggestions helped tighten up the manuscript, making it more readable and accessible. Both Harold and Dick have assisted me in many ways on this book and otherwise, helping shape my judgment professionally and personally. Dick Fenno also read earlier versions of the book, assisting particularly in helping me conceptualize the research design for Chapters 4 and 5. While in graduate school, I always enjoyed my conversations with Dick about his research travels, and these conversations have contributed greatly to this book.

In addition, three colleagues and friends I met at Rochester provided useful feedback and comments and provided important encouragement as I worked on the book. Gail McElroy provided cutting criticisms and suggestions from a comparativist's perspective, and the book is much stronger as a result of my discussions with her. Similarly, Stephen Gent, an international relations scholar, gave suggestions that helped tighten up the theoretical foundations of the book and helped me determine how to write the book in a way that would be interesting to a wider audience. Antoine Yoshinaka, a frequent co-author of mine, read most chapters of this book in multiple draft stages. His insights and interests in American politics, legislatures, and representation have shaped this work and my research as a whole.

I thank the political science departments where I have been employed for providing research time and resources for the completion of this book: Lawrence University, Vanderbilt University, and the University of Southern California. The book began in earnest at Vanderbilt, and I particularly thank my American politics colleagues that I met while there. John Geer and David Lewis encouraged me to aim high when writing and revising this book manuscript, and I benefited from their advice and guidance. Stefanie Lindquist has been a proponent of my work on voting rights since I met her at a conference at the University of Georgia, and she always encouraged me in this research area. Marc Hetherington read portions of the manuscript, and his advice to take the time to write the book well was a good one. Marc was also a mentor for other career goals as I worked on this manuscript, and I am lucky to have been the recipient of his sage advice. Pam Corley deserves extensive thanks for providing feedback on this work, for offering suggestions on how to get the book accepted for publication, and for being a good friend as we learned the

ropes of being junior faculty together. Carol Swain was always a proponent of this book, and I thank her for reading the manuscript extensively
and giving me feedback. As she is the author of the seminal work in this
area of research, I was lucky to have her as a colleague. A presentation she
asked me to give to her law school class was particularly useful toward
reshaping some of the arguments in the book. Bruce Oppenheimer is perhaps as familiar with this book as I am, having read a much older version
of it and subsequent drafts. Bruce was a great colleague while I wrote
this book, always encouraging me to do the best that I could with the
material. Not only did Bruce read this book and provide feedback, but
he read every working paper I ever asked him to – and he did so quickly.
His mentorship combined with his keen expertise in legislative studies
strengthened this book and my professional career.

My colleagues at the University of Southern California deserve thanks
for their efforts as I worked on the final revisions to the book. A talk I
gave to the department yielded incisive and difficult questions that caused
me to better shape the book's argument. In particular, comments raised
by my colleagues at USC led me to better specify the policy prescriptions
that I offer in Chapter 7. Especially those scholars of race and politics,
American politics, and political institutions at USC (Jeb Barnes, Tony
Bertelli, Ann Crigler, Howard Gillman, Ange-Marie Hancock, Jane Junn,
Mat McCubbins, Ricardo Ramirez, Jeff Sellers, Nick Weller, Janelle
Wong, and others) have been extremely welcoming and supportive of
this book or welcoming to me in general. Tony Bertelli, in particular, both
before my arrival at USC and once I arrived, encouraged me to transition
this project from draft manuscript to book. Also in Los Angeles, I want to
thank the hotel lounge at Casa del Mar in Santa Monica for allowing me
to sit for hours drinking coffee while making the final revisions.

The editors and staff at Cambridge University Press deserve thanks. It
has been wonderful – and downright easy – to work with Lew Bateman
and Anne Lovering Rounds. The copyediting staff provided by Cambridge
has done an excellent job. I am lucky to work with such a capable and
professional staff at Cambridge.

Maurice Mangum, Chris Martin, Keesha Middlemass, and Noushin
Jahanian all assisted me in some way with the interviews conducted for
the book. Maurice and Chris, in particular, participated in three different interview visits at congressional district offices during a "research
road trip" and the qualitative data gathered via these interviews was
strengthened as a result (and contributed to some of the evidence presented in Chapter 5). Keesha and Noushin were instrumental in helping

me conduct a few exploratory interviews with congressional staff in Washington that did not make it into this book, but that were useful for structuring the district interviews that followed. I am of course grateful to the members of Congress and their staff who opened their district offices to me. I would also like to thank the National Science Foundation for providing funds for the travel involved in conducting some of the interviews used in this book (Grant 0001808).

My most profuse thanks go to my wife, Sarah Ramage. As the smartest person I know, Sarah's contributions to this book are substantial (editor, colleague, critic, cheerleader), and her contributions to me personally are literally innumerable. Nothing delighted me more than when she read a draft chapter of this book and exclaimed "Unlike other things you've written, this is actually interesting!" I took this comment as a compliment and a meta-critique of the often opaque style of political science writing. Especially during my year on research leave in which I completed the revisions to the book manuscript, Sarah deserves thanks. Even though I did not have to teach or go into the office, she was always supportive of the days in which the creativity and productivity flowed late into the night or on those days in which I would wake up early in the morning to get a head start on writing. In general, her support throughout the book publication process has been amazing. I cannot bear to think what my years would have been like had I not met her, nor can I even begin to detail the love and affection I have for her. I thank her for simply being there.

Finally, I thank my family: my parents, Robert and Jacqueline Grose, and my brother, Aaron. I very much appreciate my family's constant encouragement as I have written this book and as I have pursued a career as a professor. Many phone calls home were crucial to keeping me grounded as I wrote and completed this book. I enjoyed talking about the book and the writing process with them, and I cannot thank them enough for everything they have done for me in my life. I hope they are as proud of me as I am grateful to them.

I

African-American Legislators, African-American Districts, or Democrats?

In November 2008, then-Senator Barack Obama surprised the nation and the world by becoming the first African-American president of the United States. In a country where nearly all major elected officials are white, Obama had pulled off what seemed impossible to many. Not only had no African American ever won the presidency, in a country whose voting majority is white, but very few African Americans had ever been elected to *any* federal office in constituencies where black voters did not constitute a majority. Prior to the 2008 elections, for instance, only three African Americans had ever been elected to the U.S. Senate since Reconstruction (one of whom was Obama, representing Illinois from 2004 to 2008). Dianne Pinderhughes (2009, 4), reflecting on Obama's historic electoral triumph, noted that a "number of the most high achieving, successful African Americans, whether in academic, literary or political life thought it improbable that there would ever be a president of African American ancestry."

In the U.S. House of Representatives, cracks in the racial glass ceiling had become apparent a decade before Obama won the presidency. Until the mid-1990s, nearly all African Americans elected to the U.S. House won election from districts without white majorities. However, beginning in 1996, a few black legislators – in southern states that had only decades earlier employed Jim Crow laws to disfranchise African Americans – won election to Congress in districts in which whites were a majority. It was on the shoulders of these lesser-known black members of Congress that Obama stood as he won the White House with a coalition of white, African-American, Latino, and Asian-American voters. This book is about these members of Congress and their legislative colleagues and what they mean for race, representation, and the history of the struggle for full voting rights in America.

The symbolic importance of Obama's election to the highest office in the United States is without question. However, beyond the symbolic importance of electing an African American to the presidency, does race matter? Does it matter that Obama is an African American for the substantive and policy needs of African-American voters? Does the election of African-American politicians result in better outcomes for black Americans? In this book, I argue that race matters in the U.S. Congress, but not always in ways that might be anticipated. Electing black members of Congress is important for substantive outcomes that enhance the lives of African-American constituents, but only in certain congressional activities in which legislators have significant power and control.

In the case of Obama, we will have to wait until he completes his presidency to determine whether he has made a greater substantive impact on the lives of African Americans than had his predecessors. However, we can look to late 20th-century America to get a sense of whether having black elected officials in office matters for substantive outcomes that affect African Americans. Contrary to the great expectations placed by some on Obama in 2008 to deliver for the African-American community (and the American community in general), some have raised doubts that the election of African-American officials to public office necessarily results in meaningful, substantive change that benefits African Americans. As Valeria Sinclair-Chapman and Melanye Price (2008) have noted, "Having a member of one's own group command the enormous power of the presidency is, for some, the ultimate manifestation of full integration – though [by itself it] does not satisfy requirements for accountability or responsiveness between voters and their representatives."

This quote echoes a first generation of scholars who have examined racial representation in the United States. Carol Swain (1995), arguably the most prominent scholar in the field of race and representation, contends that African-American elected officials are no better than white elected officials at delivering policy outcomes that are beneficial to African-American constituents. Legal critics, historians, political scientists, and the U.S. Supreme Court have also questioned the efficacy of drawing black-majority districts, which has often resulted in the election of African Americans to Congress.[1] Even though varied theoretically and

---

[1] For instance, see the following works, which all argue that black-majority congressional districts (which typically elect black legislators) resulted in "worse" roll-call vote outcomes

empirically, these political and legal observers generally find that the creation of black-majority districts actually hurts black interests by packing black voters into a small number of districts, leaving surrounding districts with fewer black constituents. Thus, many of these scholars claim that electing Democrats, regardless of race, will lead to better representation for African Americans. A number of cases decided by the U.S. Supreme Court have concurred with these scholars, arguing that maximizing black-majority districts is a detriment to the best aggregate substantive representation of black interests in the legislature. *Substantive representation* is defined as legislative decisions, such as roll-call votes, that serve the interest of a subset of constituents, in this case black constituents. *Descriptive representation* is defined as the election of black legislators to office.[2] Summarizing much of the first-generation conventional wisdom on the subject, Marvin Overby and Kenneth Cosgrove note that "the bad news is that there does, indeed, seem to be a significant trade-off between descriptive representation and substantive representation" (1996, 549; see also Cameron, Epstein, and O'Halloran 1996; Lublin 1997).

Most scholars point to the canonical example of the twelfth congressional district of North Carolina as an example of this dilutive effect of racial redistricting and how descriptive representation does not necessarily result in substantive representation in the U.S. Congress (e.g., Lublin 1997). The twelfth district of North Carolina was originally drawn in 1992, as required by the mandate of the Voting Rights Act extensions passed by Congress in 1982 (and as interpreted by the U.S. Department of Justice). The twelfth district, long and narrow in shape, stretched from Durham to Charlotte for about 200 miles. Its width, in parts, was no wider than a few inches. As state legislator Mickey Michaux (D-NC) noted, "[i]f you drove down the interstate with both car doors open, you'd kill most of the people in the district" (Biskupic 1993). This

---

in the aggregate for African Americans: Guinier (1994); Lublin and Voss (2003); Lublin (1997); Overby and Cosgrove (1996); Swain (1995); Tate (2003); Whitby (1997). However, see Shotts (2002, 2003a) and Kousser (1999, 275). See also Canon (1999), Haynie (2001), and Tate (2003) for pro-descriptive representation arguments unrelated to roll calls. Hutchings, McClerking, and Charles (2004), examining only white members of Congress, also suggest white legislators are able to substantively represent African Americans in the North, but less so in the South. Others have argued that certain electoral and institutional settings can yield differences in descriptive representation or substantive outcomes that benefit minorities (Austin 2002; Casellas 2009a; Meier et al. 2005; Reckhow 2009).

[2] See Hanna Pitkin (1967) for an extensive theoretical discussion of descriptive and substantive representation.

district elected Mel Watt, one of North Carolina's first black members of Congress since Reconstruction. It also, arguably, resulted in the election of white Republican legislators in the surrounding districts that had been "diluted" by removing most African-American voters and placing these voters in the twelfth district. Observers suggested that a large number of white Democratic members of Congress in North Carolina would have been better for black voters than the dual election of black Democratic legislators and white Republican legislators in surrounding districts. As I will discuss, the Supreme Court later ruled the 1992 North Carolina districting plan unconstitutional. Based on criticism from the Court and scholars, this redistricting map became the symbol of the dilutive effect of racial redistricting that resulted in the election of African-American members of Congress.

Yet those who work in politics do not necessarily agree with the contention that the election of black members of Congress via black-majority districts is harmful to black substantive interests. A disconnect between scholars of African-American representation and a conversation I had with someone who works for a congressman demonstrates this point. Congressional staffers, especially those from offices of black legislators, did not agree with and were surprised to hear of scholarly findings claiming white Democrats are better representatives of black voters in the aggregate. The following is an exchange that occurred during an interview I conducted with a black staff member working in a district office of Mel Watt:[3]

QUESTION: Do you think black members of Congress are better representatives than white members in terms of the concerns and interests of their black constituents?

ANSWER FROM STAFFER: [looking at me in quizzical disbelief] Yes, of course.... Isn't it obvious? Mel understands the [black] community in ways that someone white can't. He's from here, he lives here. Now we reach all voters – black, white, whoever – but what we do in this office is going to be different than what's done in ... [neighboring white representative's office]....Why would you even ask?

Q: Well, ... [some] academics who have written on the topic think that white and black Democrats, at least, are similar in terms of their voting records and responding to their black constituents. So having black-majority districts might not be the best way ...

A: (cutting in, laughing): What? Are they crazy? Do you think they're right?

---

[3] Interview with Tawana Wilson-Allen in Charlotte, NC, on May 9, 2002.

Q: That's what I'm here to find out and why I'm asking you these questions. But I really want to know what you think.

A: Well, I *really* want to read this book when you're done with it. And you can write down that I said they're wrong.

What do we make of her incredulous dismissal of some scholars' previous findings? Are the scholars missing something or is the staffer missing something? One reason for this disagreement is that scholars and policy makers are conceiving of a broad concept (black representation) in a relatively narrow fashion. Minority representation scholars generally measure substantive representation as roll-call voting and Washington-based activities (such as bill sponsorship, co-sponsorship, or the accumulation of leadership and committee positions) but do not address the fact that members of Congress engage in multiple activities in their districts.[4] This same staffer, at another point, when detailing for me a laundry list of how her boss works for black constituents, only rarely mentioned specific votes on a particular bill. Instead, she detailed how Watt has worked to serve black constituents through service in the district beyond roll-call voting. Yet, surprisingly, few minority representation scholars have looked at legislative behavior beyond roll calls. Even fewer have looked at behavior outside of Washington where each legislator can be pivotal. Further, few have analyzed the rational choices legislators make by connecting the electoral incentives facing legislators and their resultant decisions in both roll-call voting and activities beyond the vote.

Whereas many observers have claimed that black-majority districts and the subsequent election of black legislators in these districts has hurt African-American interests, a second generation of scholars have instead

---

[4] Canon (1999) and Tate (2003) are exceptions as they explore more than behavior in the legislative chamber. Canon, though, is primarily concerned with variation in representation within the subset of black legislators, whereas Tate focuses on symbolic representation. Sinclair-Chapman (2002), Haynie (2001), and Platt (2008a) have also looked at bill introductions and/or committee memberships, though they have not focused on district-oriented activities. Orey et al. (2007) also examines bill introductions and success at bill passage of these introduced bills. Gamble (2007) and Minta (2009, 2011) have examined committee participation by black and nonblack members of Congress, and Fraga et al. (2007) have examined priorities of minority legislators. Mansbridge (1999) and Williams (1998) have also theorized that representation is more than roll-call voting but have not tested their normative claims empirically. Others have examined the role of race, ethnicity, and/or descriptive representation in the realm of the courts (Bonneau and Rice 2009; Jensen and Martinek 2009; Killian 2008; Scherer and Curry 2010), the bureaucracy (Goode and Baldwin 2005; Theobald and Haider-Markel 2009), and the media or Internet (Cooper and Johnson 2009; Gershon 2008; Grose 2005; Wilson 2009; Zilber and Niven 2000).

argued that African-American legislators are critically important in providing substantive representation to African Americans. Katherine Tate
(2003) has made this argument, noting that black legislators provide crucial symbolic benefits for their constituents; David Canon (1999) has also
suggested that a legislator's race is important. Canon has demonstrated
that African-American legislators are more likely to propose legislation,
make statements, and prepare press releases relating to racial issues.
Further, Kenny Whitby (1997) argues that African-American legislators
share a "consciousness" with black constituents, thus providing better
public policy or substantive representation. Kerry Haynie (2001) has
argued that black state legislators enhance African-American interests via
bill sponsorship and other legislative activities (also see Orey et al. 2007;
Preuhs 2006; Rocca and Sanchez 2008; and Sinclair-Chapman 2002).

     Whereas these scholars point to the importance of African-American
legislators and descriptive representation, no one has disentangled the
effect of the race of the legislator and the African-American population of
the district in studies of race and representation in the U.S. Congress. These
scholars claiming to find that race affects legislative behavior do not consider that almost all black representatives they examine in their research
have historically hailed from black-majority districts. Kenny Whitby and
George Krause (2001, 561) have called this problem a "dilemma [that]
hampers all other research on this topic." No scholar has analyzed the
separate effect of a legislator's race from the racial population of the congressional district that elects the legislator with data that can allow for
the disentanglement of these two explanations. These scholars may claim
to find effects for a legislator's race on roll-call votes and other activities,
but this may simply be due to the demographics of the electorate voting
for these black representatives. I am able to provide a more sophisticated
analysis in this book because of the increased racial diversity of the districts that have sent African Americans to the U.S. Congress at the end of
the 20th century, and because of a natural experiment due to mid-1990s,
court-ordered redistricting.

     As mentioned previously, most scholars and practitioners who claim
that the race of the legislator has no impact do not consider activities
beyond roll-call voting. By only looking at representatives' roll-call voting,
researchers have neglected other important substantive avenues of institutional behavior in Congress and behavior that occurs in the district.
Richard Fenno (1978) first established the importance of congressional
behavior in the district, whereas others such as Bruce Cain, John Ferejohn,

and Morris Fiorina (1987) and Richard Hall (1996) have demonstrated the importance of other participation in Congress beyond roll-call voting. Morris Fiorina (1989, 39) states that members of Congress, for the most part, have three primary activities: lawmaking, pork barrelling, and casework. Lawmaking is self-explanatory, though pork barrelling and casework are worth defining. Pork barrelling is when a legislator secures federal projects or grants for constituents (examples could include grants for a new transportation project, a community center, a public park, or a small business). Casework is defined as assisting constituents with any type of service request unrelated to legislation, and these requests are usually dealt with in a member's district office. Common requests include assistance with immigration applications for family members, help in securing veterans or social security benefits, and so on. No scholars of minority representation have ever attempted to look at the second of these activities, and only a few have attempted to measure its impact on the third (Canon 1999; Swain 1995). This book examines both. Further, the scholars that have examined non-roll-call legislative actions have focused on symbolic legislative behavior (e.g., Fenno 2003; Tate 2003) or on substantive decisions in which an individual legislator is not pivotal or is unlikely to be effective. The policy activities I examine result in tangible goods and services received by African-American constituents. They are not symbolic actions but decisions with substantive impact. Symbolic activities are also important, but goods and services delivered to constituents have the potential to result in the substantive betterment of African Americans' lives. A key gap in our understanding of race and representation is whether an individual legislator can be pivotal in delivering substantive outcomes to African-American constituents.

What factors cause legislators to represent the substantive needs of black constituents in their districts as measured by roll-call voting as well as activities beyond the vote? Are legislators who are African American or who hail from districts with a large black population more likely to reach out to black constituents than other legislators? Does race matter for substantive outcomes – and not just substantive behavior – in legislatures? This book will answer these questions, attempting to shed light on this puzzle in the study of minority representation.

Specifically, I determine the effect of the following three factors on the substantive representation of black constituents: (1) electing black representatives; (2) drawing black-majority districts; and (3) electing Democratic representatives. Few scholars have disentangled the separate effects of these factors, and I do so here. I also offer a fourth factor – racial trust – that explains substantive representation. Moreover, I will answer these questions by examining different modes of substantive representation in Congress: roll-call voting, federal "pork" project allocation, and constituency service.

In addition to addressing these questions, this book is at its core about, in Gunnar Myrdal's words, the "American dilemma" of race. The book focuses on congressional districts in the U.S. South, though is also supplemented with analyses of congressional districts in the entire country. The South is the focus because it is the region in which race has been one of the most politically charged issues throughout this nation's history. As V.O. Key (1949) famously stated, "In its grand outlines, the politics of the South revolves around the position of the Negro." The South is also the region in which much of the racial redistricting described previously has occurred. Somewhat ironically given the region's tortured history with race, it is the one area of the country that has produced the largest number of black members of Congress who have won election from white-majority districts. Whereas my argument in the book is not limited to the U.S. South, it speaks to enduring debates in political science, history, and the law over the role of race in politics in this region and in the entire country.[5]

Summary of Book's Argument and Findings

The primary argument of my book is consistent with the comments offered by Mel Watt's staffer: descriptive representation yields substantive representation in Congress, when measured as activities beyond roll-call voting. To increase the substantive representation of black interests as measured by the delivery of goods and services to black constituents, the best strategy is to elect African-American legislators. Legislators like Watt have the electoral incentives to deliver targeted distributive policy benefits to African-American constituents. To increase the substantive representation of black interests as measured by roll-call voting, however, the best strategy is to elect Democratic legislators, even though the race of the legislator and the black population of the district are also important factors.

---

[5] From an empirical standpoint as well, my focus on the South suggests that my conclusions presented at the end of the book may be limited primarily to the debates over racial redistricting in that region.

However, even when the Democrats controlled the U.S. House before the 1994 elections, civil rights policy outcomes on the floor were not substantially different from other years (1995–2006) when the Republicans held the majority. Few members of Congress of any party or race are pivotal on roll-call outcomes, and oftentimes African-American legislators are less effective at passing legislation (Haynie 2001) because they are shut out of the legislative process due to racial bias (Guinier 1994; Hawkesworth 2003). The institution of the U.S. House – a legislative chamber with mostly white legislators elected from white-majority districts – favors the status quo. The decision of one legislator to influence the allocation of millions of dollars of federal funding to African-American constituents is usually more meaningful than a non-pivotal roll-call vote on the floor of the U.S. House, no matter which party is in the majority.

In addition, a key finding of this book is that the election of black legislators from politically competitive districts with black populations just under 50 percent results in the best district for the substantive representation of black interests. However, it is also important to note that white legislators from competitive districts, while less focused on the delivery of projects and services to black constituents, attempt to reach black constituents in districts with large black populations under certain conditions. Finally, again in terms of the delivery of projects and services to black constituents, there is surprisingly little difference between white Democrats and Republicans. *In sum, if we want to enhance substantive representation for black constituents, and conceive of it as roll-call voting, then electing black legislators is not very important. However, if we want to enhance service and project delivery to black constituents, then descriptive representation in Congress is crucial.*

These results speak to decisions by the U.S. Supreme Court, lower courts, and public policy debates in Congress regarding the utility of racial redistricting. In the 1990s and 2000s, the U.S. Supreme Court generally ruled against drawing black-majority districts, though has on occasion permitted race to be considered as a factor (but not the predominant factor) in the drawing of legislative districts. The U.S. Congress, both in 2006 and much earlier, passed voting rights legislation at odds with the Court's more limited interpretation of the extent that race can be allowed in drawing districting plans. Given evidence that I offer in this book regarding the importance of race in the legislative representation of African Americans, I also offer some policy guidelines that can be used by the courts and policy makers as they continue to grapple with these fundamental legal and policy questions of race in the United States.[6]

The courts and Congress have tended to debate the utility of black-majority versus black-influence districts. Instead, I propose a new category of districts be considered that I call *black-decisive districts*. These are districts that are likely to elect black legislators. In some instances, these will be districts without a black majority, whereas in other instances these districts may require a majority-black district. The determination of the likelihood of electing a black legislator is achieved by considering the local conditions and past willingness of white voters to cast ballots for black candidates. Specifically, I present evidence and argue that black-influence districts, which have generally been defined as districts ranging from 25 to 49 percent black, should *only* be encouraged when there is a strong likelihood of electing black legislators. If it is unlikely that a black legislator will win in a black-minority district, then black-majority districts of just over 50 percent should be drawn to maximize black substantive representation. In the conclusion of this book, I argue that black-decisive districts should be pursued by those advocating for stronger voting rights via congressional redistricting. These legal questions are likely to persist for decades as states must redraw their congressional districts every ten years. I argue that with careful redistricting, substantive and descriptive representation are not mutually exclusive goals.

Regarding the scholarly debate related to race and representation, these results suggest that black legislators are more likely than other legislators to make substantive decisions affecting African-American constituents, but not that black legislators are somehow different in character or nature than their white colleagues. Some, such as Mary Hawkesworth (2003), essentially argue that black legislators are distinct from their colleagues due to their personal experiences. In particular, she argues that African-American (and female) legislators are not driven by the same rational, general election vote-maximizing decisions of their white (and male) colleagues. I contend that this logic is highly problematic and not empirically demonstrated. Black legislators – like their white colleagues – are rational. If black legislators are rational actors – interested in getting reelected – then these personal experiences are much less likely to shape

---

[6] Whether my policy prescriptions offered in the book are legally or politically viable is a separate question. I leave this to legal and political experts to determine whether my policy prescriptions are able to be implemented. As Canon (2008, 4) has stated, even as these issues are in constant flux in the realms of the courts and Congress, they "are still extremely important for both legal and policy debates" that "are far from settled."

substantive and policy outcomes than are electoral goals. I argue that African-American legislators make different decisions from their nonblack House colleagues because most black legislators face different electoral concerns. Black legislators almost always rely on a larger percentage of black voter support to garner reelection – even in white-majority districts – than do white legislators. As I describe in greater detail in the next chapter, electoral constraints predict differences in non-roll-call vote decision making. However, black and nonblack legislators alike have an incentive to take issue positions and vote in a way that appeals to a majority of the voters in their congressional districts. Thus, any legislator representing a conservative, white-majority district has an incentive to take more moderate positions than a legislator representing a more liberal, black-majority district. The district's preferences – and not the race of the legislator – are the primary determinants of reelection-driven roll-call decisions. In conclusion, black and nonblack legislators are all rational actors seeking reelection and adjusting their behavior in ways to maximize their likelihoods of winning. However, the maximal strategy to rationally seek reelection differs between black and white legislators due to the composition of black legislators' and white legislators' primary and reelection constituencies. The result of this difference is that black legislators are better deliverers of substantive goods and services to black constituents.

The Book's Roadmap

These conclusions were reached based on an extensive analysis of legislators' representational decisions between 1994 and 2002. Throughout the book, I draw primarily on (1) interviews I conducted while visiting seventeen congressional districts in the U.S. South during the 106th Congress (1999–2000) and the 107th Congress (2001–02); and (2) quantitative analyses primarily from the 104th to 106th Congresses (1995–2000) of legislators' decisions in voting and beyond roll-call voting. In Chapter 2, I outline a unified theory of black representation in greater detail and note the importance of studying black legislators representing white districts, a phenomenon that occurred almost exclusively in the late 1990s. I detail why this time period (1995–2000) provides a critical window to those interested in the effect of race in Congress – and why this time period is superior to other periods studied by most scholars. By leveraging the variation in these Congresses with black legislators hailing from districts without a black majority, we can learn about differences in representation of both black and nonblack members of Congress and those legislators hailing from districts with varied black population levels.

In Chapter 3, I make the bold and controversial argument that civil rights roll-call vote outcomes in the U.S. House have changed minimally from 1969 to 2004. I show that the position of the vote-deciding, decisive 218th House member has not changed over this entire time period, though the decisive member of the majority party has. I also show that racial redistricting has a minimal effect on partisan control of the U.S. House and on the location of the majority party median. In sum, the drawing of black-majority districts and the election of black legislators has little positive or negative impact on policy outcomes on the floor of the House. I argue that studying racial representation at the level of roll-call votes in the U.S. Congress is not particularly important for assessing voting rights law given these aggregate findings. Further, I examine the effect of descriptive representation (the presence of a black legislator), the black population of a district, and two other factors (party and racial trust) on the voting records of legislators. At the level of the individual legislator, districts with large populations of black voters and districts represented by black legislators lead to more pro-civil rights voting records. However, as others have stressed, the effect of a legislator's party is by far the most important on roll-call voting. Thus, to best understand the importance of racial representation in Congress, we need to look beyond simply roll-call voting, which can be explained mostly by the effect of a representative's political party.

I turn my attention to the analysis of these factors (the race of the legislator, the black population of the district, party, and racial trust) on the delivery of targeted goods to black constituents in Chapter 4. Here, based primarily on qualitative research conducted with staff in eight states and seventeen congressional districts, I find that black legislators generally are the most responsive to black constituents in terms of constituency service. This conclusion is based on analyzing the location of district offices in predominately African-American or racially diverse neighborhoods and the relationship between this decision and reaching black constituents.

I continue the analysis of constituency service in Chapter 5 and argue that black legislators are more likely to empower their black constituents by over-hiring African-American staffers in their offices in congressional districts at levels in higher proportion than their districts' black populations. Further, I argue that black staff hired by members of Congress are more likely to have strong connections with the district's black community than do white staff. I analyze the hiring of black staffers that are involved in and are knowledgeable about the black community in their districts. Like Chapter 4, I conclude that the race of the legislator is of critical importance in providing service to African Americans. Also, though, I find that both white Democrats and white Republicans from black-influence districts make attempts to reach black voters with constituency service, but not to the same extent as black legislators from black-influence districts. Chapter 5 was written with Maurice Mangum and Chris Martin, who joined me in conducting some of the interviews in this chapter.

In Chapter 6, I focus on the delivery of federal projects to black constituents by members of Congress. Often derided as "pork" projects, distributive public policies can have a positive impact on the lives of those constituents lucky enough to receive the "pork" projects. Congressional scholars have noted the importance of distributive politics and the delivery of goods to constituents for some time, but scholars of minority representation have not looked at this topic. In this chapter, I look at which legislators are more likely to allocate federal projects to black constituents and to historically black colleges and universities (HBCUs). I find that black legislators, controlling for other factors, always give more projects to black constituents than do legislators of other racial backgrounds. Also, as we might expect, white legislators give more projects to black constituents when the black populations of their districts are larger. Interestingly, though, black legislators give more projects to black constituents when they represent black-influence districts with no black-majority population.

Finally, in Chapter 7, I offer conclusions and implications. I argue that electoral institutions matter in shaping policy outcomes. I consider how my unified theory of black representation and its empirical support illuminates the policy debate on the subject in the federal courts and in Congress. I also discuss the ability for black representatives to win in districts without a black majority and also consider the "best" districting arrangement for enhancing black interests in Congress, given the findings presented here. These conclusions are relevant to the scholarly debate regarding race in political representation. They also have clear policy implications regarding the enforcement of the Voting Rights Act and racial redistricting policies interpreted by the federal courts. I argue that the Supreme Court and states redrawing district lines should maximize *black-decisive districts*, districts that have a high likelihood of electing a black legislator but that are just at or near a black-majority district population.

A Unified Theory of African-American Representation in Congress

In 1992, Sanford Bishop (D-GA) made history. He became the first African-American congressman to represent a South Georgia congressional district. Georgia had sent African Americans to Congress before, but these elections occurred in districts in the Atlanta area. Bishop had achieved a more difficult victory: winning office in a rural district that is demographically more like Alabama than Atlanta. His 1992 election was a result of the drawing of a congressional district that was black-majority.

In 1996 and more than a decade before Barack Obama was elected president, Sanford Bishop (D-GA) made history yet again. He became the first African-American legislator elected to the U.S. Congress in Georgia in a predominately rural district in which whites were a majority. A coalition of white and African-American voters reelected Bishop to the U.S. House in a South Georgia district that includes former President Jimmy Carter's home town of Plains. In the same year, African-American Democrat Cynthia McKinney (D-GA) also garnered reelection in a white-majority district centered in suburban Atlanta. In 1995, the Supreme Court had ruled in *Miller v. Johnson* that Bishop's and McKinney's districts were unconstitutional racial gerrymanders, causing them to run in newly created white-majority districts. The same pattern was evident across a number of states in the U.S. South, as black legislators forced to run in court-ordered white-majority districts surprisingly won reelection by building a biracial coalition of white and black voters.

Following the 2000 election and much court litigation leading to a reduction in the number of black-majority congressional districts, 37 of the 435 legislators elected to serve in the U.S. House were African

American. Of these, 13 black legislators won election in districts without a black majority. Five black legislators were elected from districts with a non-Hispanic white majority. This is in stark contrast to historical patterns of African-American electoral success in the U.S. House. As David Canon (1999, 10) reports, between 1966 and 1996, 0.52 percent of all House elections held in white-majority districts led to the election of a black representative (only 35 out of 6667 elections). Before the late 1990s, white-majority districts had not tended to elect black representatives.

While these African-American legislators were breaking electoral barriers and gaining reelection in white-majority districts, a debate among scholars continued to rage regarding the effect of race on congressional representation. Some scholars have vociferously argued that the presence of African-American legislators in Congress had a positive impact on policy outcomes that favored African Americans, whereas others argued that the race of the legislator was unimportant.

Curiously, while this debate among scholars raged, these cases of African-American legislators from white-majority districts were not systematically studied. Instead, commentators focused on the beginning of the 1990s or earlier, during which nearly all black legislators were elected from black-majority districts. Even the most recent research published in the 2000s has tended to focus only on these early 1990s districts from the 103rd (1993–94) and 104th Congresses (1995–96). I argue that we can only assess the importance of a legislator's race and a legislator's constituency when we examine these new instances of black legislators hailing from white-majority districts and compare them to other black and white legislators from other types of districts.

The history-making elections of African-American legislators resulting from the 1992 redistricting have been noted by many. Perhaps more notably, though, is the fact that Bishop and a number of other black legislators in the U.S. South won reelection a few years later in districts that were majority-white or majority-nonblack. Most commentators have treated these elections as aberrations, as most black legislators have previously been successful in garnering election to the U.S. House through the support of black voters in black-majority districts. Aberrations or not, these historic elections of African Americans in white-majority districts have not been systematically examined. Perhaps these early trailblazers laid the groundwork for Barack Obama to be elected as president in a white-majority country.

Since his initial election to Congress in 1992, Sanford Bishop had always been a moderate, though he rationally altered his voting record dramatically when he needed to appeal to whites in the district. His district director noted that he faced a difficult balance as an African-American legislator in a white-majority district. The white voters in his district often assumed he would be too liberal for them, given their lack of shared racial backgrounds. Bishop's district director said: "He's got to bend over backwards to demonstrate that he's conservative." Because of the new constituency dynamics of his post-1996 white-majority district, Bishop rationally adjusted his voting record to become even more conservative.

At the same time, he still needed to keep his primary base of support within the African-American community. His district director noted that the campaign was concerned about balancing both black and white voters in the 1996 election: "We spent an awful lot of effort making sure we got the black vote out [though we also] ... needed to attract white voters." Bishop's strategy involved frequently positioning himself on roll-call votes in line with the majority of his constituents, while targeting goods and services to the African-American minority in the district.

This pattern exists in numerous congressional districts across the country. I argue that legislators – black and white – rationally respond via roll-call voting to the majority of their constituents in order to get reelected. Thus, legislators representing black-majority districts will vote in favor of legislation substantively in the interest of black Americans much more than legislators representing districts without a black majority. The race of the legislator is not as substantively important as the underlying racial makeup of the constituency when it comes to voting records. Sanford Bishop, when faced with a white-majority district, had no choice but to moderate his record (Hancock 2004, 110) in order to garner at least 51 percent of the vote in his reelection bid. Prior to 1996, when his district's majority was African American, he was able to vote more liberally on issues of interest to African Americans than when his district was white-majority.

However, I also argue that African-American legislators are much more likely to focus on the interests of African-American voters when it comes to allocating federal projects and constituency service to African Americans. We have been unable to separate the importance of these two factors – the race of the legislator and the district black population – until these historic elections of black legislators in districts without a black majority. Given these changing electoral patterns, it would be useful to examine late 1990s-era Congresses to best determine the effect of party, race, district black population, and racial trust on substantive representation. Because almost all black legislators won election from black-majority districts until the mid-1990s, the samples available to empirical scholars faced serious data limitation problems. If no black legislators came from districts without a majority-minority population, how could we know if descriptive representation leads to substantive representation? Instead of the presence of a black representative, the district constituency may simply be driving substantive representation outcomes.

John Conyers, for example, is an African-American member of Congress representing a congressional district based in Detroit, Michigan. His congressional district is about 61 percent black in population. Conyers has long been recognized as a prominent proponent of black interests in Congress and has pushed for a discussion of slavery reparations and restoring the right to vote for former felons who are disfranchised, which disproportionately impacts African-American men (Koch 2008; Merida 1999; Thomas 2005; Yoshinaka and Grose 2005). However, it is difficult to determine whether Conyers is a strong proponent of black interests due to his race or due to the racial composition of his district. Thus, analyzing recent Congresses with black legislators from both black-majority and black-minority districts is useful toward understanding black representation in Congress. Whereas some have begun to look at how black elected officials are able to win in electoral settings without a black majority (Bositis 1998; Bullock and Dunn 1999; Grose, Husser, and Yoshinaka 2010; Hajnal 2007; Highton 2004; Jackman and Vavreck 2010; Voss and Lublin 2001), no scholar has used the variation from these 1990s-era elections to address questions about racial representation in Congress. Moreover, because the black legislators who won in white-majority districts had previously been elected in black-majority districts, this era provides a natural experiment suitable for testing these questions. I present a theory of African-American representation in this chapter and then describe how this theory can be tested with these new historic cases.

The Unified Theory of African-American Representation in Congress

The combination of institutional rules within the legislature and electoral coalitions within the districts predicts when legislators will engage in substantive representation for African Americans. Recall from Chapter 1 that substantive representation is when legislators work to provide substantive results for African-American constituents. Given the reelection incentives of members of Congress, legislators rationally work to reach out to black constituents through different activities, depending on the extent of their black electoral support and which activity they are engaging in. In the remainder of this chapter, I will sketch out this theory of minority representation focusing on (1) differing expectations of legislator behavior based on the type of activity (roll calls, constituency service, and project delivery); and (2) the importance of electoral coalitions in determining substantive representation for these three activities.

Three Competing Theories of Racial Representation in Congress

There are three factors likely to explain legislators' attempts to represent black constituents (in addition to a fourth factor I also offer). A legislator's political party, the racial population of the district (the percent black) and the race of the legislator (the presence of a black legislator) have also been demonstrated, or sometimes asserted, to affect legislative outcomes related to black substantive representation.

These three competing theories are relatively straightforward. In Table 2.1, I present a visual explication of the theories, indicating which factors have been hypothesized to lead to higher or lower substantive representation. Substantive representation typically is considered as a continuous concept; although in the table, two dichotomized categories of "high" and "low" suffice to convey the direction of the relationship.

First, as detailed previously, the prevailing research has indicated that the political party of the representative has an effect on the substantive representation of black constituents. Democrats are more likely to support the interests of black constituents in Congress, as African-American voters overwhelmingly support Democratic legislative candidates.[1] Republicans, drawing on very little support from black voters, are not expected to substantively represent the interests of African-American constituents.

Second, the race of the legislator has been theorized or asserted to be an important factor in substantive representation outcomes by many scholars, but it has rarely been demonstrated empirically in studies that also

---

[1] For instance, see Cameron et al. (1996); Endersby and Menifeld (2000); Hutchings et al. (2004); Lublin (1997); Swain (1995); Whitby (1997).

TABLE 2.1. *The Substantive Representation of African-American Constituents*

Political party effects:
Democratic legislators → High substantive representation
Republican legislators → Low substantive representation

Race of legislator effects:
Black legislators → High substantive representation
White and other nonblack legislators → Low substantive representation

Black district population effects:
Low black population districts → Low substantive representation
Black-influence districts → Moderate substantive representation
Majority-black districts → High substantive representation

---

control for the black population of the district.[2] In cases in which the race of the legislator has been empirically examined along with the racial composition of the district, the impact of a legislator's race has been questioned (Swain 1995). The theory is that African-American legislators, all else being equal, are more likely to substantively represent the interests of African-American voters than are nonblack legislators. Also, as a result, white, Latino, Asian-American, and Native American legislators are less likely to be responsive to the needs of black constituents. Even for those African-American legislators representing white districts, we may expect black legislators to better represent black interests. Kerry Haynie (2001, 7), borrowing from W.E.B. DuBois's insights, argues that a "duality dilemma" exists for African-American legislators who are "living, working, and participating in the dominant white society while attempting to maintain an identity and connection with the African American community." This duality dilemma may be the most acute for those black legislators representing districts without a black majority, given electoral pressures.

Some scholars claim this link between black legislators and black voters exists due to descriptive commonality and a shared fate between black legislators and black constituents. Black consciousness has been found to explain voter participation (Shingles 1981), but the link between elite behavior and black consciousness has been hypothesized more than

---

[2] For instance, see Bratton and Haynie (1999); Bratton, Haynie, and Reingold (2007); Canon (1999); Davidson and Grofman (1994); DiLorenzo (1997); Dovi (2002); Gamble (2007); Grose (2005); Guinier (1994); Haynie (2001); Mansbridge (1999); Minta (2009); Owens (2005); Parker (1990); Preuhs (2006); Tate (2003); Wielhouwer and Middlemass (2005); Williams (1998). Nearly all of this work does not control for both district black population and race of legislator.

demonstrated. James Conyers and Walter Wallace (1976) and Kenny Whitby (1997) have suggested black consciousness may explain black elected officials' behavior. More strongly, Mary Hawkesworth (2003) has put forth what I consider to be an essentialist argument that black female legislators have distinct experiences, which lead to actions in Congress not predicted by either a behavioral or a rational choice model of decision making. In contrast, I argue that rational decisions guide all legislators – black or otherwise – and these rational decisions are shaped by electoral incentives. Further, differences between black and white legislators that may exist in Congress are primarily attributable to differences in electoral coalitions, as I describe later in this chapter.

Third, some researchers have indicated that constituency factors are paramount, and thus the racial demography of the district will predict substantive representation results.[3] Generally, the higher the black population is in a district, the more likely that district will elect a legislator who responds to the needs of black constituents. Legislative districts are generally classified into three groups: black-majority districts, black-influence districts, and districts with a low black population. Black-majority districts are defined just as they sound: any district that is greater than 50 percent black in population. Legislators from these districts have been found to substantively represent black constituents more than in other surrounding districts. Black-influence districts are districts that have a large proportion of black constituents, but not a majority. Generally, influence districts are those with a black population of approximately 25 to 49 percent, though scholars differ on the exact definition. These districts have been endorsed by the U.S. Supreme Court in *Georgia v. Ashcroft* (2003), though Congress in 2006 extended the Voting Rights Act in a way that discourages the drawing of these influence districts (a classic example of Congress attempting to override the court's decision; see Barnes 2004). Sandra Day O'Connor, writing for the majority regarding a legislative redistricting plan drawn in 2002, suggested that districts in which black legislators were able to carry influence though not necessarily a numerical majority were constitutional. These districts are expected to also produce legislators who substantively represent black interests, though at a lesser level than districts with a

---

[3] See Bullock (1981); Combs, Hibbing, and Welch (1984); Endersby and Menifeld (2000); Fleisher (1993); Grose (2005); Herring (1990); Hood and Morris (1998); Hutchings (1998); Hutchings et al. (2004); Lublin (1997); McKee (2004); Overby and Cosgrove (1996); Sharpe and Garand (2001); Whitby (1985); Whitby and Gilliam (1991).

black majority. Some also argue that black-influence districts are just as sufficient as black-majority districts for achieving substantive representation. And legislators from districts with a low population percentage of African Americans have, not surprisingly, been found to be least responsive to black constituents, all else being equal.

In sum, three predictors are suggested: (1) Democratic representatives lead to higher substantive representation; (2) black legislators lead to higher substantive representation; and (3) the higher the black population of a district, the higher the substantive representation. However, no scholar has adequately examined these three at the same time when studying the U.S. Congress. I argue that all three factors explain representational decision making by members of Congress, but not all equally for all legislative activities.

Racial Trust between Black Voters and Black Legislators

A fourth and final hypothesis related to racial trust needs to be tested in addition to these three, and this hypothesis gets at the electoral basis for how descriptive representation affects substantive representation. The interactive relationship between the race of the legislator and the black population of the district needs to be considered if trust affects substantive representation. Vincent Hutchings, Harwood McClerking, and Guy-Uriel Charles (2004, 451) have noted that the effect of "black constituency size will vary." Claudine Gay (2002) has shown that black voters trust black legislators more than legislators of another racial background, and also that white legislators face a trust deficit from their black constituents. John Griffin and Patrick Flavin (2007) have found that levels of accountability and information access differ for white and African-American voters, and that this relationship is conditional on the race of the legislator. Additionally, Katherine Tate (2001) has shown that black constituents rate black members of Congress higher in terms of satisfaction than they do their white counterparts in Congress (see also Brunell, Anderson, and Cremona 2008). As a result, whereas white legislators may generally not be as responsive to black constituents as black legislators, the effect of the district black population may be more pronounced within the subset of white legislators. White legislators representing black-influence districts may be much more likely to act in ways to benefit black voters compared to white legislators from districts with a smaller black population. The actions of black legislators are more likely to be consistent across districts of differing black populations due to the trust, electoral support, and high levels of turnout that most black legislators receive from black voters.

This trust is demonstrated by the differential levels in turnout seen between black and white voters. Turnout and political interest among African Americans have been found to be higher when comparing black voters represented by black elected officials to black voters represented by nonblack elected officials (e.g., Bobo and Gilliam 1990; Griffin and Keane 2006; Herron and Sekhon 2005; Voss and Lublin 2001; Washington 2006; Whitby 2007; though Sinclair-Chapman, Gillion, and Walker 2009 find little difference between whites and blacks on levels of participation). Even among those scholars that have not found a robust relationship between black elected officials and increased black turnout (e.g., Gay 2001; Lublin and Tate 1995; Tate 1993, 2003), there is some evidence of higher black turnout relative to that of whites when represented by black elected officials.[4] Whereas the scholarship is mixed as to whether the presence of black elected officials is always associated with higher black turnout, the evidence is much more clear when considering the *differential* levels of black and white turnout under both black and white elected officials. For instance, Gay (2001) finds that white voters are less likely to participate when represented by a black legislator than by a white legislator, even though she finds no relationship among black voters.

In terms of electoral support, Bullock and Dunn (1999) have shown that black legislators from black-influence districts are somewhat less likely to receive white support compared to white legislators from the same party and from similar districts. Crayton (2007) similarly finds that black Democratic incumbents receive less white support than do white candidates running concurrently for other statewide offices. All else equal, black members of Congress are more likely to have a larger percentage of

---

[4] Tate (2003, 136–37), in an examination of African-American voter turnout, found that self-reported turnout among African Americans was about 12 percentage points higher when the respondent was represented by an African-American legislator instead of a white Democratic legislator. This relationship was not found, however, in her multivariate analysis. Tate (1993) found black turnout increased in Jesse Jackson's 1984 bid for the presidency, but not in 1998. Moreover, Lublin and Tate (1995), in a study of mayoral elections, found that black turnout is higher only when a black candidate is running for the first time but not in subsequent elections. See Whitby (2007) for an excellent discussion of this research on turnout. Examining Latino turnout, Barreto, Segura, and Woods (2004) find that turnout is increased when a Latino resides in a majority-minority district. Ramirez (2007) finds that appeals to increase Latino turnout can be effective in majority-Latino precincts.

black voters in their winning electoral coalitions than are white members of Congress. Perhaps more importantly, based on the interviews I conducted with staff in congressional offices of black members and white Democratic members, there is a perception that black legislators are more reliant on black voters than are white legislators, even of the same party. As a result, black legislators may not alter their levels of substantive representation dependent on the black population of their districts to the same extent that white legislators might.

This racial trust explanation does not contradict the "district black population" and the "race of legislator" explanations; it simply suggests that the interaction of these two factors could also have an effect on substantive representation. As Carol Swain (1995) reports, white representatives from black-influence districts were often given less leeway from black constituents than black representatives were. Charlie Rose, a white Democrat and former congressman from North Carolina, concurred in an interview with Swain (1995, 167):

> When confronted with a new white boy, black voters will require that a white politician do all kinds of things to prove his loyalty. They will push him almost to the breaking point to prove that he's loyal.

Rose's comment implies that white legislators face more of an onus to prove their muster with black constituents and thus suggests that substantive representation outcomes differ for white legislators than for black legislators as the black population of the district increases. Thus, the interaction of the race of the legislator and the black population of the district (which I term racial trust) needs to be included as an explanation of substantive representation outcomes in a unified theory. This final portion of the theory is more nuanced than the three separate hypotheses detailed earlier. This racial trust explanation further suggests, contrary to that of Mary Hawkesworth (2003), that black legislators are rational seekers of reelection and that they make substantive decisions in Congress based on electoral constraints. If the differential response of black legislators compared to white legislators is also dependent on the black population of their districts, then electoral considerations are likely to be at work. If a nonelectoral, nonrational personal experiences explanation was the primary consideration differentiating black legislators from other legislators, then there would be no difference in black legislative response regardless of the size of the district's black population (the slope of the line for black legislators would not differ from the slope of the line for white legislators in regards to levels of responsiveness contingent on districts' black populations).[5]

On their face, all four of these theories or explanations appear to be reasonable predictors of minority representation in Congress, and most have been empirically supported in some way. However, no one has attempted to test these theories at the same time and on multiple representational activities as I do here. Further, no one has suggested that all of these factors may predict different levels of representational actions due to legislators' rational responses to existing institutional and electoral constraints. I offer a broader, more compelling approach than those presented by previous scholars. Drawing on these three competing paradigms and the additional fourth hypothesis on racial trust, I develop a unified theory of the substantive representation of black interests in legislatures. As I describe later in this chapter, I expect that all of these factors will affect minority representation outcomes in Congress. However, the magnitude of their effect will vary dependent on what legislative activity is being explained: behavior on the floor of the House or activities beyond roll-call voting. Also, their effect will vary based on the electoral effects present in certain districts. Moreover, by drawing on the theoretical expectations from the spatial model and behavior in the U.S. Congress, we can better theorize about minority representation outcomes.

Congressional Decision Making, Political Parties, and Race

The underlying assumption in the unified theory is that members of Congress are rational: they are interested in reelection, and the decisions they make on roll-call votes, project delivery, and constituency service will be related to this desire for reelection (Mayhew 1974; Tate 2003, 51). The electoral and constituency connections of roll-call behavior have been well-established.[6] Further, legislative scholars have shown that legislators also have an incentive to give pork projects and engage in constituency service in order to try to achieve reelection.[7] Legislators may be

---

[5] It is, of course, possible that black legislators seeking to provide greater levels of constituency service and federal project allocation to black voters are driven by their own personal or enduring preferences and not necessarily by electoral factors (e.g., Burden 2007; Hawkesworth 2003; Haynie 2001; Whitby 1997). If this is the case, the interaction term may prove insignificant in subsequent analyses.

[6] See Arnold (1990); Fiorina (1974); Kingdon (1989); Miller and Stokes (1963); Powell (1982).

[7] See Anagnoson (1982); Ansolabehere, Gerber, and Synder (2002); Arnold (1979); Bertelli and Grose (2009); Cain, Ferejohn, and Fiorina (1987); Fenno (1978); Ferejohn (1974); Lazarus and Reilly (2010); Mayhew (1974); Stein and Bickers (1995).

interested in policy and other goals, but they can only achieve these goals if they are reelected.

Whereas reelection is a motivating factor behind these different legislative activities, the amount of individual control that a representative has over each is very different. With roll-call voting and policy making on the floor of the House, members of Congress have very little personal control over the agenda (see Sinclair-Chapman 2002). Legislation that is voted on must work its way through the committee system and often needs the blessing of party leaders for consideration. The individual legislator can choose which way to vote on legislation, but the agenda-setting power is simply not available for most members, as party and ideology are likely to be key variables in explaining policy making on the floor of the House.[8] This is not to say that constituency factors and other factors specific to individual legislators (such as their racial backgrounds) will not have an impact on their votes on legislation, but simply that party or ideology will play a dominant role in roll-call voting outcomes.

With constituency service, on the other hand, and to a lesser extent with project delivery, these institutional constraints are less prevalent and legislators have substantial control over decisions beyond the wishes of their political parties in the legislature. With constituency service decisions, other than constraints related to budgetary allotments for staff and offices, legislators are able to have complete control over decisions related to serving constituents with casework. National party leaders in the House and inside-the-Beltway politics do not dictate who should be hired, where a legislator holds office hours in the district, or where to put district offices, for example. Similarly, the relative unimportance of the party label among constituents and the importance of candidate-centered elections when voters evaluate incumbents have been well-established (Jacobson 2003). In terms of racial representation, David Canon (1999), Kerry Haynie (2001), Valeria Sinclair-Chapman (2002), and Katherine Tate (2003) examine roll-call voting and bill sponsorship, finding that party constrains the roll-call voting records of members of Congress but not bill sponsorship (an agenda-setting activity). I expect a similar pattern when looking at roll-call voting and activity beyond the halls of Congress such as constituency service.

With project allocations, members of Congress do not have complete individual control over decisions, as there are constraints on the funding

---

[8] For instance, see Aldrich (1995); Binder (1997); Cox and McCubbins (1993, 2005); Lawrence, Maltzman, and Smith (2006); Nokken (2000); Rohde (1991); Sinclair (2002); Snyder and Groseclose (2000); Yoshinaka (2005).

TABLE 2.2. *Selected List of Individual Federal Projects Requested by Congressman Harold Ford, Jr. (D-TN), 109th Congress (2005–06)*

- LeMoyne – Owen College/SoulsvilleUSA Community Development, $1.5 million – "To build affordable homes in central Memphis to address the growing demand from professionals moving to areas bordering higher education institutions."
- National Civil Rights Museum, $1,112,300 – "To enhance and expand educational programming. The requested funding would enable the museum to continue its vital mission of teaching current and future generations the lessons of the American civil rights movement."
- Tennessee Best Buddies, $250,000 – "This nonprofit organization is dedicated to fostering the social integration of individuals with intellectual disabilities. Best Buddies seeks to expand programs in Tennessee for the more than 170,000 children and adults residing in the state who have an intellectual disability. This funding would help Best Buddies open an office in Memphis to help 24 students with intellectual disabilities, fund 96 group outings and countless one-to-one outings."
- Northwest Treatment Plant technology replacement project, $3 million – "For reconstruction of its 8-year-old Northwest Wastewater Treatment Plant to update its existing treatment technology. The treatment plant improvements will protect the environment and water of the Wolf River."
- Rhodes College NASA Stars, $1,021,372 – "For the NASA Stars Teacher Training Curriculum to help improve elementary and middle school science teachers."
- Literacy Education and Ability Program, $1 million – "To continue and expand its effective intervention program for at-risk youth in under-performing schools in Memphis and Baton Rouge, La."

Source: Quoted from Theobald (2006).

and number of projects. However, most legislators can expect to receive some projects that are requested for their districts, and then it simply becomes a question of which groups within their districts they will work with to secure projects. For instance, Table 2.2 shows some of the individual requests for projects made by Congressman Harold Ford, Jr. (D-TN) in the 109th Congress (2005–06). Some project requests are funded, and some are not, but typically every legislator receives some of their requests. Ford made his request list public to a Tennessee news source (Theobald 2006 is the source for the list in Table 2.2), though most legislators have historically not done so (and earmark requests were not publicly available during the time studied in this book).

Party may be an important factor in explaining project allocations (Lazarus and Reilly 2000; Stein and Bickers 2000) at the point of passage for distributive policy legislation, but individual members are personally

TABLE 2.3. *Congressional Parties and Legislative Behavior*

	Roll-call Voting & Legislative Organization	Constituency Service & Project Delivery
Party	Large effect	Small effect
District constituency (black population of district)	Important effect, though perhaps less than party	Large effect
Legislator characteristics and personal preferences (race of legislator)	Small effect	Large effect

responsible for determining which projects they attempt to have inserted into these bills (e.g., Ford's list of requests is his own to determine). Also, individual members can bypass the House floor and assist constituents with project grants by directly taking their cases to the federal bureaucracy (Bertelli and Grose 2009). Legislators can work with bureaucrats so that a project grant receives more serious consideration. Often, the chair and ranking member of a particular congressional committee, regardless of party, will be the most important partners in assisting a legislator in securing a project for his or her district. Thus, project delivery gives legislators an opportunity to personally intercede at multiple stages on a constituent's behalf with only some influence from their political party leaders in the House. Specifically, I argue that legislators are likely to allocate pork projects to constituents in their primary constituency as a way to reward the most motivated voters who turn out in large numbers.

In sum, especially with constituency service and also with project delivery, legislators have much more individual control over their decisions. This has implications for the substantive representation of black constituents, as constituency factors (such as the black population of the district) and factors related to the individual member (such as the race of the legislator) will have more explanatory power than party in non-roll-call legislative decision making. Legislators have leeway to focus on specific subconstituencies or interests (Bishin 2000, 2009; Miler 2007) in their districts when the area of attention is constituency service or project delivery. In Table 2.3, I provide a visual description of these theoretical expectations.

In addition to these agenda-setting explanations for different expectations in the types of legislative behavior, it is important to consider the monitoring of roll-call voting by potential opponents or by constituents in general. Any activity conducted by a member of Congress that can be viewed or monitored by all constituents in the district will likely be driven by district-wide constituency factors in addition to the political party. Roll-call voting would be the most prominent example of this. Whereas few constituents may be aware of individual vote decisions by legislators, it is more likely that they are generally aware of the basic ideological position of their elected officials (Stimson 1990). Also, Douglas Arnold (1990) has demonstrated that the threat of a challenger raising the issue of an incumbent's lack of ideological fit with the district is a powerful incentive to keep the incumbent generally in line ideologically with the majority of constituents. If legislators vote contrary to their districts' preferences, they will face negative consequences at the ballot box (Bovitz and Carson 2006; Grose and Oppenheimer 2007).

Thus, on roll-call votes, something monitored districtwide, the ideology of legislators will generally favor the median voter of the district (Downs 1957; Peress n.d.): if black constituents are in the minority, the likelihood of roll-call voting that enhances substantive representation is reduced, controlling for party and the partisanship of nonblacks in the district. However, if black constituents are a majority, the likelihood of substantive representation from roll-call voting is increased. Again, legislators are rational – they are simply going to respond to the demands of a majority of their constituents in their roll-call voting records.

On activities beyond the vote, however, this districtwide monitoring is not possible. Whereas high-profile projects are generally trumpeted districtwide, most federal projects are smaller and geared toward specific subsets of constituencies, be they geographic, racial, or otherwise. It is unlikely that even a congressional challenger will have enough information to determine which groups of voters in the constituency receive more projects and casework assistance than other groups. Without this monitoring, a legislator has more leeway to reach out to constituents that are a numerical minority without fear of reprisal from other constituents for not getting their "fair share." In this scenario, the legislator can allocate service and projects to black constituents, helping their electoral prospects with this constituency, without the knowledge of most nonblack voters in the district. This same legislator, in a district with a white majority, though, may not be able to vote substantively in the interest of black constituents on the floor as often as a legislator from a black-majority district may. Thus, project delivery and casework can be used by the legislator to reach black constituents even in those districts where the legislators are unable to always vote in favor of black interests on roll-calls.

In sum, voting rights advocates, judges ruling on redistricting plans, and scholars of black legislative representation need to consider multiple modes of legislative activity. Like Morris Fiorina (1989), I suggest that roll-call voting, constituency service, and pork project delivery are the most important roles of a legislator in the eyes of constituents. Due to institutional constraints in the legislature with roll-call voting, party will be the most important factor explaining this measure of substantive representation. Due to the electoral conditions and the lack of institutional constraint with project delivery and constituency service, I expect that the race of the legislator, the black population of the district, and the interaction of these two factors (racial trust) will have the greatest explanatory power for these measures of substantive representation beyond the vote.

Electoral Coalitions, Turnout, and Substantive Representation

The second piece of the theory, then, focuses on the makeup and the dynamics of legislators' electoral coalitions. The impact of the hypothesized factors – political party, race of the legislator, black population of the district, and racial trust – will be affected by the role of black constituents in legislative elections.

The differences in the electoral coalitions of Democratic and Republican legislators, as well as the differences among black and white legislators, are important in understanding whether a legislator will work in the interests of black constituents. Since the passage of the Voting Rights Act in 1965 and the subsequent enfranchisement of black voters in the South, Democratic legislators have generally been more responsive to black voters (Grose and Yoshinaka n.d.). Black voters overwhelmingly support Democrats in legislative elections, typically at levels of 85 to 95 percent on election day.[9] Thus, obviously, Republicans receive very little support from black voters. This pattern of overwhelming black support for Democrats is generally consistent regardless of the race of the legislator and regardless of the black population of the district. Similarly, black voters are very important in the primary elections of Democratic legislators and, depending on the black district population, may make up a majority of primary voters. Democrats from black-majority districts receive overwhelming general election support from black voters, as do Democrats from districts with few black voters. For this reason, the party explanation of substantive representation outcomes seems to be important, as we

[9] See Black and Black (2002); Bullock and Dunn (1999); Dawson (1994); Glaser (1996); Grose et al. (2010); Stanley and Niemi (1999); Tate (1993); Voss and Lublin (2001).

should expect black voter support for Democrats to lead to Democratic legislative support of black voters in the House.

However, to understand whether and how black voters are rewarded for this support in Congress, we also need to consider the size of the black population of the district. Earl Black and Merle Black (2002, 385) unambiguously describe the importance of the black population of a district in determining the actual percentage of the vote that Democratic incumbents receive from black voters. They compare the 1994 election results for John Spratt, a South Carolina Democrat hailing from a white-majority district and John Lewis, a Georgia Democrat from a black-majority district:

Lewis was reelected [with 69 percent of the vote in his district]. If he received the entire black vote in a district in which blacks were 58 percent of the voting-age population, blacks accounted for 83 percent of his total vote. Spratt secured 52 percent of the vote in a district that was 28 percent black. Assuming that he obtained 90 percent of the black vote, blacks cast 44 percent of Spratt's total vote.

Given these percentage point differences that black voters provide as the margin of victory in these example districts, the size of a district's black population undoubtedly affects representational outcomes as well. A legislator like Lewis who receives 83 percent of his support from black voters is more likely to focus primarily on the representation of black interests than a legislator like Spratt, who needs to balance the needs of both black and white constituents more evenly.

Also, though, legislators of different races will have different electoral coalitions and differential levels of voter turnout by race in their districts. Scholars have long suggested that black candidates receive less white support than comparable white candidates receive (Grofman and Handley 1989; Parker 1990; Reeves 1997; Terkildsen 1993). Their argument is that white voters are much less likely to support black candidates, thus requiring black candidates to make up this difference with increased black voter turnout. Studies looking directly at congressional elections have questioned this empirical assertion, pointing out that black candidates can win a substantial share of the white vote (Bullock and Dunn 1999; Highton 2004; Voss and Lublin 2001). Charles Bullock and Richard Dunn (1999), examining congressional elections from 1992 to 1998, show that black Democrats generally receive about one-third of the white vote, contrary to some previous scholars' expectations. Even though a numerical minority of white voters will support black legislators, Bullock and Dunn also demonstrate that white voters are less likely to support black legislative incumbents than white legislative incumbents. They found that "whites drew about ten percentage points more of the white vote than did a comparable black" candidate in congressional elections. Charles Bullock (1984) similarly finds that successful black municipal candidates must draw on both a minority of white voter support and large support and heavy turnout among black voters (also see Grose 2007). Further, African-American citizens are more likely to participate when they "have greater access to policymakers" (Platt 2008b), and this access may be more likely with black elected officials.

This gap in support between white and black legislators indicates that black legislators rely more on black voters than do comparable white legislators who still receive black support. Similarly, in a Democratic primary, black candidates are much more likely to rely on black voter support than are white candidates (Branton 2009; Bullock and Dunn 1999; Canon 1999). As David Canon (1999) and Kareem Crayton (2007) have argued, these dynamics change when black candidates run against one another; a winning strategy for a black candidate can be to appeal to a majority of whites and a subset of blacks in order to win a Democratic primary. However, in any district with a large black population, this candidate still has to rely on the overwhelming support of black voters in the general election (Lublin et al. 2009). In the 2002 primary between black Democratic incumbent Cynthia McKinney and black Democratic challenger Denise Majette, for example, this strategy worked for Majette in her primary defeat of McKinney (Bullock, Gaddie, and Smith 2005). Majette's victory in the subsequent general election contest, though, was predicated on her ability to gain the support of the majority of black voters in the district, many of whom initially supported McKinney. In 2004, Majette unsuccessfully ran for the U.S. Senate, and McKinney was once again elected in a 53 percent black district. McKinney was subsequently defeated again in a 2006 primary by black Democratic challenger Hank Johnson.

As a result, legislators' rational responses to electoral considerations are a key cause of the substantive representation of black interests in Congress (and the elite behavior of legislators). If a black legislator is substantively representing black interests more than a comparable white legislator, this is likely due in part to differential support and turnout among white voters. Thus, a black legislator's electoral coalition is likely to include more black voters than a white legislator's electoral coalition, even when controlling for party and district black population.

The dynamics of race in elections are more than simply differences in black and white voter support for legislators, however. Differentials in turnout by race can also have an impact in shaping an incumbent legislator's voter coalition – and thus the legislator's substantive representation of black interests. Here is where racial trust again becomes important.

Studies of race and representation have examined what leads to increased voter turnout, but rarely has anyone posited the link between minority turnout and substantive representation. Black turnout varies substantially depending on whether a black or white incumbent is running and depending on whether the district is black-majority or not (Brace et al. 1995). Claudine Gay (1997, 2001) has shown that white turnout is substantially lower when a black legislator is running for Congress. Matthew Jacobsmeier (2009) has shown that white voters misperceive that black candidates are out-of-step with the voters' ideological positions (perhaps explaining less white mobilization or white support for black candidates). Whereas black legislators can and do receive white voter support, the absolute level of support is often smaller than what white legislative incumbents receive due to these differential levels of turnout. Thus, the substantive representation of black interests, especially as measured by constituency service and project delivery, will differ depending on the black-white differential in support between black and white legislators *and* the black population of the district. Because of the secret ballot, we do not have reliable national data on black versus white turnout at the level of the congressional district. In lieu of precisely measuring turnout by race, the racial trust hypothesis and its associated variable (the interaction of the legislator's race and district black population) is a proxy that will capture this concept of differential turnout by race of legislator and across congressional districts of varying black populations.[10]

Similar to James Glaser's (1996) argument that campaign strategies are contingent on the black population of congressional districts, I summarize my own voter support and turnout expectations for different legislators in Table 2.4. In order to understand the role of electoral coalitions and turnout, we need to establish the effects of each of these in different

---

[10] Ideally, we could collect data on turnout by race in each district to include as an independent variable in models of substantive representation. Unfortunately, the data are often unavailable and the methods required to gain such estimates (ecological inference) are too cumbersome to estimate for large numbers of congressional districts over time. Also, critics have noted that ecological inference estimates, which would be required to examine turnout in a multivariate model of black representation, cannot be properly used in second-stage regression models as this practice can result in inconsistency, bias, and incorrect coefficient signs (Herron and Shotts 2003).

TABLE 2.4. *Electoral Coalitions and Turnout Differentials*

	Low Black Population Districts, < 25% Black	Black-influence districts, 26–49% black	Black-majority districts, > 50% black
Black Democrats	–	Black support crucial; some white support also crucial High black mobilization level relative to whites	Black support crucial; white support not crucial Moderate level of black mobilization relative to whites
White Democrats	Black support is important and perhaps crucial; white support also crucial Low black mobilization relative to whites	Black support crucial; some white support also crucial Moderate level of black mobilization relative to whites	–
White Republicans	White support crucial; black support not crucial Low black mobilization relative to whites and black turnout unimportant	White support crucial; little black support occurs Low black mobilization relative to whites	–

types of districts. In the table, I specify (1) the electoral coalitions and (2) the turnout differentials between black and nonblack voters for black Democrats, white Democrats, and white Republicans in districts with varying black population percentages. Note that of the nine cells in the table, three are blank. These blank cells are not detailed, as empirically there are almost no cases that fit in these cells, and thus the possible electoral coalitions and turnout differentials cannot be examined. As of this writing, there are no white Republicans elected in districts with a black majority or black Democrats elected in districts with a black population less than 25 percent. From 1992 to 2002, there was one white Democrat that was elected in a 52 percent black district in Pennsylvania, though the district was redrawn to have a black minority in 2002. In 2006, white Democrat Rep. Steve Cohen was elected in a 59 percent black district in Tennessee. Given the paucity of cases in the blank cells, I will detail the electoral coalitions and racial turnout differentials for the remaining six types of legislators: black Democrats elected in black-influence districts; black Democrats elected in black-majority districts; white Democrats elected in districts with small black populations; white Democrats elected in black-influence districts; white Republicans elected in districts with small black populations; and white Republicans elected in black-influence districts. Here, I will motivate the importance of electoral factors, and I will provide further evidence later in this book.

In the top part of each cell, I explain the role of black versus white support in the electoral coalition of each legislator, depending on party, race, and the black population of the district. Here, party clearly plays the key role. Democrats, white and black, rely on black voters for reelection. This is true for Democrats from black-majority districts, from black-influence districts, and from districts with a low black population. Alternatively, white Republicans do not rely on most black voters for reelection, though they benefit from higher levels of white turnout relative to black turnout. Regardless of turnout, most black voters are simply not in Republicans' electoral coalitions, but they are almost always in Democrats' coalitions (Glaser 1996). These results are consistent and indicate that Democrats will substantively represent black voters in Congress.

However, note the second portion of each cell in Table 2.4. Here, I detail the levels of turnout by race that each type of legislator can expect to receive. Unlike simple voter *support* by blacks versus whites, there is substantial variation in expectations of *turnout differentials* by race.

First, consider districts with a small black population, 25 percent or lower. Because black voters are unlikely to be a majority of voters in a Democratic primary and because white legislators are usually the only candidates in this sort of district, then relative mobilization levels are likely to be low for black voters. In terms of substantive representation, we should expect that white Democratic legislators from these districts will need to reach the minority of black voters, but they will particularly need to focus on the district's large white majority as black voter mobilization for these white Democrats is likely to be low.

Similarly, white Republicans from districts with low black populations will typically not substantively represent black voters in any way. Black voters are not typically in Republicans' electoral coalitions, and levels of black mobilization will be unimportant to the outcome of an election anyway. Even if black voters are mobilized highly in this sort of district, a Republican has little to worry about if he or she is taking care of the white voters in the district. Thus, the focus of roll-call voting, service, and project delivery will not be on black constituents.

In column 2 of the Table 2.4, I detail the electoral coalitions and turnout levels by race for legislators in black-influence districts. In these districts, black constituents will not be in the majority but will be large enough to possibly exert some influence on any election outcome, depending on turnout. Black Democratic legislators from these districts will rely primarily on black voters and a numerical minority of white voters to secure election –they will also rely on substantially higher levels of black turnout relative to whites. As a result, these legislators will likely represent black interests more than white legislators also hailing from black-influence districts. This will be very important in a general election but will also be crucial in a Democratic primary, in which black legislators may face opposition from white opponents. Thus, these black voter turnout levels will be rewarded, as black legislators will work to deliver projects and constituency service to this descriptive constituency.

White Democratic legislators from black-influence districts will have virtually identical support coalitions by race as will black Democratic legislators, though black turnout will not be as high relative to white turnout. White legislators will also generally receive a higher percentage of the white vote than will black legislators in black-influence districts. As a result, white legislators from these districts will find it necessary to balance the needs and concerns of white and black constituents, and black constituents will receive less substantive representation from these white representatives. Basically, these legislators will work to reach black voters but not to the detriment of maintaining a sizable group of white voters in their coalitions. Thus, we can expect that white Democrats from black-influence districts will generally vote in the interests of black constituents (given the expectations related to political party), though they may not engage in constituency service and project delivery to the same extent that black legislators from black-influence districts will. White Democrats are able to appeal to a broader base of white voters than can black Democrats, though they are unlikely to rouse the excitement of their base of black voters in the same way that black legislators can.

White Republicans from black-influence districts, on the other hand, are fearful of a serious challenge from a Democrat, black or white, given the size of the black vote in a black-influence district. As a result, white Republicans in these districts who are successful will be able to mobilize large numbers of white voters relative to black voters (or alternatively, demobilize black voters by not giving African-American voters a reason to strongly oppose the incumbent). As the United States has become more diverse, there is some evidence that the Republican party has attempted to make appeals to African Americans, even if these appeals may be "cosmetic" (Philpot 2008). This result may have met some, albeit limited, success at the ballot box. Black and Black (2002) note that Republican incumbents in the South are able to win some support from black voters, even though these incumbents are generally not voting substantively in the interests of black constituents.[11] Republican legislators are still unlikely to substantively represent black constituents through their roll-call votes in Congress. However, compared to white Republicans from low black population districts, white Republicans from black-influence districts may engage in some constituency service to black constituents so that black voters will be less likely to mobilize against them in future elections, or even occasionally vote Republican. Even the once-segregationist Senator Strom Thurmond made nonpolicy overtures to African Americans later in his career. Once African Americans gained the right to vote in Thurmond's state of South Carolina following passage of the Voting Rights Act, Thurmond moderated his views on race and actively sought to reach black voters through constituency service and other means (Stanley 1987, 142).

Finally, in the last remaining cell at the top right of Table 2.4 are black Democrats from black-majority districts. Black voters in these districts will be the majority of both the general election and primary election electorates. As a result, black Democrats almost always win in these districts, and at least some (if not most) black support is crucial in this sort of district. Thus, substantive representation will be high in these districts. However, black turnout, especially in "supermajority" black districts with populations well over 60 percent black, is likely not to be as important to black legislators representing these districts. Unlike black legislators representing black-influence districts, black legislators from black-majority districts do not need to mobilize large numbers of black voters to offset a potential deficit in white voter support. Thus, activities beyond roll-call voting will be engaged in, but there is no clear indication as to the extent that they will be conducted (especially compared to black legislators from black-influence districts). Ironically, the trust that many black constituents may give a black legislator in a majority-black district combined with these districts' electoral dynamics may cause black legislators

---

[11] In terms of policy outreach, Hutchings et al. (2004, 466) find that "[northern] Republicans do appear to make some conscious efforts to court black support, given the moderately higher influence of black constituency size." However, other than this work, most scholarship suggests that Republicans are not reaching out to black constituents on policy grounds. Furthermore, much of my study is focused on the South.

to focus less on reaching out to black constituents. Carol Swain (1995) demonstrated this in the "historically black" districts she examined with supermajority black populations. Still though, it is likely that these black legislators from black-majority districts will engage in greater substantive representation of black interests than white colleagues from black-influence and low black population districts.

In conclusion, there are a few assumptions regarding electoral coalitions and turnout that underlie this analysis. First, it is assumed that Democratic incumbents will receive overwhelming support from black voters. Second, it is assumed that the size of the black population in a district will directly relate to how important black turnout will be in an election. If a district is overwhelmingly black or overwhelmingly white, then an incumbent of any race or party is unlikely to rely on black voter support to provide the *margin of victory*. However, Democratic candidates in black-influence districts or in districts that are just under or at 50 percent black will need to rely on a strategy of both increased turnout among black voters and black support. Finally, it is assumed that the presence of a black legislator often results in higher black turnout relative to whites, regardless of district black population (or that legislators perceive this to be the case). All of these previously demonstrated electoral assumptions further suggest that the four predictors – party of the legislator, the race of the legislator, the district black population, and racial trust (the interaction of the legislator's race and district black population) – will impact substantive representation outcomes both in roll-call voting and in legislative activity beyond the vote.

Black Faces, White Districts: The Supreme Court and Racial Redistricting

To test this unified theory of African-American representation, the recent increase in African-American legislators representing white-majority districts is extremely important. A number of black House members were elected to white-majority districts because the U.S. Supreme Court and other courts ruled many black-majority districts unconstitutional in the mid- to late-1990s. Following these court cases, such as *Miller v. Johnson*, African-American legislators previously elected in black-majority districts ran for reelection and – surprising political observers and sometimes themselves – won historic elections from a number of white-majority districts. To understand how these elections occurred, we need to gain a greater understanding of the Voting Rights Act and racial redistricting.

In 1982, the U.S. Congress extended the Voting Rights Act, amending it in a way that had serious implications for the election of black officials and black representation in Congress. The legislative culmination of years of civil rights struggles, the Voting Rights Act was initially passed in 1965 so the federal government would force states to enforce the Constitution and remove formal barriers to the right to vote for minority citizens (Davidson and Grofman 1994; Thernstrom 1987). The 1982 amendments extended this enfranchisement beyond formal barriers by focusing on the claims of vote dilution in redistricting. Vote dilution is defined as "the practice of reducing the potential effectiveness of a group's voting strength by limiting its ability to translate that strength into the control of (or at least influence with) elected public officials" (Engstrom 1980, 197). The 1965 Voting Rights Act enforced the ability for all citizens to cast a ballot, whereas the 1982 amendments were about "the right to representation" for minority citizens (Grofman, Handley, and Niemi 1992, 23). Proponents of the 1982 amendments asked: "What use was the right to vote if the preferred candidate of those previously disfranchised was regularly defeated at the ballot box?" The 1982 Voting Rights Act extensions were reapproved by Congress in 2006, so this law is likely to continue to be enforced until 2032 unless the Supreme Court curtails the law's impact.

In terms of vote dilution at the congressional district level, the most common claim was that of gerrymandering to dilute the power of minority citizens to affect the outcome. In much of the United States, the electoral choices of white and minority voters have often been divergent (Dawson 1994; Kousser 1999; Reeves 1997; Tate 1993). As a result, states have drawn congressional district plans that spread out minority voters throughout districts (a practice termed "cracking") so that no congressional district has a significant percentage of minority voters. Alternatively, states "pack" minority voters into one congressional district, leaving surrounding districts overwhelmingly white. In both scenarios, the claim has been that minority voters' opportunity to affect the outcome of elections is significantly reduced, even though the right to cast a vote is not prohibited.

The 1982 and 2006 voting rights extensions were designed to combat these claims of vote dilution. Every ten years, congressional districts are reapportioned and redistricted according to population shifts in the United States. Before the 1982 amendments, few districts with a majority of black voters existed outside of northern, urban areas. Following the 1982 amendments, the U.S. Department of Justice was instructed to examine districting plans for states that were covered by the Voting Rights Act to determine whether their plans maximized the number of majority-minority districts. By drawing majority-minority districts, the intent of the 1982 amendments would be fulfilled, easing the ability of minority voters to elect a "candidate of choice," who is often (though not necessarily) African American. In addition to increased descriptive representation, though, there were many consequences, both legal and political.

The first congressional redistricting maps affected by the 1982 amendments were those drawn after the 1990 census. Following this census, in primarily southern states, new majority-minority districts were drawn for the 1992 elections. In 1990, seventeen districts had a black majority, whereas in 1992, the number of black-majority districts increased to thirty-two. These new black-majority districts elected black representatives, in many cases forcing white Democrats into retirement, some by choice and others unwillingly at the polls. After 1992, for the 103rd Congress, thirty-eight black legislators were serving in Congress, and most were elected from black-majority districts (only two came from districts with an outright white majority, and one of these was Republican Gary Franks, elected with little black support in a district with only a 5 percent black population).

Almost as soon as this new class of black members of Congress was elected, swelling the ranks of the Congressional Black Caucus, lawsuits were filed in states alleging that these district plans impermissibly used race in violation of the Fourteenth Amendment. The districts created in order to solve the problem of "cracking" minority groups into many districts now faced legal challenges on the grounds of diluting the voting rights of whites in these majority-minority districts. A minimalist reading of these lawsuits indicate that the plaintiffs claimed that state legislatures who had drawn these districts at the behest of the George H.W. Bush, Justice Department had constitutionally overstepped the intent of the 1982 amendments. Another interpretation of these lawsuits was that the 1982 amendments violated the Fourteenth Amendment altogether.

Throughout the 1990s and early 2000s, the U.S. Supreme Court and lower courts considered a number of these lawsuits and in most cases ruled that these new black-majority districts were unconstitutional. In 1993, the Supreme Court first considered the case against North Carolina's majority-black twelfth district. Perhaps the most litigated congressional district in history, the Court raised serious concerns over the district but did not actually overturn the district at that time. In *Shaw v. Reno*, Justice Sandra Day O'Connor wrote for the majority, claiming these districts "balkanize

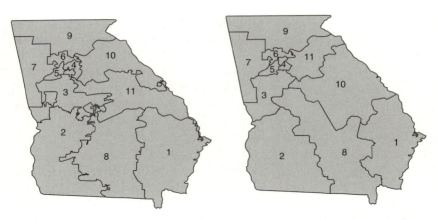

Georgia congressional districts in the   Georgia congressional districts in the
1992 U.S. House Elections   1996 U.S. House Elections

FIGURE 2.1. Georgia's 1992 and 1996 congressional district maps.
Source: Map generated by author using publicly available federal data provided
by U.S. census.
Note: Three black-majority districts in this redistricting plan used for the 1992
and 1994 elections elected black representatives: the 2nd district (57% black), the
5th district (62% black), and the 11th district (64% black). The 2nd district, which
elected Sanford Bishop, and the 11th district, which elected Cynthia McKinney,
were required to be drawn due to the 1982 Voting Rights Act extensions. The
1996 redistricting plan is a re-map of Georgia's congressional districts following
the Supreme Court's ruling in *Miller v. Johnson* (1995). The number of black-
majority districts in this map is only one (the 5th district). Black Democrat
Sanford Bishop successfully sought reelection in the 2nd district in 1996, with his
district's black population reduced to 39%. Black Democrat Cynthia McKinney
also successfully sought reelection in the 4th district in 1996, which took in part
of her former district and had a 37% black population.

us into competing racial factions." Two years later in *Miller v. Johnson*
(1995), the Court clarified its stance on majority-minority districts, finding that any maps drawn with race as the "predominant factor" were
unconstitutional. As a result of the decision in *Miller*, Cynthia McKinney's
black-majority eleventh district was redrawn, as were most of Georgia's
other districts including the black-majority second district represented
by Sanford Bishop (Hood and McKee 2009, 679–680). Figure 2.1 displays the 1992 Georgia map along with the 1996 Georgia map reducing the number of black-majority districts. The black-majority twelfth
district in the 1992 North Carolina map was discussed in Chapter 1 and
is displayed in Figure 2.2. The redrawn 1998 and 2000 North Carolina

NC 12 in the 1992 U.S. House Elections

NC 12 in the 1998 U.S. House Elections

NC 12 in the 2000 U.S. House Elections

FIGURE 2.2. North Carolina's twelfth district in 1992, 1998, and 2000.
Source: Map generated by author using publicly available federal data provided by U.S. census.

twelfth-district maps (which were redrawn to be white-majority districts) are displayed in Figure 2.2 as well.

In total, between 1992 and 2001, congressional district plans in ten states were altered in some way after initial redistricting in 1992, in some cases more than once (see Table 2.5 for a list of these states, the court action that led to new lines, and the year the changes were made). Of

TABLE 2.5. *The Courts and Congressional Districts, 1993–2001*

State	Case(s)	Date	Impact
FL	*Johnson v. Mortham*, 926 F. Supp. 1460	1996	Ruled black-majority 3rd district, represented by Corrine Brown, an unconstitutional racial gerrymander; redrew map before 1996 elections.
GA	*Johnson v. Miller I*, 864 F. Supp. 1254 (affirmed by U.S. Supreme Court in *Miller v. Johnson*, 515 U.S. 900; 1995)	1994	Ruled black-majority 11th district, represented by Cynthia McKinney, as an unconstitutional racial gerrymander; did not redraw map at this point.
	Johnson v. Miller II, 922 F. Supp. 1552 and 922 F. Supp. 1556 (affirmed by U.S. Supreme Court in *Abrams v. Johnson*, 117 S. Ct. 1925; 1997)	1995	Ruled black-majority 2nd district, represented by Sanford Bishop, unconstitutional; redrew map for both 2nd and 11th districts for 1996 elections.
LA	*Hays v. Louisiana*, 839 F. Supp. 1188	1993	Ruled that the Z-shaped black-majority 4th district, represented by Cleo Fields, was unconstitutional; state legislature then redrew map for 1994 elections.
	Hays v. Louisiana, 936 F. Supp. 369	1996	Ruled that the second incarnation of the black-majority 4th district, which followed I-49 from Shreveport to Lafayette, was also unconstitutional; the district court enacted a new plan devised by the legislature (the third of the decade).
ME	*In re 1993 Apportionment*, No. SJC-93-229, Maine Sup. Jud. Ct. (unpublished)	1993	The legislature did not pass a new map for the 1992 elections, so the state Supreme Court intervened and a new map was established for the 1994 elections (Maine's two districts have small black populations).
MN	*Growe v. Emison*, 507 U.S. 25	1993	U.S. Supreme Court threw out map from 1992 elections, which was drawn by a federal district court; the new map instituted for the 1994 elections was one initially drawn by the state (Minnesota's districts all have tiny black populations).

State	Case	Year	
NC	*Shaw v. Hunt (Shaw II)*, 116 S. Ct. 1894	1996	The U.S. Supreme Court overturned a district court decision upholding the state's infamous 12th district, represented by Mel Watt, calling it a racial gerrymander; the decision was preceded by *Shaw v. Reno*, 509 U.S. 630 (1993) in which the Court laid out criteria for how minority-majority districts violated the Fourteenth Amendment; though the *Shaw v. Hunt* decision was in 1996, the districts were not redrawn until the 1998 elections; the black majority 1st district was also redrawn, as were most surrounding white-majority districts.
	Hunt v. Cromartie, 526 U.S. 541	1999	The plan used in the 1998 elections was overturned as an earlier proposed plan following *Shaw II* was ruled not to be a racial, but a partisan, gerrymander; the 12th district and surrounding districts were redrawn yet again for the 2000 elections.
NY	*Diaz v. Silver*, 978 F. Supp. 96 (E.D. N.Y. 1997)	1997	The majority-Latino 12th district, represented by Nydia Velázquez, was thrown out; district was redrawn for the 1998 elections with just a 49% Latino population; some surrounding black-majority districts and other districts were also altered for the 1998 election.
SC	*Statewide Reapportionment Advisory Committee v. Theodore*, 508 U.S. 968	1993	The legislature failed to enact a new plan in 1992, so a court-ordered 1992 plan was redrawn for the 1994 elections; however, changes between the 1992 and 1994 plans were very small, and the black population of the state's one black-majority district was unchanged.
TX	*Bush v. Vera*, 116 S. Ct. 1941	1996	U.S. Supreme Court affirmed a lower court ruling that declared the majority-minority 18th, 29th, & 30th districts unconstitutional; thirteen total districts were redrawn for the 1996 elections.
VA	*Meadows v. Moon*, 117 S. Ct. 2501	1997	Affirmed a district court ruling overturning the majority-black 3rd district, represented by Bobby Scott; the 3rd district was redrawn with a smaller 54% black population for the 1998 election (four surrounding districts were also redrawn).

Source: Minnesota State Senate (www.senate.leg.state.mn.us/departments/scr/redist).

these cases, seven states' districting plans were overturned on voting rights grounds. In Florida, Georgia, Louisiana, North Carolina, Texas, and Virginia, majority-black districts were ruled unconstitutional. In Louisiana and North Carolina, the districts were redrawn twice following their initial districting plans passed in 1992. A majority-Latino district, represented by Nydia Velàzquez, was also overturned in New York on voting rights grounds.[12]

In each of these states, majority-minority districts were redrawn with smaller minority populations, and in most cases, with populations of 50 percent black or less. These court decisions resulted in anger from the voting rights community and from some of the black legislators faced with the daunting prospect of reelection in very different districts. Laughlin McDonald, a voting rights attorney with the ACLU, apocryphally stated that the Supreme Court was "sending us back to the dark days of the 19th century" (quoted from Holmes 1997). Incumbent black legislators declared that they had little chance of winning in their reconfigured black-influence districts with white majorities. Corrine Brown, a black Democrat initially elected in a black-majority district (55 percent black), claimed she would face a difficult reelection when her district was redrawn following a court invalidation caused in part by litigation from a former white opponent: "The bubba I beat couldn't win at the ballot box, so he took it to the court."[13] However, Brown was elected in her new white-majority district, which had a 47 percent black population.

In Table 2.6, I list the congressional districts that were substantially redistricted due to court order between the 103rd and 107th Congresses (1993–2002) and that were represented by an African-American legislator. Even though these court cases have received extensive attention, few have systematically examined representation in congressional districts following the court-mandated redistrictings. I study this natural experiment and exceptional moment in history in which numerous black members of Congress – even in the South – represented white-majority districts (with the redistricting following the 2000 census, many of these black legislators once again saw the black populations of their districts increased, making the mid-to-late-1990s era even more important for analysis). The black Democrats who saw the black population of their districts reduced in the mid- to late-1990s are listed in Table 2.6. Black Democrats Corrine

---

[12] South Carolina's districts also slightly changed, but the changes were so minimal they do not warrant discussion.

[13] David Grann, "Whose Bishop?" *New Republic* 4 November 1996.

TABLE 2.6. *African-American House Members Representing Districts that Changed Due to Court-Ordered Redistricting, 104th to 107th Congresses (1995–2002)*[1]

District	Representative before Redistricting (race, party)	Representative after Redistricting (race, party)	Year of 1st Election with New District	Black Population Change in District	Latino Population Change in District
FL3	Corrine Brown (B, D)	Corrine Brown (B, D)	1996	55% to 47%	3% to 3%
GA2	Sanford Bishop (B, D)	Sanford Bishop (B, D)	1996	57% to 39%	2% to 2%
GA11/4	Cynthia McKinney (B, D)	Cynthia McKinney (B, D)	1996	64% to 37%	1% to 3%
LA4	Cleo Fields (B, D)	Cleo Fields (B, D)	1994	66% to 58%	1% to 1%
LA4	Cleo Fields (B, D)	Jim McCrery (W, R)	1996	58% to 32%	1% to 2%
NY10	Edolphus Towns (B, D)	Edolphus Towns (B, D)	1998	61% to 56%	20% to 18%
NY11	Major Owens (B, D)	Major Owens (B, D)	1998	74% to 67%	12% to 12%
NC1	Eva Clayton (B,D)	Eva Clayton (B,D)	1998	57% to 50%	1% to 1%
NC12	Mel Watt (B, D)	Mel Watt (B, D)	1998	57% to 36%	1% to 1%
TX18	Sheila Jackson-Lee (B, D)	Sheila Jackson-Lee (B, D)	1996	51% to 45%	15% to 23%
TX30	Eddie B. Johnson (B, D)	Eddie B. Johnson (B, D)	1996	50% to 45%	17% to 18%
VA3	Robert Scott (B, D)	Robert Scott (B, D)	1998	64% to 54%	1% to 3%

[1] Also, congressional districts in South Carolina and Virginia were redrawn for the 1994 elections, but the changes were extremely minimal and did not result in any change in black district populations. For this reason, I do not include them in this table. Only black population data – and not black voting age population data – were available for some districts, so I only report district black population.

Brown (FL-3), Sanford Bishop (GA-2), Cynthia McKinney (GA-11), Eva
Clayton (NC-1), Mel Watt (NC-12), Sheila Jackson-Lee (TX-18), Eddie
Bernice Johnson (TX-30), and Robert Scott (VA-3) were all forced to run
for reelection in districts with a smaller black population than the districts
they were initially elected from, due to suits to their states' black-majority
districts (with the exception of Scott, all had to run in new districts that
were 50 percent black or less). Some New York black legislators also
ran in districts with smaller black populations due to Nydia Velázquez's
nearby majority-Latino district being thrown out, though they all retained
black majorities. In Louisiana, one black incumbent, Cleo Fields, saw the
black population of his district reduced twice. Initially elected in 1992 in
a district with a 66 percent black population, his district was redrawn in
1994 with a 58 percent black population. Then, having won reelection in
this new district, he chose not to seek a third term in 1996 when the district was redrawn with a substantial 66 percent white majority. In all of
these cases, the black incumbents who ran in their reconfigured districts
were able to win reelection, mostly with a substantial base of support
from black voters and a minority of white voters in the district (Bullock
and Gaddie 2006).

   Why are some black legislators now able to win elections in districts
that are not black-majority, contrary to the expectations of many observers? Some, such as Abigail and Stephan Thernstrom (1997), claim that
white racial attitudes have moderated, allowing black candidates to seek
and win office in white-majority districts. Others suggest the power of
incumbency, questioning whether the same black candidates could have
won in these districts without having had the opportunity to serve (Bositis
1998; Carter 1998; Highton 2004; Voss and Lublin 2001). Lending support to the incumbency explanation, Mark Rush (1993) has found that
voters who are placed into a new incumbent's district following redistricting are more likely to vote for an incumbent even if of a different
political party than their previous representative. Corrine Brown has
concurred with this view. She thinks that her incumbency allowed white
voters to evaluate her differently than had she been an unknown congressional challenger: "People get an opportunity to see your good works."[14]
Cynthia McKinney also claimed that her incumbency was the key to her
victory and stated the following: "To the pundits who will try to draw
conclusions from our victory and misuse it as a justification to disman-
tle all minority districts, I say, 'Think again.' I won because of – not in

---

[14] Mark Johnson, "Blacks in Congress Defy Dire Predictions." *Tampa Tribune* 8 March 1998.

spite of – a majority-minority district, which gave me a chance to prove myself."[15] Of course, there is one additional, very prominent example of a successful black candidate who has won open-seat elections in white-majority settings: Barack Obama surprised many analysts of race and voting by winning both the 2004 U.S. Senate election in Illinois and the 2008 presidential race (Anderson and Junn 2010; Grose et al. 2010; Jackman and Vavreck 2010; Philpot, Shaw, and McGowen 2009).

Also, it is important to note that not all black legislators from districts without a black majority are elected in white-majority districts resulting from court decisions. Some black legislators have won in districts with a black plurality, and David Lublin (1999) and Jason Casellas (2009b) have shown that black House members can win more easily in districts with a combined black and Latino majority than in white-majority districts. Black legislators in districts with a minority-majority (but not black-majority) population can build coalitions with Latino or Asian-American voters; these minority coalitions explain victories by some black Democrats in districts without a black majority, especially by black legislators outside of the South who win in racially and ethnically heterogeneous districts. For instance, Charles Rangel, a black Democrat from New York, has represented a Harlem-based district since 1970. In the 2000s, the district was only 31 percent black and 48 percent Latino. Long considered a major player in New York and congressional politics, he has also been a prominent promoter of African-American interests since winning his first congressional race in a black-majority district. The size of the Puerto Rican and Latino communities in his district has increased over the years, though, and he has begun to focus on this growing constituency (Carter 2001). He has been noting his partial Puerto Rican heritage to Latino constituents and was a proponent of Latino Bronx Borough President Fernando Ferrer's 2001 and 2005 New York City mayoral bids (Dineen 2001; Fernandez 2005). Combined with strong black support and significant Latino support, Rangel has been able to win reelection easily (though in 2010, Rangel faced ethics charges yet he won again in a fairly competitive primary race). More and more frequently, black legislators like Rangel are able to win in districts without a black majority because of coalitions built with other minority voters.

The purpose of this book, though, is not to explain why black legislators are now more frequently winning elections in districts without black

---

[15] Charmagne Helton, "McKinney, Bishop Show Blacks Can Win in White-Majority Districts." *Atlanta Journal-Constitution* 7 November 1996.

majorities, but instead to utilize these formerly unusual occurrences to investigate other questions about race and representation in Congress. With black legislators now residing in more white-majority districts and more racially heterogeneous districts than ever before, we can better test the competing theories that others have not been able to. The question that I hope to answer is whether legislators like Charles Rangel or Corrine Brown, due to the lack of a black majority in their district, devote less time and resources to the representation of black constituents than black legislators from black-majority districts. Or does their race trump the lack of a black majority in the district, and do they therefore still represent black interests? Or finally, do race and the district black population interact to affect substantive representation outcomes? I argue that legislators rationally respond to the nonblack majority of their districts with roll-call votes but target individualistic service and allocation activities to African-American constituents.

White Legislators and Black-Influence Districts

I also test the differences in the substantive representation of black constituents by white and black legislators hailing from districts with similar levels of black population. Unfortunately for purposes of empirical analysis, very few white legislators represent black-majority districts and few black legislators represent districts without a significant black population. However, also due in part to the court-ordered redistricting in many states, there are now both white and black legislators from black-influence districts in large enough numbers to allow for direct comparison.

Many of those who commented extensively on the impact of these court-ordered districting plans on black incumbents missed the impact of these changes on white legislators who were initially elected in surrounding districts with a small percentage of black voters. Suddenly, some white legislators were faced with larger black constituencies. In the same way that the increased numbers of black legislators serving in districts without a black majority allows us to test theories of racial representation, the increased numbers of white legislators from districts with significant black minorities is also important.

Some white Republicans faced especially difficult initial elections following the court-ordered redistricting. In Georgia, for example, all four white Republicans with new districts saw the black populations of their districts increase by an average of more than 10 percent. Charlie

Norwood, a white Republican member of Congress from Georgia, was first elected in 1994 in a district with just an 18 percent black population. He had to run for reelection in 1996 following *Miller v. Johnson* in a district that was 38 percent black. Describing the substantial black population of his redrawn district, Norwood said: "They typically vote Democratic; we know that. Our message is a very good message for working black people. [But] we don't expect we're going to get a lot ... [of black voter support]."[16]

Norwood achieved reelection, but by a much smaller margin (4 percent) than his earlier victory in 1994 over a Democratic incumbent (30 percent). As a legislator in a black-influence district, did Norwood work at all to reach African-American constituents, especially compared to other white legislators from districts that have fewer African-American voters? Or as a Republican with black voters outside of his electoral coalition, was the substantive representation of African-American interests not an interest of his? White Republicans representing black-influence districts, like Norwood, also can help address the research questions.

Why No One Has Examined *Both* a Legislator's Race and a District's Black Population

Why are cross-sectional data including these court-ordered districts so useful? The data are useful because previous researchers have not had enough variation in their samples to test competing theories of racial representation in Congress. Scholars, lawyers, and voting rights advocates have made broad conclusions regarding the best arrangement of voters in districts and the effect of a legislator's race and party on congressional outcomes. However, those who have tried to divine the differential effects of (1) electing black representatives; and (2) the overall black population of districts on the substantive representation of black constituents typically run into a methodological "brick wall" of observational equivalence: as noted earlier, until recently, nearly every black legislator was elected from a majority-black district. As a result, scholars were unable to determine if black-majority districts or black legislators were the key factors in explaining substantive outcomes to African-American constituents.[17]

---

[16] Tom Corwin, "Challenges Await Incumbent." *Augusta Chronicle* 7 January 1996.
[17] The correlation between these two variables was typically so high (> 0.9) that quantitative scholars have been forced to choose just one variable to include in models. Multicollinearity is typically a problem in that it causes standard errors between

Previous scholars examining racial representation in Congress have faced this problem simply due to the lack of variation that has histori-cally existed between these two key variables (race of legislator and black district population). Table 2.7 details thirteen cross-sectional studies of substantive black representation in Congress, focusing particularly on (1) the substantive outcome studied (the dependent variable); (2) the samples of legislators analyzed; and (3) the explanatory variables included (race of legislator, district black population, or political party). Of note, most of these studies only examine the effect of a legislator's race *or* district black population on roll-call voting in Congress. The scholars are not to blame, though, as only in the mid-1990s has variation between these two key variables existed.

Most of these scholars conclude that the black district population and party are the main factors predicting the substantive representation of black interests in Congress. These prior results need to be reconsidered with the new mid-to-late-1990s court-ordered districts that can allow for full tests on all three factors (race of legislator, black district population, and party of legislator). Twelve of the previous studies analyze the effect of party on substantive representation, whereas eleven of them examine the effect of the black or minority population (Cameron, Epstein, and O'Halloran 1996; Canon 1999; Fleisher 1993; Hood and Morris 1998; Hutchings 1998; Lublin 1997; Overby and Cosgrove 1996; Sharpe and Garand 2001; Swain 1995; Whitby 1985; Whitby and Krause 2001). However, only six examine the effect of the legislator's race on roll-call voting (Cameron et al. 1996; Canon 1999; Swain 1995; Tate 2003; Whitby 1997; Whitby and Krause 2001), and none examine all three variables (party, race, and black district population) in one model except for Canon (1999).[18] Also, none examine racial trust – or the interactive effect of a legislator's race and district black population.

As a result of these pre-*Miller v. Johnson* district limitations, these scholars are unable to appropriately analyze all factors theorized as being relevant to substantive representation in one model. Many scholars,

---

correlated variables to become inflated even when the variables may in fact be significant. In fact, the so-called multicollinearity problem is simply a problem of sample size and of lack of variation among observations, as Achen (1982) has stated: "[M]ulti-collinearity violates no regression assumptions. Unbiased, consistent estimates will occur. ... The only effect of multicollinearity is to make it harder to get coefficient estimates with small stan-dard errors."

[18] Swain (1995), in her book's appendix, describes a model with all three variables but does not present results. In the book's text, she reports the results of a regression with only party and district black population variables.

TABLE 2.7. *Legislator's Race or Legislator's Black District Population? Selected Previous Analyses of Substantive Representation in Congress*

Study	Measure of Substantive Representation (Dependent Variable)	Sample	Independent Variables Related to Racial Representation Examined in Quantitative Analyses
Cameron et al. (1996)	• Roll-call votes (Leadership Conference of Civil Rights, LCCR, scores)	103rd Congress	• Race • Black voting age population of district • Party • Looks at race and black voting age population by stratifying sample (not in one equation)
Canon (1999: 178)	• Roll-call votes (LCCR scores) • Bill sponsorship • District activities	103rd Congress	• Race • Black population of district (not significant in LCCR analysis) • Party
Fleisher (1993)	• Roll-call votes (Americans for Democratic Action, ADA, scores; party unity scores)	97th–100th Congresses, Democrats only	• Black population of district • Party controlled for by only examining Democrats
Hood and Morris (1998)	• Roll-call votes (ADA scores)	98th–102nd Congresses, southern MCs only	• Minority population of district • Party
Hutchings (1998)	• Roll-call votes (focus on amendments)	101st Congress	• Black population of district • Party

(continued)

TABLE 2.7. *(continued)*

Study	Measure of Substantive Representation (Dependent Variable)	Sample	Independent Variables Related to Racial Representation Examined in Quantitative Analyses
Lublin (1997, chap. 5)	• Roll-call votes (Poole and Rosenthal's 1997 nominal three-step estimates, or NOMINATE scores)	92nd–102nd Congresses	• Black population of district • Party
Overby and Cosgrove (1996)	• Roll-call votes (American Federation of Labor-Congress of Industrial Organizations Committee on Political Education, COPE, scores)	103rd Congress, white incumbents only	• Change in black population • Party
Sharpe and Garand (2001)	• Roll-call votes (ADA scores)	103rd Congress, returning MCs only	• Black population of district • Change in black population • Party
Swain (1995, chap. 1)	• Roll-call votes (LCCR, others) • District activities	100th Congress	• Black population of district • Party
Tate (2003, 86–87)	• Roll-call votes (key legislation)	103rd and 104th Congresses	• Race • Party
Whitby (1985)	• Roll-call votes (LCCR scores)	91st–97th Congresses	• Black population of district • Party
Whitby (1997, chap. 4)	• Roll-call votes (LCCR scores)	93rd–102nd Congresses	• Race • Party
Whitby and Krause (2001)	• Roll-call votes (LCCR scores and other key votes)	104th Congress	• Party • Looks at race and black population separately

facing this previously intractable problem, simply drop an explanatory variable. For instance, Kenny Whitby (1997, Ch. 4), in his seminal work on black representation, theorizes that both a legislator's race and the black district population are important, but he only analyzes the effect of a legislator's race and drops the black population of the district from his analysis.

Most other studies, alternatively, examine only the black district population and not the race of the legislator. For example, in another seminal work on the subject, David Lublin (1997) examines the effect of the racial population of the district on legislators' ideologies, but he does not include the race of the legislator as an explanation. David Canon (1999) is the only one who considers and reports the full results of a model with both the race of the legislator and the district black population in the same regression examining roll-call voting. However, Canon (1999, 178) does not find the black district population to be a significant predictor of civil rights voting records. This counterintuitive result is certainly due to this problem of almost all black legislators being elected from black-majority districts during the time period he studies. In sum, few studies have considered and none of these prior studies have found that both the race of the legislator and the black district population are significant predictors of substantive representation when measured as either general ideological or pro-civil rights voting indices.

In conclusion, given the contrary results in which scholars pick and choose only certain explanatory factors to study, it is time to examine the historic elections of legislators like Sanford Bishop in white-majority districts. Does a legislator's race matter in providing substantive representation? Does the district black population matter? Or do they both matter? Which of these two is most important? By addressing these questions during the natural experiment of the mid-1990s redistrictings, we can learn about race and representation both in roll-call voting and beyond roll-call voting – and we can determine the relative impact of all theoretically specified explanations.

3

The "Hollow Hope" of Civil Rights Change in the U.S. House

"What really happened during the 1990s redistricting round[?] ... [B]lack interests suffered as a result of this [racial redistricting maximization] ..."
                                    –David I. Lublin and D. Stephen Voss (2003)

"If you go from a safe [black majority congressional] seat [to a black influence district], that is backsliding."
                        –Justice John Paul Stevens, during questioning
                        in *Georgia v. Ashcroft*, 2003 (from Cook 2003).

"Racial redistricting results in the election of some liberal representatives, thereby shifting the House median to the left."
                                          –Kenneth W. Shotts (2003a, 226)

"I don't want to ... [increase my district's black population]. I believe it should be unconstitutional, if it's not, to stack black people in political ghettos."
                        –Rep. Jim Clyburn, black Democrat from South Carolina's
                        sixth district (from Associated Press 2001)

Do majority-minority districting plans cause more liberal or more conservative civil rights policy outcomes in the aggregate U.S. House? Or is it possible that majority-minority districting plans have little to no impact on civil rights outcomes in the aggregate U.S. House? Whereas substantial debates have occurred over these questions in the fields of history, political science, law, and on the Supreme Court, there has always been an assumption that these districting plans have either benefited or harmed African Americans.

In this chapter, I argue that these districting plans have neither harmed nor helped African Americans and other minorities when we examine aggregate civil rights outcomes on the floor of the U.S. House before and after these districting plans were implemented. Instead, I argue and show that they have had virtually no impact on the location of the decisive legislator in the U.S. House over time. In fact, a somewhat dismal conclusion is reached. If we examine the policy preferences of the median legislator in the U.S. House – the vote-deciding 218th House member (of 435) – the position of this decisive legislator has changed minimally from the late 1960s to the present. Borrowing terminology from Gerald Rosenberg (1991), the U.S. House has been nothing more than a "hollow hope" for civil rights advocates during most of the last three decades.

However, I also show that the decisive legislator within the majority party that controls Congress has changed during this time, and thus agenda-setting power on civil rights is much more conservative since the Republicans took control of the House in the 104th Congress (1995–96). Whereas racial redistricting may have helped elect some Republicans in districts surrounding newly created black-majority districts, it was not decisively responsible for the Republican takeover in 1994. Thus, even though the party median has shifted concurrent with the increase in racial redistricting, racial redistricting was not the primary cause of this shift in the location of the party median. Instead, the broader competitiveness in the South and the entire United States contributed to the GOP takeover, which has hurt African-American interests in the legislature. This is because political party, and not a legislator's race, is the key individual-level predictor of pro-civil rights records in the U.S. House. The conclusion of this chapter is that the drawing of black-majority districts neither helps nor harms African Americans when we examine aggregate policy making on the floor of the U.S. House. Thus, the majority-minority districting debate is substantially overblown, at least when we examine civil rights policy outcomes. Party control of the legislature is basically what matters for promoting civil rights outcomes, and racial redistricting has had only a small impact on party control.

Thus, to evaluate the efficacy and the effects of black-majority districts as well as the election of black legislators to Congress, we must examine policy and other substantive decisions that occur off the floor of the House. These other substantive congressional decisions – such as constituency service and "pork" project allocation – are examined in subsequent chapters.

The conventional wisdom regarding the effect of racial redistricting on aggregate policy outcomes in the interest of African Americans can be summed up by returning to the case of North Carolina and its districting plan in the 1990s. Many commentators have alleged that this plan led to aggregate voting that hurt black voters. Prior to the 1992 redistricting, most of the members of the congressional delegation in North Carolina were white Democrats, and none of the members of Congress hailing from North Carolina were African American. In 1992, as detailed earlier, two black-majority districts were drawn. Following the 1992 elections, North Carolina elected eight Democrats and four Republicans; two of the eight Democrats, Mel Watt and Eva Clayton, were African American, and both were elected from black-majority districts. The Democrats – both the African-American and white legislators – generally supported civil rights votes in Congress. However, in 1994, due in part to the "bleaching" of surrounding districts to create the black-majority districts that Watt and Clayton were elected from, the number of Democrats elected in North Carolina dropped from eight to four. Further, the voting records of the eight Republican-four Democrat congressional delegation became much more conservative on civil rights. Critics of racial gerrymandering, including the defeated white Democratic incumbents, blamed racial redistricting and the Republican realignment in the South for this outcome in North Carolina and other states. Former Georgia Senator Sam Nunn noted that the Republican tide that occurred in 1994 had "been coming, frankly, since … 1972." Nunn added that the "[creation of whiter] predominately Republican districts and black districts" accelerated this change in southern states (McConagha 1995).

This question has been the subject of dozens of Supreme and lower court cases in the United States. In rulings such as *Shaw v. Reno* (1993) and *Miller v. Johnson* (1995), the Supreme Court declared that the packing of black voters in districts was evidence of an unconstitutional racial gerrymander. In *Georgia v. Ashcroft* (2003), the Court suggested that black-influence or coalitional districts – districts without a black majority – may be better for the aggregation of public policy outcomes in the interests of African Americans under Section 5 of the Voting Rights Act. In response to this case, Congress in 2006 altered the Voting Rights Act in order to require majority-minority districts under Section 5. In *Bartlett v. Strickland* (2009), in a somewhat incoherent plurality opinion, the Court concluded that state legislatures are not required to draw coalitional districts, yet they are not prohibited (at stake in the case was a state legislative district just under 40% black that was drawn to enhance minority interests). The bulk of Supreme Court decisions over the last two decades suggest that black-majority districts lead to a dilution of minority influence in surrounding districts, whereas legislation coming out of Congress during this time has favored the drawing of black-majority districts in the interests of voting rights.

Contrary to those arguing that black-majority districts enhance African-American policy representation and contrary to those arguing that these districts hurt minority interests, I show that the districts are neither particularly harmful nor helpful to enhancing civil rights policy outcomes on the floor of the U.S. House. Essentially, the entire racial redistricting debate as it relates to roll-call voting is overstated. Instead of perverse effects or beneficial effects arising from racial gerrymanders, I suggest racial redistricting results in *minimal effects* on the floor of the U.S. House. It is important to note that my argument does not dispute that state delegations may have become more conservative following the 1992 redistricting plans within a handful of specific southern states, but that a broader analysis of the entire U.S. House during this time is warranted. Instead of focusing on the handful of districts in states like North Carolina where racial gerrymandering was important in affecting the eventual winners, we need to also examine the more common districts that were drawn with no racial gerrymandering imperative.

Why are the findings in this chapter significant? First, the debate thus far about the policy consequences of various U.S. House districting plans has centered on the alleged aggregate change in policy at the congressional level. Whereas some argue minority gerrymanders cause more conservative outcomes in the aggregate and others argue they cause more liberal outcomes in the aggregate, no tests have been conducted on civil rights policies that are supported by African-American voters with all 1990s-era congressional districts. The analyses of policy change in the aggregate typically focus on general left-right ideological voting, and I depart from this practice by estimating a civil rights issue space.

Second, no one has estimated a scale-comparable civil rights issue space over time (though see Espino 2007 for an estimate of a Hispanic voting dimension during the 103rd Congress). I offer new civil rights ideology scores for House members over three decades, which likely will be used by scholars, practitioners, and the courts to answer other research questions beyond the scope of this book. Most scholars and practitioners attempting to assess civil rights voting typically rely on the Leadership Conference on Civil Rights (LCCR) voting indices in each Congress. However, these "LCCR scores" are not technically comparable across Congresses (see Poole 2005; Groseclose, Levitt, and Snyder 1999; and Treier 2006 for discussions of interest group rating comparability). Further, if a legislator votes with the LCCR 100 percent of the time, this assumes that the legislator is on the far left of the civil rights voting spectrum. However, some legislators may actually be even more liberal than the LCCR, but the existing scale does not pick this up. One advance in the measures offered in this chapter is that the civil rights issue space allows legislators to be to the left of the LCCR as well as to the right. It is possible that some legislators vote contrary to the LCCR for liberal reasons (e.g., if they perceive proposed civil rights legislation as not being strong enough). Another advantage of these new estimates is that they do not weight all roll calls equally for all legislators, which the existing LCCR scores do.

Whereas some scholars have examined civil rights voting records and specifically LCCR scores to address questions related to racial redistricting (e.g., Whitby 1997), none have examined the extent of civil rights voting over such a long period of time. I analyze civil rights voting in the U.S. House from 1969 to 2004 (91st through 108th Congresses), whereas others have looked at shorter time periods (e.g., Canon 1999; Grose 2005; Hutchings 1998; Hutchings, McClerking, and Charles 2004). Prior to this book, the most exhaustive study of civil rights voting records in Congress was Whitby (1997), who examined twenty-two years of roll-call voting from the 93rd through the 103rd Congresses. The time period I study includes thirty-four years of roll-call voting on civil rights.

Perverse Effects, Beneficial Effects, or Minimal Effects? Does Racial Gerrymandering Affect Median Civil Rights Policy Outcomes in the U.S. House?

This chapter addresses a puzzle in the literature on racial redistricting and minority representation. If we are interested in questions about American democracy and concerned about how best to enhance minority representation, what arrangement of black voters in a district maximizes the representation of black interests via public policy – black-influence districts as suggested by cases such as *Georgia v. Ashcroft* or black-majority districts as suggested by the Voting Rights Act extensions of 1982 and 2006?

I suggest that racial redistricting plans have neither perverse nor beneficial effects but, instead, minimal effects. Even if states are required to maximize majority-minority districts, they are limited by geography and demography. The districts drawn for the 1992 elections likely represent the highest number of majority-minority districts geographically possible unless and until the demographics of the United States shift extensively. In the 104th Congress (1995–96), for instance, only 32 of the 435 congressional districts in the U.S. House had a black population of 50 percent or greater. Of the thirty-two black-majority districts used in the 1992 elections, only thirteen of these districts were newly drawn in southern or border states (I use the term South in this chapter to encompass both southern and border states).[1] If the dilutive effect is occurring – even in all of the southern districts racially gerrymandered in 1992 – then at most ten to twenty districts are "bleached" in a dilutive manner (McKee 2004). Although this is a large number, it is still not the bulk of congressional districts in the United States – more than 80 percent of the House members will ultimately be elected from districts that are drawn with no bearing on African-American gerrymandering. Legislators from congressional districts in Minnesota and Montana will dominate civil rights votes in Congress, and this handful of legislators from states with racial gerrymanders will not. Redrawing black-majority districts in a few states will simply result in rearranging the deck chairs in the U.S. House.

Essentially, my argument is that scholars' obsession with roll-call voting outcomes (e.g., Cameron, Epstein, and O'Halloran 1996) in a few state delegations misses the broader point of how policy is made on the floor of Congress. Because the bulk of U.S. states' congressional districting plans do not require preclearance under Section 5 of the Voting Rights Act, the median legislator in the 435-member U.S. House is unlikely to change dramatically with the addition – or subtraction – of a few black-majority districts in the states that are covered by Section 5.[2] Further,

---

[1] In this chapter, when I use the term "South" I mean all states below the Mason-Dixon line, instead of referring to the eleven states of the Old Confederacy as is the typical definition of the South in other work on southern politics. I use the broader term to encompass southern and border states because the racial gerrymandering maximization imperatives from the Department of Justice caused these southern and border states to increase the number of black-majority districts. Only two nonsouthern states, New York and Pennsylvania, also added one black-majority district in their 1992 congressional redistricting. In New York, a district already represented by an African-American legislator had the black population increased to higher than 50%. In Pennsylvania, a white legislator initially elected in a black-minority district won reelection in a redrawn district that was 52% black. When I discuss new black-majority districts in this chapter, I am considering only those districts in the southern and border states and not those in New York and Pennsylvania (as these latter two did little to alter the composition of their state delegations and partisan control).

[2] No states are allowed to draw discriminatory districting plans under Section 2 of the Voting Rights Act. However, state districting plans that maximized majority-minority districts due to the Justice Department's interpretation of Section 5 have been most frequently criticized as racial gerrymanders that dilute black voting power in surrounding districts. See Kousser (1999) and Middlemass (2001) on Justice Department enforcement. Moreover, given the Supreme Court's decision in *Bartlett v. Strickland* (2009), the drawing of black-influence districts (instead of black-majority districts) is neither prohibited nor required under Section 2, meaning the legal restrictions to draw black-majority districts under Section 2 is weaker than under Section 5, given the *Georgia v. Ashcroft* "fix" of Section 5 passed in the 2006 Voting Rights Act extension.

TABLE 3.1. *Hypothetical Legislature with Seven Legislators*

Five legislators are elected from districts in states where racial gerrymandering is
not possible, and these legislators are moderates on civil rights. These legislators are indicated by M_1, M_2, M_3, M_4, M_5 (M stands for moderate legislators).
These positions indicate where these legislators are located on the civil rights
ideological space, with those closer to the left being more pro-civil rights.
Two legislators, L_1 and L_2, are elected from a state where racial gerrymandering
is possible.

Scenario 1, no majority-minority districts:

←- - - - - - - - - - - - -M_1 - - L_1 - M_2 - -M_3 - - L_2 - - M_4 - --M_5 - - - - - - - - →
Left = liberal on civil rights   Right = conservative on civil rights

Scenario 2, Legislator L_1 elected in black-majority district and L_2 elected in nearby
"bleached" white-majority district:

←- - L_1 - - - - - - - - M_1 - - - - - M_2 - - M_3 - - - - - - M_4 - - M_5 - - - - - L_2 - - - -→
Left = liberal on civil rights   Right = conservative on civil rights

---

this suggests that the debate over black-majority versus black-influence
districts and districting's effects on policy outcomes is relatively unimportant once we examine aggregate policy outcomes in Congress for all
House members from all state delegations. When we consider legislators'
policy preferences from states without racial redistricting imperatives
in conjunction with legislators' policy preferences in states where racial
redistricting was required, the aggregate policy outcomes in Congress are
likely to be dominated by the large supermajority of legislators hailing
from states without racial gerrymandering.

   In the spatial model of voting in legislatures, there are certain pivotal
legislators in Congress that can dominate policy outcomes (Krehbiel 1998).
To understand why the median legislator is important, consider a hypothetical and stylized legislature with seven members (see Table 3.1). Imagine
that five of the seven House members are elected from moderate districts
without regard to racial gerrymandering (a reasonable assumption given
that the U.S. public outside of the South is generally moderate in terms
of public opinion on civil rights). The other two legislators are elected in
the same state where racial gerrymandering is a possibility. Under a plan
with two black-influence districts and no black-majority districts (labeled
Scenario 1 in Table 3.1), two moderate legislators will be elected who also
cast moderate votes on civil rights (these legislators are designated L_1 and
L_2 in the table). However, the median legislator – who will cast the decisive
vote on any close bills (because she is in the middle) – is M_3.

Under a racial gerrymandering plan (labeled Scenario 2 in Table 3.1) with a heavily black district and a heavily white district, these two districts will elect one very liberal and one very conservative legislator on civil rights. L_1 is elected from the black-majority district and thus votes liberally on civil rights, while L_2 wins in a "bleached" white-majority district and is a conservative on civil rights. Under this plan, even though L_1 and L_2 are now at different policy locations in a civil rights one-dimensional space, the median legislator will still remain the same (legislator M_3). For any pro-civil rights legislation to pass (conditional on the location of the status quo), the three legislators on the left will need to convince legislator M_3 to support civil rights proposals. The location of the moderate, median legislator becomes critical – and the districts drawn in states where racial redistricting is possible are simply rearranging the location of the extremists who have less control over the final vote outcomes.

This stylized legislature is simply used to motivate a similar reality in the actual U.S. House of Representatives. In the U.S. House, where 218 of 435 votes are required to pass legislation on the floor, the median legislator – the 218th legislator – on a left-right issue dimension is the critical legislator for determining roll-call outcomes in the legislature as a whole. The theoretical device of the decisiveness of the median legislator is used to motivate a broader point. In reality, given some uncertainty over legislators' preferences, one individual at the middle of the chamber will not be decisive on every roll call, but instead a small group of legislators in the middle of the ideological distribution of the House will be decisive. Those on the extremes (i.e., the Maxine Waters [D-CA] and the Lynn Westmorelands [R-GA] of the world) will have a very low probability of being decisive.

Racial redistricting scholars have tended to focus on a few state delegations instead of assessing the policy outcomes in Congress as a whole based on the location of the median legislator. Kenneth Shotts (2002, 2003a) is the only scholar who has used the logic of the spatial theory of voting in analyzing racial representation, and he finds that majority-minority districts may move policy outcomes to the left under some conditions. However, he (2003a, 2003b) also notes that majority-minority districts may move policy outcomes to the right in the aggregate legislature under other conditions (e.g., in nonsouthern states with liberal voter preferences). Contrary to Shotts, David Lublin and Steven Voss (2003) argue that racial redistricting and black-majority districts will shift the median legislator in Congress to the right. No one has empirically examined the ideological positions of members of the House on the ideological dimension of civil rights within the framework. The debate between Shotts (2003a, 2003b) and Lublin and Voss (2003) and others has examined how black-majority districts cause shifts leftward and rightward on a general left-right ideological dimension.

What Are Black Interests on Roll Calls?

However, African-American voter preferences are not consistently liberal on general public policies, even though this is an underlying assumption in the ideology measures used in much of the work measuring substantive representation as roll-call votes (e.g., Fleisher 1993; Grose 2005; Haynie 2001; Lublin 1997; Lublin and Voss 2003; Overby and Cosgrove 1996; Rocca, Sanchez, and Nikora 2009; Sharpe and Garand 2001; Shotts 2003a). In fact, there is great diversity of public opinion within the black community (Swain 1995, 10; Whitby 1997, 8), and thus using general left-right ideological measures of policy outcomes in Congress may not be the best proxy for policies in the interest of African Americans. As David Canon (1999, 30) has emphasized, "Blacks have the same preferences as whites on non-racial issues, irrespective of political party."[3]

However, there is one issue area in which public opinion surveys suggest a high level of unity among African Americans. Canon (1999) and Tate (2003) note that African-American voters do, in fact, have distinct – and more liberal – policy preferences on civil rights issues than white Americans. Given the evidence that the primary differences in public opinion between African Americans and whites are on civil right issues, I will use original estimates of the ideological positions of members of Congress on only civil rights issues to determine if the median legislator in Congress has changed over time.

In sum, I expect there will be minimal civil rights change, whereas others suggest otherwise. Ken Shotts has argued that *drawing majority-*

---

[3] Haynie (2001) and Lublin (1997) have argued that there are important commonalities in African-American public opinion favoring broad social welfare policies, as well as more objective criteria suggesting that liberal social welfare policies are in the interests of African Americans. Although they may be correct, there are two reasons I do not examine broader social welfare questions. First, the existing preference measures of social welfare such as NOMINATE scores include roll calls on social welfare policies and on other policies in which the African-American community have much more diverse public opinion preferences. Second, we know that civil rights/racial policy preferences differ between African Americans and whites. Thus, I rely on the measure of policy preferences, civil rights, that is certainly favored by a large majority of African Americans.

minority districts results in more liberal outcomes in the aggregate legislature (when racial gerrymandering occurs in southern states where racial groups of voters have distinct preferences). Notably, whereas Shotts has argued that racial redistricting affects the aggregate location of the median House member in the legislature (see quotation introducing this chapter), the only empirical evidence Shotts (2003a, 2003b) offers is based on the U.S. South. His model is supported when examining southern House delegations, but he does not examine the aggregate location of the U.S. House median (of all 435 House members), even though his theory suggests an examination of the U.S. House as a whole.

David Lublin and Steven Voss (2003) argue that *drawing majority-minority districts results in more conservative outcomes in the aggregate legislature.* Like Shotts, Lublin and Voss have presented evidence primarily based on southern congressional districts. I do not quibble with their argument that racial redistricting may have been one of the factors resulting in the Republican gains in some southern states in the 1990s. However, like Shotts, they do not analyze policy positions among legislators in all U.S. House districts. David Lublin (1997) and other scholars examine roll-call voting in the U.S. House as a whole, but the focus is mostly on the individual district-level predictors of liberal-conservative vote outcomes and not on civil rights votes. In contrast, I argue that *racial redistricting has resulted in minimal effects in terms of civil rights policy outcomes on the floor of the U.S. House: drawing majority-minority districts will have no discernible impact on aggregate civil rights outcomes as most House members are elected from state delegations where majority-minority districting is not required or is not feasible (given a paucity of minority constituents).*

Before proceeding any further, I want to point out that I intend to discuss the role of majority party control of the legislature but at a latter point in the chapter. We know that Democrats are better representatives of the policy interests of African Americans than Republicans on general ideological issues (Grose 2005; Lublin 1997; Swain 1995; Whitby 1997) and on civil rights (Grose 2005; Hutchings 1998; Whitby 1997). A case can also be made that racial gerrymandering in southern states played some role in the 1994 GOP takeover of the U.S. House (Lublin and Voss 2003), though the movement of white voters toward the Republicans is also critically important (Aistrup 1996; Black and Black 2002; Bullock, Hoffman, and Gaddie 2005; Clark and Prysby 2004; Fenno 2000; Hayes and McKee 2008; Hood, Kidd, and Morris 2004, 2008; Lublin 2007;

Overby and Brown 2002; Petrocik and Desposato 1998; Shafer and Johnston 2001, 2006; Stanley 1987; Wink and Bargen 2008). At this point in the chapter, I am only interested in assessing the location of median policy outcomes on civil rights (regardless of which party controls the chamber), but I will address partisan control later.

How Can We Determine Legislators' Preferences on Civil Rights?

I estimate the civil rights issue space in the 91st Congress (1969–70) through the 108th Congress (2003–04). For technical details regarding the estimation process, which is computationally intensive, please see Appendix 1. The estimation is based on the civil rights votes of House members during these Congresses. These civil rights ideological positions are comparable across time periods and vary over time for legislators who serve over multiple Congresses. For instance, if a legislator serving in the 102nd Congress continues to serve in the 103rd and 104th, we can examine the estimate of her ideological location in the civil rights issue space to determine if she became more liberal or more conservative when voting on civil rights. I estimate all legislators' positions on a scale on which negative indicates more liberal positions on civil rights and positive numbers indicate more conservative positions on civil rights. The canonical measures of legislator ideology, Poole and Rosenthal's (1997) DW-NOMINATE scores, have been used in prior studies, as have LCCR scores. Whereas DW-NOMINATE scores are comparable over time, they are constrained by a linear trend. As Shawn Treier (2006, 6) notes, this linear trend "restriction would be inappropriate for testing whether or not a congressman alters his position in a given year" and makes assessments of change between just two Congresses nearly impossible (also see Garretson 2009). Furthermore, DW-NOMINATE scores measure general ideology and not civil rights. The other measures typically used by scholars examining racial redistricting and ideological change are LCCR scores, but they are not comparable over time.

My ability to make across-time comparisons of legislative roll-call voting records relies on assumptions similar to the extant work measuring ideal point estimates over time. The technique described in Appendix 1 for placing all legislators on the same civil-rights ideological scale over time is similar to the techniques used in other work that scales raw roll-call data into legislator preference estimates based on assumptions about certain actors' or roll-call locations on the underlying scale in order to identify the space (e.g., Bailey 2007; Bertelli and Grose 2006, 2009; Clinton, Jackman, and Rivers 2004; Martin and Quinn 2002; Poole and Rosenthal 1997; Treier 2006).

Thus, I am able to assess whether the positions of legislators change over time. If maximizing black-majority districts in 1992 led to more conservative aggregate policy outcomes on civil rights in the legislature or if maximizing black-majority districts in 1992 led to more liberal aggregate policy outcomes, we can examine whether (1) the location of the median House member; and (2) the distribution of legislator preferences on civil rights has changed between the 102nd, 103rd, and 104th Congresses (and all other Congresses between 1969 and 2004 as well).

The 102nd (1991–92), 103rd (1993–94), and 104th (1995–96) Congresses present natural experiments to assess the importance of racial gerrymandering on aggregate civil rights outcomes in the U.S. House. The 102nd Congress (1991–92) was controlled by Democrats, but the new majority-minority districts required by the voting rights extension to Section 5 "covered" – and mostly southern – states had yet to be drawn. The 103rd Congress (1993–94) was also controlled by Democrats, but a number of states now had legislators elected from more black-majority districts following redistricting in 1992. For the 103rd Congress, ten states saw an increase in the number of black-majority districts, and all but two of these were below the Mason-Dixon line (Alabama, Florida, Georgia, Louisiana, Maryland, New York, North Carolina, Pennsylvania, South Carolina, Texas, and Virginia). The 104th Congress (1995–96) was controlled by Republicans and still retained numerous black-majority districts in covered states.[4] Thus, by examining the ideological locations of members of Congress during these Congresses, a natural experiment can be conducted to assess whether the legislators' preferences on civil rights in the aggregate legislature shifted dramatically. I also examine the 91st through 108th Congresses (1969–2004) broadly to provide baseline comparisons for pre-1992 Congresses when majority-minority districting was not required in any states.

---

[4] As noted in Chapter 2, beginning with the 105th Congress, black-majority districts were reduced in a number of states due to court order. By the logic of those claiming majority-minority districting leads to more conservative aggregate policy outcomes, we may expect to see more liberal aggregate records starting in the 105th Congress. If my minimal effects argument holds, though, we should expect to see little meaningful aggregate shifts in the 105th Congress and later as well.

Has the Civil Rights Policy Space in Congress Changed Over Time?

Table 3.2 displays the location of the median House member along this civil rights dimension over time. To create Table 3.2, I arranged all the House members in each Congress by the order of their civil rights ideal point estimates. The ideal point estimates, and the names associated with them, are those that are the median value preference point estimate in that specific Congress. The range of ideal point estimates for all legislators serving during this time is from about -2 (very liberal) to the +2 (very conservative).

Statistically, the position of the median – or middle, decisive legislator – has not changed between the 1969–70 session of Congress and the 2003–04 session of Congress. The point estimates of the median House member on civil rights vary slightly, with these point estimates becoming slightly more conservative over time (but given the uncertainty estimates, these slight variations in point estimates are not statistically meaningful).

For instance, in the first Congress studied, the 91st Congress, the median legislator (Rep. John Erlenborn, R-NY) is located at 0.014, which is a moderate position as the estimates range from approximately -2 to +2. Jumping ahead ten years, the median ideal point estimate is -0.059 (Rep. Tim Carter, R-KY), which is approximately the same value as Erlenborn's preference estimate in the 91st Congress (based on the uncertainty estimates in parentheses). Again, looking at Table 3.2, this moderate position persists into the 1980s, 1990s, and 2000s. In the 100th Congress, for instance, Tim Penny's (D-MN) preference estimate is -0.089, whereas in the 107th Congress, the median's preference point estimate is 0.220 (Chris Shays, R-CT). In general, the point estimates from the 91st through 106th Congresses fall within a narrow and moderate range of -0.2 and 0.2, whereas they shift to become slightly more positive in the latter Congresses (e.g., with the median in the 108th Congress having an ideal point estimate of 0.311).

However, these are simply point estimates, and over the entire time period the median member of one Congress is statistically indistinguishable from other median members in other Congresses. This statistical indistinguishability is apparent through an examination of the uncertainty estimates displayed in Table 3.2 (in parentheses following the point estimates in the column labeled "median civil rights position").[5] Whereas

---

[5] These uncertainty estimates are the highest posterior density regions (HPD regions) displaying the 10% lower bound and the 90% upper bound of the distribution of MCMC iterations from which the point estimate was calculated. See Appendix 1 for more details.

TABLE 3.2. *Position of the Decisive Legislator (the Median Legislator) on Civil Rights Roll-Call Votes in Congress, 91st to 108th Congresses (1969–2004)*

Congress (years), Majority Control	# Districts > 50% Black	Median Civil Rights Position[a]	Name of Median Legislator
91st (1969–70), Dem	10[b]	0.014 [−0.23, 0.16]	John Erlenborn (R-NY)
93rd (1973–74), Dem	12	−0.030 [−0.29, 0.24]	Joseph Gaydos (D-PA)
94th (1975–76), Dem	12	−0.163 [−0.56, 0.22]	Samuel Stratton (D-NY)
95th (1977–78), Dem	12	−0.036 [−0.38, 0.26]	Clarence Long (D-MD)
96th (1979–80), Dem	12	−0.059 [−0.44, 0.21]	Tim Carter (R-KY)
97th (1981–82), Dem	17	0.077 [−0.18, 0.32]	Steve Neal (D-NC)
98th (1983–84), Dem	15	−0.170 [−0.52, 0.12]	Bill Alexander (D-AR)
99th (1985–86), Dem	16	−0.073 [−0.37, 0.21]	John Breaux (D-LA)
100th (1987–88), Dem	16	−0.089 [−0.39, 0.23]	Tim Penny (D-MN)
101st (1989–90), Dem	16	−0.054 [−0.26, 0.19]	John LaFalce (D-NY)
102nd (1991–92), Dem	17	−0.056 [−0.29, 0.16]	James Moran (D-VA)
103rd (1993–94), Dem	32	−0.088 [−0.28, 0.11]	James Barcia (D-MI)
104th (1995–96), GOP	32	0.138 [−0.02, 0.34]	Christopher Smith (R-NJ)
105th (1997–98), GOP	26	0.157 [0.02, 0.34]	Jack Quinn (R-NY)
106th (1999–2000), GOP	25	0.189 [0.01, 0.36]	John Sweeney (R-NY)
107th (2001–02), GOP	25	0.220 [0.04, 0.39]	Christopher Shays (R-CT)
108th (2003–04), GOP	25	0.311 [0.08, 0.53]	Jack Quinn (R-NY)

[a] The first value is the ideal point estimate, and the values in the parentheses are uncertainty estimates (HPD regions). Based on the uncertainty estimates, the median civil rights positions are statistically indistinguishable for all time periods.

[b] Data on the number of black-majority districts for the 91st Congress were unavailable, so the number of African-American members of Congress is included instead for this observation.

it appears there has been a very slight rightward shift in the ideological location of the floor median in Congress on civil rights issues, the uncertainty estimates reveal that there is no meaningful difference between the median over the entire time period examined. The substantive implication of this result is that civil rights floor outcomes have not changed much since the 1970s.

Because the median legislator can be pivotal for floor outcomes, these results suggest that (within a middle swath of legislators that is likely to include the median on any given roll call), there are not substantial differences in the kinds of policies adopted by the chamber for those bills that make it to the floor. Although contrary to the conventional wisdom, it is not necessarily surprising that civil rights median floor preferences have been so stable and moderate over this time period. Going back to the major pieces of civil rights bills in the 1960s (the Civil Rights Act in 1964 and the initial passage of the Voting Rights Act in 1965), the biggest blockade to passage had been the Senate in which a supermajority is needed to end a filibuster. On the floor of the House, though, a simple majority of House members is needed to pass legislation. A coalition of House liberals, moderate Democrats, and moderate Republicans formed on the floor to support some civil rights bills during the period examined in Table 3.2. This floor coalition was evident on major pieces of legislation, such as the 1982 extension of the Voting Rights Act (Thernstrom 1987). This coalition of liberal Democrats and moderates of both parties has persisted into the 1990s and 2000s as well. The 1991 Civil Rights Act was passed with most Democrats and some moderate Republicans, whereas the 2006 extension to the Voting Rights Act was passed with a coalition of Democrats and Republicans.[6]

The Relative Unimportance of the South for Civil Rights Floor Outcomes in the House

The median legislator has regularly been a moderate legislator from states outside of the U.S. South and typically from states where racial gerrymandering has not occurred. Based simply on the examination of the point estimates in Table 3.2, with the exception of 1981–86 and 1993–94 (when Steve Neal of North Carolina, Bill Alexander of Arkansas, John

---

[6] The motives of some Republicans on the 1982 and 2006 extensions may have been to support the legislation with the hope that black-majority districts would be drawn that would "bleach" surrounding districts.

Breaux of Louisiana, and Jim Moran of Virginia were the median legislators on civil rights), the median legislator on civil rights is someone from a northern state without the demographic possibility for racial gerrymandering. Northeastern moderates like John Sweeney (R-NY) and Jack Quinn (R-NY) show up as the decisive legislator on civil rights in Table 3.2. Again, these nonsouthern legislators (Sweeney and Quinn hail from upstate New York) are the ones who are most likely to be decisive on civil rights votes that reach the floor. No gerrymandering based on race is required in their states' regions. Because there are many districts like Sweeney's and Quinn's that cannot be racially gerrymandered, either due to demographic constraints (because the population is heavily white) or due to lack of Section 5 Voting Rights Act coverage (Sweeney's and Quinn's districts are not covered by Section 5 of the Voting Rights Act), racial gerrymandering turns out to have a relatively minimal impact on median civil rights policy outcomes on the floor of the U.S. House.

The implication of these findings is that a legislator like Quinn is likely to be more important in recent Congresses when it comes to the final outcomes of civil rights floor votes than any member of, for instance, the North Carolina congressional delegation. Even though western New York congressional districts were never under litigation due to voting rights, his ideological position on civil rights proves critical in two recent Congresses (the 105th, 1997–98; and the 108th, 2003–04). Quinn is a moderate Republican who served in Congress from 1992 to 2004 and who represented Buffalo, New York, congressional district. His district has been overwhelmingly white during his entire tenure (his district's black population was never higher than 17 percent). The bulk of the district's constituents are pro-union white ethnics who are economically liberal and socially moderate to conservative. Quinn regularly cast some votes with Democrats and others with Republicans, including civil rights votes. He invited civil rights hero and Congressman John Lewis (D-GA) to speak in his district in 1998, and Lewis described Quinn as a "good friend."[7] His record is one of semi-frequent support of civil rights, and this record has nothing to do with racial gerrymandering in his district or surrounding districts.

I offer this example of Quinn, not to suggest that he was the individually most powerful member of Congress or to suggest definitively that he was the median legislator, but simply to motivate the results of Table 3.2.

[7] Robert J. McCarthy, "Rights Figure Says 'Agitating' is Necessary for Today's Issues." *Buffalo News* 23 June 1998.

Of course, the floor medians' ideological locations displayed in Table 3.2 are simply *estimates* that these legislators are the 218th decisive legislator. I do not claim that these legislators are the "true" or decisive floor medians on every single vote on civil rights. Being the median legislator based on these revealed preference estimates does not guarantee that this legislator is on the winning side of every single roll call in the House, nor necessarily the median legislator on every individual roll call.[8] What these estimates mean is that, probabilistically, these members have a very high chance of providing the decisive vote on many roll calls, though other members also near the center of the distribution of ideal point estimates will also have a good chance of being decisive as well. An additional estimation of which legislators had the highest probabilities of being the floor median (not presented here) revealed that most legislators likely to be the median were not southern.

Moving past the discussion of the floor median, the preference estimates on civil rights roll calls provide evidence regarding the location of other, nonmedian members of the House. Members of the House serving in the 1990s and 2000s can be compared on the same scale to legislators who served in earlier eras. Perhaps surprising to some, there are a few House members in the 1990s who were about as conservative on civil rights as segregationist members who served in Congress during the late 1960s and early 1970s. Due to space limitations, I do not include the civil rights ideal point estimates for every legislator in the text. These point estimates are available on my Web site.

Based on this evidence, the extensive debate over the efficacy of majority-minority districts on civil rights policy outcomes may be overstated. Whether districting plans maximize black populations in a handful of black-majority districts or whether districting plans spread black voters out in a number of black-influence districts has little bearing on the location of the most pivotal member's revealed preference on the floor of the House. Looking specifically at the 102nd (1991–92), 103rd (1993–94), and 104th (1995–96) Congresses, in which the natural experiment of an increase in black-majority districting (from the 102nd to 103rd) and a change in partisan control (from the 103rd to 104th) occurred, we can

---

[8] For instance, in Table 3.1, John LaFalce (D-NY) is the estimated median in the 101st Congress. Yet an amendment he introduced to the civil rights bill that was passed during that session was defeated (Hutchings 1998). However, LaFalce was on the winning side in many other roll calls during that session – and his role as a self-described centrist on civil rights was well known to civil rights advocates and Democrats who tried to first work with him, and then around him, in order to defeat his amendment to the civil rights bill.

draw some conclusions. The location of the House median in these three Congresses is not dramatically different. Even when we examine a situation in which Republicans controlled the legislature under a scenario with numerous black-majority districts (the 104th Congress), the median legislator in Congress as a whole has only slightly become more conservative on civil rights based on the point estimates displayed in Table 3.2 – and this median legislator is statistically indistinguishable from the median legislator in the Democratically controlled 103rd Congress (1993–94) based on the uncertainty estimates in Table 3.2.

Examining the distributions of legislators' ideological locations between the 103rd and 104th Congresses (not displayed) does reveal what most scholars have already noted – that the number (and density) of conservative legislators increased. However, the density of legislators hovering near the middle of the scale during the 104th Congress is also quite large. Thus, whereas it is possible that conservative Republicans may have been elected to the 104th Congress because of "bleached" districts in some southern states, the median legislator on civil rights remained moderate. Remarkably, the ideological location of legislators on civil rights has only marginally changed between the early 1970s and the present day – and regardless of whether black-influence districts or majority-black districts predominate – and regardless of whether Republicans or Democrats control the House.

Civil Rights Ideological Shifts in State Delegations Due to Racial Redistricting

Although racial redistricting was not responsible for a shift in civil rights ideological locations on the floor of the House, it may have been a factor in changes in legislator preferences in specific state delegations. Thus, I also examine how and whether civil rights preference change occurred in a variety of individual state delegations. This section again focuses on the 102nd through 104th Congresses due to the natural experiment embedded in these three Congresses.

Figure 3.1 shows the median civil rights ideal point estimates for a selection of six southern and border states. Four of these states – Alabama, Georgia, North Carolina, and Virginia – are represented in the figure by dashed lines and had an increase in the number of black-majority districts in the 103rd Congress.[9] Alabama and Virginia added one new

---

[9] I choose these states as they are representative of the southern states that added black-majority districts in 1992.

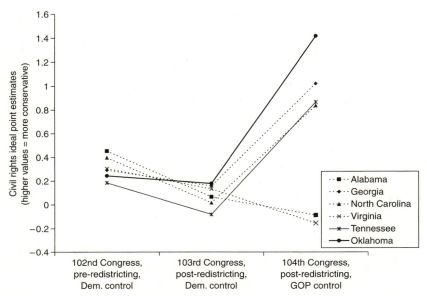

FIGURE 3.1. Shifts in civil rights policy preferences in selected state delegations.

black-majority district each, while North Carolina and Georgia added two new black-majority districts each. In all four states, the median member of each state delegation shifted leftward on civil rights from the 102nd to the 103rd Congresses, though these shifts were small. However, in North Carolina and Georgia in the 104th Congress, the median in each state delegation became much more conservative on civil rights as Republicans replaced more moderate-to-liberal white Democrats in the districts that were "bleached" surrounding newly drawn black-majority districts. This evidence implies that racial redistricting did have an effect on a rightward shift in legislator preferences in these two states (supporting Lublin and Voss 2003). Interestingly though, in Alabama and Virginia, civil rights preferences continued to move slightly leftward even in the 104th Congress, suggesting that racial redistricting in these states may have improved black substantive representation within these state delegations (supporting Shotts 2003a).

In Figure 3.1, as a comparison, I also show the shift in the median civil rights preferences in the state delegations of Tennessee and Oklahoma. Neither of these states redrew their congressional districts to add black-majority districts in 1992 (though Tennessee retained one black-majority district in the Memphis area). The shifts in their state delegations on

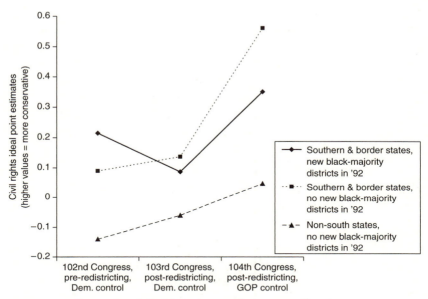

FIGURE 3.2. Increasing civil rights conservatism across all regions.

civil rights are strikingly similar to the shifts seen in North Carolina and Georgia. This would imply that the shifts in North Carolina and Georgia are attributable less to racial redistricting and more to the realignment among whites that occurred in all southern states.

To pursue this point further, I examine the mean value of state delegation ideal point estimates on civil rights in the entire country separated into three groups: (1) the southern and border states that added black-majority districts in 1992; (2) other southern and border states that did not add black-majority districts; and (3) nonsouthern states.[10] As is apparent in Figure 3.2, state delegations in the South became more conservative in the 104th Congress, regardless of whether the states increased the number of black-majority districts. Outside of the South, state delegation civil rights preferences shifted rightward as well, though to a much smaller extent than in southern states. The results displayed in Figure 3.2 provide some limited evidence that racial redistricting moved policy preferences in southern states in a more conservative direction, but it is difficult to disentangle the extent that this was

[10] I first calculated the state delegation median in each state and then took the mean of these values for each of the three groups.

due primarily to redistricting or due to the realignment of southern white voters toward the Republican party. Interestingly, in the southern states where black-majority districts were increased, the move toward conservatism was smaller than in other southern states. This suggests southern realignment toward the Republican party played the greatest role in shifting southern legislative civil rights ideological estimates to the right. Finally, whereas state delegations may have shifted their ideological positions, in the aggregate, they had little overall impact (recall Table 3.2).[11]

Political Parties, Agenda Setting, and Civil Rights Voting Records in Congress

In terms of voting on the floor of the U.S. House and the location of the median legislator, racial redistricting has clearly had a minimal impact. However, Gary Cox and Matthew McCubbins (2005), among others, have argued that the party median is responsible for setting the agenda. Whereas the floor median is dominant for legislation that has reached the floor, legislation may never reach the floor if the party median does not favor it. In the 109th Congress (2005–06), there was an informal rule used by then-Speaker Dennis Hastert (R-IL) and the majority party leadership to not bring a bill up for a vote on the floor of the House if a "majority of the majority" party does not want the bill brought up. Thus, the decisive legislator within the majority party – the majority party median – is important for deciding what bills may or may not be considered on the floor.

Table 3.3 shows the location of the majority party median preference on civil rights from 1969–2004. In the Congresses examined in Table 3.3, the Democrats controlled the House from the 91st Congress (1969–70) to the 103rd Congress (1993–94), and the Republicans were the majority party since the 104th Congress (1995–96). As shown in the table, the location of the majority party median has moved with the change in partisan control following the 1994 elections. An implication is that electing Democrats is very important for setting the agenda on civil rights, given the locations of the Republican party medians since 1995 when the Republicans took control of the chamber. Interestingly, the Democratic majority party medians are statistically indistinguishable

---

[11] The mean of the state delegation median obscures the fact that many of the largest states (e.g., California and New York) have many liberal members.

TABLE 3.3. *Position of the Decisive Legislator within the Majority Party Caucus (the Democratic Median Legislator from 91st to 103rd Congresses and the Republican Median Legislator from 104th to 107th Congresses)*

Congress (years), Majority Control	# Districts > 50% Black	Majority Party Median Civil Rights Position[a]	Name of Majority Party Median Legislator
91st (1969–70), Dem	10[b]	−0.588 [−0.82, −0.26]	Gus Yatron (D-PA)
93rd (1973–74), Dem	12	−0.424 [−0.64, −0.09]	Charles Carney (D-OH)
94th (1975–76), Dem	12	−0.575 [−1.01, 0.00]	Robert Mollohan (D-WV)
95th (1977–78), Dem	12	−0.523 [−0.89, −0.14]	Les AuCoin (D-OR)
96th (1979–80), Dem	12	−0.556 [−0.96, −0.02]	Samuel Stratton (D-NY)
97th (1981–82), Dem	17	−0.626 [−0.96, −0.27]	Frank Annunzio (D-IL)
98th (1983–84), Dem	15	−0.702 [−1.06, −0.24]	Mike Synar (D-OK)
99th (1985–86), Dem	16	−0.990 [−1.53, −0.13]	Les Aspin (D-WI)
100th (1987–88), Dem	16	−1.043 [−2.10, −0.12]	Kika de la Garza (D-TX)
101st (1989–90), Dem	16	−0.708 [−1.61, −0.11]	Nick Mavroules (D-MA)
102nd (1991–92), Dem	17	−0.711 [−1.17, −0.26]	Frank McCloskey (D-IN)
103rd (1993–94), Dem	32	−0.683 [−1.03, −0.28]	James Bacchus (D-FL)
104th (1995–96), GOP	32	0.907 [0.44, 1.26]	Tom Bliley (R-VA)
105th (1997–98), GOP	26	0.976 [0.72, 1.26]	Joe Barton (R-TX)
106th (1999–2000), GOP	25	1.008 [0.63, 1.45]	Van Hilleary (R-TN)
107th (2001–02), GOP	25	0.996 [0.38, 1.39]	Ed Schrock (R-VA)
108th (2003–04), GOP	25	1.063 [0.60, 1.47]	Stevan Pearce (R-NM)

[a] The first value is the ideal point estimate, and the values in the parentheses are uncertainty estimates (HPD regions). Comparing the period of Republican control (104th–108th Congress) to the period of Democratic control (91st–103rd Congresses), the civil rights positions are statistically distinct. However, within these specific time periods, they are indistinguishable.

[b] Data on the number of black-majority districts for the 91st Congress were unavailable, so the number of African-American members of Congress is included instead for this observation.

from one another during the entire time period. Also, each Republican majority party median is statistically similar to the other GOP medians. However, the Democratic majority party medians and the Republican majority party medians are distinct, and this has important implications for agenda setting.

Whereas the redistricting based on race in 1992 had no impact on the location of the floor median, racial redistricting correlates with the change in the location of the majority party median (the decisive legislator for agenda setting). Based on Table 3.3, we cannot yet reject the claim that racial redistricting increases in 1992 led to the shift in the location of the party median. However, Table 3.3 also does not provide enough evidence to confirm that racial redistricting caused the conservative shift of the majority party median.

Counterfactual Analysis

What would have happened if there was no new racial redistricting in 1992? What if the same southern members of Congress from racial-redistricting states elected in 1990 to the 102nd Congress remained in office in the 103rd and 104th Congresses? Would the party median not have shifted so dramatically? We can assess what would have happened had the southern and border states required to draw additional black-majority districts for the 1992 elections *not* drawn those districts and the same members of Congress serving in these states in the 102nd Congress continued to serve in the 103rd and 104th Congresses.

To do this, I conduct a counterfactual analysis. I take the civil rights ideal point estimates for the 102nd Congress, the 103rd Congress, and the 104th Congress, but replace the values from the 103rd and 104th Congresses with those legislators' ideal point estimates from the 102nd Congress in only those states that increased the number of black-majority districts for the 1992 elections. In the counterfactual analysis, I assume that those states with increases in black-majority districts beginning with the 1992 elections instead retained the same state delegation from the 102nd Congress for the 103rd Congress and 104th Congress. For instance, in the case of South Carolina, this assumes no black-majority district was added and all districts remained majority-white as they had been during the 102nd Congress (e.g., white Democrat Robin Tallon still represented the white-majority sixth district instead of black Democrat Jim Clyburn representing a black-majority sixth district). The idea is that had the same legislators from the 102nd Congress not been forced to run in reconfigured districts (or not have been forced to retire due to recon-figured districts), then it is unlikely the legislator ideology estimates in these states would have shifted much. This means, for instance, in states like North Carolina and Georgia, there would have been few "bleached" heavily white districts from which conservative Republicans would have made gains.

Given that members of Congress do not shift their ideologies substan-tially over time (Poole and Rosenthal 1997) and that the civil rights esti-mates are comparable over time, it is not an unreasonable assumption.[12] If critics of racial redistricting are correct, the counterfactual analysis should yield more moderate or liberal ideology estimates for pivotal congressional actors than the actual estimates displayed in Table 3.2 and Table 3.3. If my argument that racial redistricting results in mini-mal effects on aggregate policy change is correct, then there will be little difference between the counterfactual and actual estimates.

Figure 3.3 shows the "actual" values of the floor medians and party medians across the 102nd, 103rd, and 104th Congresses (these are the same values displayed in Tables 3.2 and 3.3). The actual floor median is indicated by the solid line with diamonds, and the actual majority party median is indicated by the solid line with triangles. Figure 3.3 also displays the counterfactual values of the floor median and majority party median as if no new black-majority districts were added for the 103rd Congress. In states with no increase in black-majority districts, I use the actual ideal point estimates of civil rights voting in each congress, but the states with new black-majority districts after 1992 are replaced by their state delegation's ideal point estimates from the 102nd Congress for the 103rd and 104th Congresses.[13] The counterfactual floor median is indicated with

---

[12] It is of course a strong assumption, as even if districts were not changed before and after 1992, it is likely that some of the legislators serving in the 102nd Congress may have lost in either 1992 or 1994. Of course, given the GOP sweep that occurred in 1994, especially in the southern states in which the counterfactual analysis is conducted, any losses likely would have been Democrats replaced by conservative Republicans. Thus, the counterfactual analysis is, if anything, biased in favor of finding differences between the counterfactual and the actual preference data. If I do not find differences, we can feel comfortable that the aggregate policy effect of racial redistricting was minimal.

[13] I do not include New York and Pennsylvania in the counterfactual analysis because, whereas they both added a black-majority district, as I discussed earlier, the dilutive effect of racial redistricting has only been alleged in southern states (Lublin 1997). The addi-tional black-majority district in New York was in New York City, where nonblack voters in surrounding districts are overwhelmingly Democratic. Similarly, the newly drawn 1992 black-majority district in Pennsylvania is in Philadelphia (represented by white Democrat Bob Brady in 1992), where the white voters are also overwhelmingly Democratic.

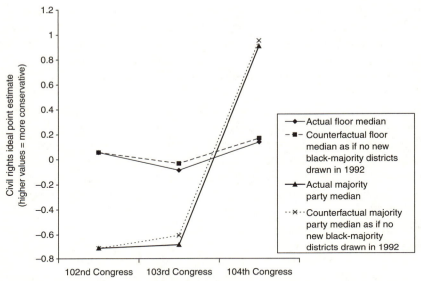

FIGURE 3.3. What if no black-majority districts were drawn in the South in 1992?

a dashed line and squares, whereas the counterfactual party median is indicated with a dashed line and an "x" for each time period.

It is clear from Figure 3.3 that there are minimal differences between the counterfactual and the actual values for the floor and party medians. Had adding black-majority districts in 1992 in a number of southern states led to more conservative shifts in civil rights policy in Congress, then the counterfactual floor and party medians would be to the left of the actual values. Instead, the counterfactual floor median (a Congress with no new black-majority districts) is just barely to the right of the actual floor median (a Congress with new black-majority districts) in both the 103rd and 104th Congresses. The same is true for the majority party median. This rejects the argument that has become conventional wisdom that the maximization of black-majority districts led to a meaningful conservative shift in civil rights policy preferences in the aggregate in Congress.

Did the Creation of Black-Majority Districts in 1992
Give the House to Republicans?

Now that I have provided evidence to show (1) that the floor median did not shift due to racial redistricting; and (2) that aggregate shifts in the location of the majority party median are not the direct result of racial redistricting, the only remaining possible harmful effect of black-majority districts on roll-call outcomes in the U.S. House would be on agenda setting due to party control of the chamber (Rohde 1991; Cox and McCubbins 2005; Sinclair 2000). Even though, based on the counterfactual analysis in Figure 3.3, racial redistricting did not cause a direct shift in the location of the party median, it is possible that racial redistricting could have indirectly affected the location of the party median by causing the Republicans to take over the House in 1994. Because Republican members of Congress tend not to vote in the interests of African Americans (Cameron et al.1996; Swain 1995), it is possible that majority-minority districts may still be a bane for aggregate minority substantive representation.

The conventional wisdom is that racial redistricting in the South helped lead to these Republican gains in Congress during the 1990s. However, if the Republicans picked up only a few seats in a handful of southern states that had increases in black-majority districts, this does not necessarily mean that party control of the chamber would shift. To assess this question, I compare Democratic House seat losses potentially attributable to racial redistricting to Democratic House seat losses attributable to other factors in Figure 3.4. The top of this figure shows the number of seats in the House that the Democrats lost between the 102nd Congress and the 104th Congress in the southern states that were required to draw at least one additional black-majority district.[14] Thirteen seats changed hands from the Democrats to the Republicans, which is not an inconsequential gain for the Republicans. This does not presume that all thirteen of these Democratic seat losses are directly attributable to the new black-majority districting, but it suggests a ceiling on the number of districts that could have been lost by the Democrats in these southern states that added black-majority districts in 1992.

Is it possible that a shift of thirteen seats swung party control in the U.S. House to the Republicans? By itself, this thirteen-seat shift away from the Democrats would not have been decisive. If these were the only seats the Democrats lost between the 102nd and 104th Congresses, the Democrats would have still maintained a large majority in the House. In

---

[14] As mentioned earlier, in this chapter I use the phrase 'southern states' to include southern and border states below the Mason-Dixon line. The states in the South that had an increase of at least one black-majority district in 1992 are Alabama, Florida, Georgia, Louisiana, Maryland, North Carolina, South Carolina, Texas, and Virginia.

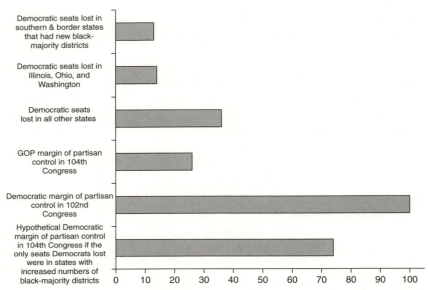

FIGURE 3.4. The small effect of black-majority districting on the Republican takeover in 1994.

fact, Democratic losses were much greater in a number of other states, both in the South and outside of the South, where there was no racial redistricting increase in 1992.

For example, in Figure 3.4, I show the Democratic seat losses in three arbitrary non-southern states, Illinois, Ohio, and Washington. In these three states, no new black-majority districts were drawn. Yet the Democrats lost fourteen seats (one more than the thirteen lost in new-black-majority districted southern states) in these three states between the 102nd and 104th Congresses, due to partisan gerrymandering and the massive Republican tidal wave that swept over the entire country in 1994.

Much as the shifts in the aggregate ideal point estimates on civil rights in recent congresses are dominated *not* by southern members of Congress in states with increases in black-majority districts but by other legislators, so was the GOP takeover of the House in 1994. Whereas the Democrats lost thirteen seats in southern and border states that increased the number of black-majority districts in their 1992 redistricting plans (Alabama, Florida, Georgia, Louisiana, Maryland, North Carolina, South Carolina, Texas, and Virginia), more than forty-five Democratic seats were lost in states in which black-majority districting did not increase or was not even an option. Had only the thirteen seats in states with increases in black-majority districts changed from the Democratic to Republican party, the Democrats still would have controlled the House after the 1994 elections (as can be seen at the bottom of Figure 3.4).

I am not the first to point out that the number of Democratic seats lost due to racial redistricting was relatively small (e.g., Bullock 1995; Engstrom 1995; Hill 1995; McKee 2004, 13). This is not to say that racial gerrymandering imperatives in states like Georgia and North Carolina did not increase Republican gains in those specific states. North Carolina lost three Democratic seats between the 102nd and 104th Congresses, while Georgia lost five Democratic seats during the same period (Whitby 1997). However, to claim that the Democratic losses in these states led to the Republican takeover of the U.S. House seems misplaced given the huge majority that the Democrats had controlled in the Congresses prior to 1994. In the 102nd Congress, Democrats maintained a one-hundred-seat majority. The Democratic margin of control of the House would have been by an impressive seventy-four seats (see Figure 3.4) in the 104th Congress if only these thirteen districts in southern states with new black-majority districts had switched parties. The bulk of the blame for the GOP takeover – and thus the shift in the party median to the right in the 104th Congress (see Table 3.3) – is attributable to the Republican sweep in states that did not have an increase in black-majority districts.

Summary: Racial Redistricting in 1992 and Aggregate Policy Outcomes in the U.S. House

Given all of this evidence, a conclusion is in order. The maximization of racial redistricting in 1992 had no direct effect on the shift of the floor median or the party median on civil rights policies in the U.S. House, and it had no decisive effect on the shift in party control to the Republicans in 1994. Whereas the racial redistricting was likely important for the loss of Democratic seats in a few states, enough seats were not lost in these states to shift the House to the Republican party (see Figure 3.4). The credit for the Republican takeover of the U.S. House in 1994 does not lie at the feet of racial redistricting. Instead, it is due to the massive shifts in Republican support in both the South and the non-South in the mid-1990s.

What this means for racial redistricting and the U.S. Congress is the following: The alleged dilution in roll-call voting due to racial gerrymandering is wildly overstated. Therefore, substantive representation in the aggregate is not reduced by the drawing of black-majority districts, and it is not reduced by the election of African-American legislators.

What About at the District Level? Does Party or Race Matter More?

Having established that the decisive legislator among the 435 voting on the floor of the U.S. House on civil rights has not changed and that racial redistricting has a relatively minimal impact on changes in the majority party median and partisan control in the House, we should also examine the dynamics of voting at the level of the individual legislator. Do the four factors specified in the theory laid out in Chapter 2 have an impact on roll-call voting records on civil rights? Does the district black population, the race of the legislator, the party of the legislator, or racial trust (the interaction of the district black population and the race of the legislator) have an impact on individual legislator's roll calls on civil rights? If so, which is more important? This question, although addressed many times previously, has not sufficiently been answered due to a thorny methodological problem. The two key factors – race of legislator and district black population – have been so highly correlated with one another because almost all black legislators were elected from black-majority districts that scholars have been unable to examine both factors at the same time (see the discussion in Chapter 2).

With the court-ordered redistricting that occurred in the 1990s, we can use mid-to-late-1990s congressional districts to finally assess these questions. Thus, I examine the impact of these four variables on civil rights voting records (LCCR scores) in the 104th through 106th Congresses (1995–2000). I only look at this short time period, as this is the era when African-American legislators were most frequently elected in white-majority districts thus allowing the inclusion of both a race of legislator variable and a district black population variable in the analysis of individual-level roll-call vote outcomes. To be consistent with the past work on this topic, I use LCCR scores ranging from 0 to 100 in this portion of the analysis, where a 100 means a 100 percent pro-civil rights voting record and a 0 means a 0 percent pro-civil rights voting record.

In other work (Grose 2005), I estimated a statistical model predicting LCCR scores. Based on this model, I have been able to determine the effect of race and party on civil rights voting records at the level of the individual legislator, and I summarize these results in Table 3.4. Table 3.4 assesses the impact of black-majority districts, black legislators,

TABLE 3.4. *The Effect of Both Race and Party on Individual Civil Rights Voting Records*

	Percentage-Point Increase in Pro-Civil Rights Record (Using LCCR Score, 0 to 100% Scale)
Effect of change from 0% black district population to 50% black district population	+22
Effect of change from nonblack to black legislator	+5
Effect of change from Republican to Democratic legislator	+55

Note: These are predicted values based on estimates from an OLS model of LCCR scores, including variables for party, race of legislator, district black population, and other control variables.

and Democratic legislators on civil rights voting records.[15] Civil rights records are 22 percentage points more pro-civil rights if a legislator represents a 50 percent black district compared to a district with a 0 percent black population, which is substantively significant. The effect of race, though, is quite small. When controlling for the district black population and the party of the legislator (and other factors), black legislators are only about 5 percentage points more pro-civil rights in their individual civil rights voting records than are nonblack legislators. However, the effect of political party is quite important. Democratic legislators have much stronger civil rights records than Republicans: A district with a Democratic legislator, all else equal, compared to a Republican legislator results in a civil rights voting record that is 55 percentage points higher. Though not shown here, racial trust (the interaction of district black population and the race of the legislator) had no impact on civil rights voting records at the individual district level.

The implications of this individual-level analysis are clear. Unlike some scholars, even when variables for the district black population and party are included, I find that the presence of an African-American legislator leads to statistically significantly greater substantive representation of

[15] The figures are predictive values based on a regression model of LCCR scores, where I control for both the race of the legislator, the district black population, and party (all three variables are statistically significant predictors of LCCR scores). For the regression model, see Grose (2005). An interaction variable for racial trust was statistically insignificant, so it was not modeled here.

black constituents via roll-call voting. However, the substantive impact is quite minimal. A trade-off between electing African Americans and electing Democrats exists at the individual district level, as many have shown. The substantive impact of having a Democrat in office is much more important than having a black legislator for increasing the individual-district level substantive representation of African Americans via roll-call voting. This finding echoes many other arguments (e.g., Lublin 1997 and Swain 1995), but no one has ever reached this conclusion analyzing all relevant factors at the same time.

Further, it critiques the work of Katherine Tate (2003), David Canon (1999), Kerry Haynie (2001), and Kenny Whitby (1997), who suggest that the race of the legislator is a critical predictor of policy outcomes. It is a predictor, but it is clearly the least important predictor of civil rights votes. The district black population and particularly political party have much greater effects on individual civil rights voting records (though these scholars also note the importance of party).[16]

Implications for the Future of Majority-Minority Districts

The aggregate implications of the district-level analysis are that districting plans that maximize the number of Democrats, regardless of race or the black population of each district, are the best for achieving substantive representation. Unlike previous work, I was able to estimate all relevant factors in one statistical model. Thus, we can safely conclude that both (1) electing black legislators; and (2) having districts with large black populations does *statistically* significantly affect legislator ideology separate from the effect of political party. However, the *substantive* effect of these two variables is simply much smaller than the effect of party.

Finding that party is the most important predictor of roll-call voting does not offer any surprising refutation of past literature on the subject, though. Thus, if the maximization of legislators with higher pro-civil rights roll-call scores are the preferred measures of substantive representation, then the "best" districting arrangement is one that elects Democrats first (regardless of race) and then possibly black Democrats as well (see Lublin 1997; Swain 1995; Whitby 1997). The aggregate analyses of civil

---

[16] One caveat regarding these results is in order. Because of the observational equivalence of two of the variables (black legislator and district black population) prior to the 1990s, it is not possible to estimate a model with both variables in earlier time periods with any confidence. However, it is theoretically possible that the race of the legislator played a much larger role in earlier time periods than I find for the 1995–2000 time period.

rights ideological estimates also suggest that a simple Democratic majority is more important than maximizing the number of Democratic-held
seats, and it also suggests that racial gerrymandering of any sort will have
little impact on shifting floor and party median preferences in Congress.

Further, and perhaps more importantly, the aggregate analysis of civil
rights voting records presents even more surprising – and perhaps dismal – findings for those concerned about enhancing the substantive representation of African Americans. The "best" districting arrangement may
be an ephemeral goal given demographic constraints present in states with
low minority populations: The aggregate civil rights outcomes in the U.S.
House will be dominated by legislators from districting plans in which
majority-minority gerrymanders are neither legally required nor demographically possible. Gerald Rosenberg (1991) argues that liberals and
others hoping for social change have misplaced their hopes in the Courts,
and specifically the U.S. Supreme Court. I argue that those hoping for roll-
call policy change via racial redistricting in Congress have also misplaced
hope in this electoral institution. The choice of districting schemes has
minimal impact on civil rights policy outcomes on the floor of the U.S.
House because there simply are not enough opportunities to draw U.S.
House districts to shift aggregate civil rights preferences. Those interested
in civil rights policy change via the U.S. Congress should focus on swaying
public opinion, especially in districts with few black voters represented by
moderates near the median of the House floor. Change may be more likely
via public opinion – which will be reflected by representatives in moderate
districts – than through the manipulation of district lines in a few states.
Because my analysis is limited to the U.S. Congress, it is still possible that
racial gerrymandering may have effects in state legislatures.

The effect of racial redistricting on the ideological positions of legislators in the aggregate may be overstated in previous work. If racial redistricting was responsible for the Republican takeover in the U.S. House in
1994 (Lublin and Voss 2003), then these majority-minority gerrymanders
hurt overall minority interests (given the majority party median positions). However, the evidence suggests that these districts had a limited
effect and were certainly not decisively responsible for the GOP takeover
of the House in 1994. Further, based on civil rights policy floor outcomes
alone (as measured by the position of the 218th decisive House member),
racially gerrymandered districts are not particularly harmful *or* beneficial.
These results imply that both critics and supporters of majority-minority
districts may be mistaken to suggest that civil rights outcomes are affected
by black-maximization districting schemes.

This research suggests that scholars' reliance on roll-call voting indices to measure substantive representation may not be the best way to get at substantive representation. Given that civil rights outcomes as measured by the position of the median legislator in Congress have not changed substantially under regimes of majority-minority gerrymanders and without these gerrymanders, we should look at other measures of substantive representation beyond roll-call voting to assess the benefits or harms of redistricting plans.

These results also have implications for legal scholarship in this area and court decisions regarding the constitutionality of majority-minority districts. As mentioned earlier, the Supreme Court endorsed the concept of black-influence or coalitional districts (I define influence or coalitional districts as districts with a 25 to 50 percent black population) in 2003. This court endorsement was based in part on research showing that redistricting plans drawing black-majority districts lead to aggregate policy outcomes harmful to African Americans. Many in the voting rights law community, though, have criticized this decision, suggesting that majority-minority districts may still be needed. For instance, Jocelyn Benson (2004) argued that *Georgia v. Ashcroft* was the impetus to push for stronger protections for majority-minority districts. Heather Gerken (2005, 1189) notes that the legal debate over *Georgia v. Ashcroft* centers on "the tradeoff between 'influence' and 'control.'" In 2006, Congress agreed with these scholars when they extended the Voting Rights Act. In the extension, a "fix" or override (Barnes 2004) was included that essentially nullified much of the court's ruling in *Ashcroft* and once again more strongly encouraged the drawing of black-majority districts. My findings suggest that African Americans' influence in specific districts does not trickle up to the aggregate legislature and that this trade-off may be much ado about nothing.

This analysis also offers a benchmark by which we can interpret what comes in the following chapters. In the remaining chapters, I analyze the effect of the party of the legislator, the race of the legislator, the district black population, and racial trust on project delivery and constituency service. It will be important to compare and contrast these results presented in this chapter (with legislator civil rights ideology as the dependent variable) with the results on activities beyond the vote. Only then can we have a full understanding of the impact of racial representation on congressional behavior.

4

Location, Location, Location

Delivering Constituency Service to African Americans

"The constituency service piece [of representation] is the most critical."

This comment is from a district staffer for a member of Congress who told me that a strong constituency service operation was the key to her legislator getting reelected. I asked her for some examples of constituency service that she, the staff, or the representative she worked for might engage in, and she detailed the "usual suspects": helping someone track down an errant social security check, assisting a constituent in procuring veteran's benefits, and the like. She also regaled me with some of the more exotic assistance her office has engaged in on behalf of the legislator's constituents over the years: hiring a private investigator to locate a constituent's stolen Boston Terrier; sending in a Medivac helicopter to a sick constituent honeymooning in Bermuda; and intervening on behalf of an eighteen-year-old constituent who got into some legal trouble in Jamaica. All in a day's work for a staffer who works hard answering all kinds of requests from constituents.

Later revealed in my conversation with her was that most of these stories she told of constituency service that went above and beyond the call of duty were for white constituents. The legislator she worked for was interested in assisting all constituents, regardless of race, in any way possible. However, the white constituents tended to contact the legislator as he was also white, whereas many black constituents contacted a nearby black member of Congress for assistance. Part of the problem may have been that the legislator's two district offices were located in predominantly white suburbs, where black constituents were less likely to walk into the office. Once the white member's staff realized this, they attempted to drum up support in black neighborhoods in his district: "We did everything but knock on people's doors and say 'What can we do for you today?'"

How common is this across other congressional districts? Do some legislators do a better job reaching black constituents with constituency service? Do black legislators engage in more service for black constituents than do white legislators? Democrats more than Republicans? What roles do the district's black population and racial trust between legislator and constituents play in a legislator's constituency service allocation decisions? These are the questions that will be examined in this chapter, and we will learn whether the election of African-American politicians has resulted in better constituency service delivered to African-American constituents.

One of the purported purposes of the Voting Rights Act and its extensions was to give both minority and white voters the right to cast effective ballots. By this, the assumption is that an elected official should be responsive to the demands of all constituents regardless of the racial backgrounds of these constituents: essentially to ensure that both black and white constituents have the same opportunity for their representatives to track down lost Boston Terriers or lost social security checks. Thus, constituency service is another way that the substantive representation of black constituents can be measured in Congress.

However, if legislators have different constituency bases of support, then we may expect that legislators will focus on different constituency groups in their districts when delivering service. As I detail in this chapter, the race of the legislator plays a key role in service allocation decisions in congressional districts. African-American legislators, all else being equal, are more likely to make decisions that enhance their ability to deliver constituency service to black constituents. The black population of the district and racial trust also play a role in constituency service allocation decisions to black constituents. The larger the black population in a district, the more likely a legislator will work to serve black constituents.

The party of the legislator is somewhat important, though as we will see, white Democrats and white Republicans do not always engage in substantially different levels of constituency service to their black constituents. However, on some (but not all) measures, Democrats reach black constituents via constituency service more than Republicans.

Constituency Service as Substantive Representation

As indicated in the previous chapter, the effect of a legislator's race on roll-call voting is rather small. However, roll-call outcomes are heavily influenced by the political party of the legislator and the party control of the chamber. Throughout this work, it has been my contention that legislative behavior "beyond the vote" is often a better indicator than roll-call voting for measuring the importance of electing black legislators and drawing black-majority districts on the substantive representation of black interests. Moreover, examining constituency service to black constituents can clearly be conceived of as substantive representation. What is constituency service? Bruce Cain, John Ferejohn, and Morris Fiorina (1987, 3) define it broadly as "service and allocation responsiveness." They continue by explaining that it is "an important means by which representatives earn personalized electoral support – votes based not on party membership or association with a particular government but on the individual identities and activities of the candidates." Robert Hopkins, district director for John Spratt (D-SC), remarked to me that constituency service was primarily engaging in casework for constituents, adding that "casework itself, for the most part, is a little bit of everything."

However defined, congressional scholars have long shown the importance of constituency service in terms of providing connections between legislator and constituents. In addition to Cain, Ferejohn, and Fiorina (1987), many scholars have examined the link between electoral factors and constituency service (Evans Yiannakis 1981; Fiorina 1981; Grose and Middlemass 2010; McAdams and Johannes 1988; Middlemass and Grose 2007; Serra and Cover 1992). Even though not all of these studies show a direct link between constituency service and electoral margins of incumbents, all agree that members of Congress *perceive* that constituency service has an effect on their chances for reelection. Thus, consistent with the theory in Chapters 1 and 2, I expect that certain legislators will have more of an incentive to reach black constituents with constituency service based on electoral factors.

Few scholars, though, have examined racial representation in Congress through the lens of constituency service. Two that have are Carol Swain (1995) and David Canon (1999). Swain (1995), in her in-depth analysis of nine black Democratic legislators and four white Democratic legislators, clearly considered constituency service as part of her conception of substantive representation, though it was not the centerpiece of her study.

Her findings indicated that white Democratic legislators were as good at constituency service to black constituents as were most black Democratic legislators. Canon (1999, 201–242) also considered constituency service and racial representation in the 103rd Congress, looking at measures such as the racial background of staff in Washington, racial content of members' newsletters, and other measures. Others have studied this topic outside of Congress: Thomas (1992) surveyed black and white city council members, finding that black elected officials are much more likely to report that it is important to serve minority constituents.

I assess constituency service in this chapter by examining where legislators choose to open their district offices and by analyzing what connections are made with African-American constituents via the location of these district offices (Canon 1999; Swain 1995). I examine these service allocation and presentation decisions through the lens of race. Are district offices located in predominately African-American neighborhoods, predominately white neighborhoods, or neighborhoods that are not predominately one race? Is there a link between descriptive representation (African-American legislators) and substantive representation (making service decisions that tangibly benefit African Americans)?

The Importance of Race: Helping Constituents in the District

As detailed in previous chapters, I am interested in examining the effects of race and party on the representation of black constituents. Legislators have more leeway in helping constituents via service than with roll-call voting. Thus, I expect that race will play an important role in constituency service decisions. Specifically, I expect the black population of the district to positively affect constituency service to African-American constituents. Members of Congress in districts with large black populations, due to electoral incentives, will be more likely to allocate service to black constituents. Second, black legislators, all else being equal, will be more likely than white legislators to make decisions regarding constituency service that favor black constituents (e.g., locating offices in predominately black neighborhoods).

Third, racial trust will be an important factor in constituency service allocation decisions. Many of the districts were redrawn by court orders in the mid-1990s. As a result, many districts represented by white legislators were substantially redrawn to include larger black constituencies. Additionally, many black legislators also faced redistricting that left them in districts with a much larger percentage of white voters (in most cases, a majority). Thus, given deficits of trust between black constituents and white legislators and between white legislators and black constituents, we may expect constituency service relationships to differ based on the interaction of the district's black population and the race of the legislator. It may be likely that white legislators representing black-influence districts, for example, are more likely to reach out to black voters in terms of constituency service, especially if they are not "representing" these voters to the same extent as black legislators via other means, such as roll-call voting. Similarly, black legislators representing white-majority districts may have more conservative voting records and thus may work more assiduously to reach black constituents via service than other black legislators from black-majority districts. Thus, we may expect that black legislators and white legislators will respond differently to districts with varying levels of black population.

Finally, party may affect the representation of black constituents via constituency service as well. As black voters are typically in Democrats' electoral coalitions and not in Republicans' coalitions, Democrats are more likely to hire black staff, locate offices in predominately black geographic areas, and present themselves to constituents in a way that is more likely to appeal to African-American voters.

Talking with Congressional Staff to Assess Constituency Service to African Americans

For the bulk of this chapter and the subsequent chapter, the analysis is qualitative. I conducted numerous interviews in the field, talking primarily to congressional staff who work in members' district offices. By focusing on staff in the districts and not in Washington, I was able to better measure how constituents are reached and thus how constituency service is conducted in the districts. I personally visited seventeen congressional districts in the U.S. South during the 106th and 107th Congresses (1999–2002). When scholars conduct field research, they are forced to limit their sample. Ideally, cases would be distributed across relevant explanatory variables, and a random sample of congressional districts could be visited and interviews conducted in each. However, given the costs involving travel to districts and the need for variation across key factors, I was forced to select a nonrandom sample with these key independent variables in mind: party of legislator, race of legislator, black population of the district, and racial trust (the interaction of race and district black population). I visited districts that included black Democratic legislators, white Democratic legislators, and white Republican legislators from a variety of district types (black-majority districts, black-influence districts, and low black population districts).

Other factors likely to explain constituency service to African-American constituents, such as legislator seniority and region, are controlled for by minimizing the variation of the sample across these dimensions. Thus, in this qualitative sample, most of the legislators studied are relatively junior, having served for less than ten years. Most of the districts examined include rural areas mixed with suburban or smaller urban areas (e.g., Tallahassee, FL; Chesapeake, VA; and Albany, GA), allowing for more direct comparison across some districts. Also, in the qualitative sample of districts, I look only at southern congressional districts. There are substantive as well as practical reasons to study just southern districts.

Scholars interested in racial representation have been drawn to the study of southern congressional districts. Portions of the Voting Rights Act initially focused only on the South. Additionally, partisan changes of white voters from the Democratic Party to the Republican Party have occurred consistently across the South and allow for useful comparisons of districts with various degrees of black Democratic voters, white Democratic voters, and white Republican voters. Most importantly, with few exceptions, the black legislators that hail from white-majority districts during this period are from southern congressional districts. Thus, in order to examine the variation in constituency service based on variation of the district's black population, southern districts are worth analyzing. Finally, whereas other parts of this book examine national samples of congressional districts, it is simply not practical to travel to multiple congressional districts across the country while keeping these districts comparable enough across other dimensions so that we can be comfortable that alternative explanations are controlled for.

Whereas much is gained in terms of context and interpretation from the study of a subset of these seventeen congressional districts, an important caveat must be noted. As with all qualitative research, my inferences are only as representative as the cases I examine. The study of congressional representation and racial representation specifically has been enhanced greatly by the close, qualitative examination of case studies by visiting the legislator's district and "soaking and poking" (Fenno 1978). The works that have most extensively used qualitative analysis in a legislator's district to examine questions of racial representation are written by Swain (1995), who qualitatively examined thirteen congressional districts; Glaser (1996), who qualitatively examined six congressional districts;

and Fenno (2003), who qualitatively examined four congressional districts. Importantly, my study builds on this past work and examines a larger number of cases than these scholars did. Nevertheless, like Fenno, Glaser, and Swain have noted in their own works, we should be cognizant of limitations of generalizing from case studies. As Fenno (2003, 10) said, "... in the end, all generalizations, both across and within districts, are unusually tentative ... [and this] condition, it is hoped, will serve to encourage – not discourage – more research of this nature."

Furthermore, because I only examine the South in this qualitative chapter (for reasons outlined previously), the inferences are limited to members of Congress from the South. Although I think some of my conclusions may be generalizable to districts both in the South and non-South, we cannot know this for certain given the cases studied. Because of these data limitations, in subsequent chapters I supplement the interview findings from seventeen southern congressional districts with broader findings from a national sample of districts. As will be revealed, the data uncovered in the qualitative analyses are consistent with the quantitative analyses. This provides greater assurance that the qualitative cases are fairly representative of the broader sample, yet we should always be cognizant of the limitations of generalizable inferences from case studies.

Table 4.1 lists the seventeen legislators in the qualitative sample, categorizing each legislator by party, race, and type of district. There are six Republicans (all white) and eleven Democrats (white and black). In terms of race, six of the seventeen were African-American legislators (all Democrats). Looking at party and race together, there are six white Republicans, five white Democrats, and six black Democrats. The white Republicans are JoAnn Davis (VA-1); Virgil Goode (VA-5); Randy Forbes (VA-4); Robin Hayes (NC-8); Jack Kingston (GA-1); and Mark Sanford (SC-1). Goode was initially elected as a Democrat but switched his party identification to Independent (Grose and Yoshinaka 2003; Yoshinaka 2005) before I visited his district office. Once he became an independent, though, he caucused with the Republicans, so I include him in the list of Republican legislators in the sample.

The districts represented by white Democrats where staff interviews were conducted are as follows: Allen Boyd (FL-2); Bob Etheridge (NC-2); Mike McIntyre (NC-7); David Price (NC-4); and John Spratt (SC-5). Of the black Democrats in the sample, three were from districts with a black-majority population: Harold Ford, Jr. (TN-9); Earl Hilliard (AL-7); and Bill Jefferson, (LA-2); and three were from black-influence districts with a white-majority population: Sanford Bishop (GA-2); Corrine Brown

TABLE 4.1. *Districts/Legislators Visited*[a]

	Low black population districts Districts with a black population of 25% or less	Black-influence districts Districts with a 26–49% black population	Black-majority districts Districts with a 50% black population or higher
Black Democrats	–	Sanford Bishop, GA-2, 107th, 39% black Corrine Brown, FL-3, 107th, 47% black Mel Watt, NC-12, 107th, 45% black	Harold Ford, Jr., TN-9, 107th, 59% black Earl Hilliard, AL-7, 107th, 67% black Bill Jefferson, LA-2, 107th, 61% black
White Democrats	Allen Boyd, FL-2, 107th, 24% black Mike McIntyre, NC-7, 107th, 24% black David Price, NC-4, 107th, 21% black	Bob Etheridge, NC-2, 107th, 28% black John Spratt, SC-5, 107th, 31% black	–
White Republicans	JoAnn Davis, VA-1, 107th, 19% black Virgil Goode, VA-5, 107th, 25% black[b] Mark Sanford, SC-1, 106th, 20% black	Randy Forbes, VA-4, 107th, 39% black Jack Kingston, GA-1, 107th, 31% black Robin Hayes, NC-8, 107th, 28% black	–

[a] District offices were visited during the Congress listed in the table. Black population percentages from Duncan and Nutting (1999) and Nutting and Stern (2001).
[b] Virgil Goode was actually an independent, though I code him as a Republican because he caucused with the House Republicans during the 107th Congress.

(FL-3); and Mel Watt (NC-12). With this variation across the black population of the district, the hypotheses regarding black population of the district and racial trust can be tested. Clearly, the variation by party and race also allow for tests of these hypotheses.

A number of the white legislators of both parties were also elected from black-influence districts to allow for direct comparison with black legislators from white-majority districts. Three white Republicans hail from black-influence districts (Forbes, Hayes, and Kingston) and three from districts with lower black populations. Two of the white Democrats are also from districts that could be classified as black-influence districts (Etheridge and Spratt). The variation among white legislators also allows for tests of the party, black population, and racial trust hypotheses. No white legislators were elected from black-majority districts in the qualitative sample, as not a single black-majority district in the South elected a white legislator during the 106th or the 107th Congresses (and only one outside of the South, PA-2, elected a white legislator).[1]

Finally, I did not immediately bring up race during my interviews. I introduced myself by explaining that I am a political scientist working on a project about constituency service in congressional districts and how members of Congress reach various parts of their constituencies. I then began my interviews by asking general, more-or-less innocuous questions about the district, about supporters and opponents of the member in the district, constituency service allocation decisions, and so on. Through these questions, I gauged how quickly the interviewees raised the racial demographics of their districts. By giving them an opportunity to first raise the topic in conversation, it indicated the extent to which race played a role in constituency service decisions in the district. Also, it gave an opening for me to ask follow-up questions about race, representation, and constituency service that some staffers may have had difficulty addressing initially.

If they did not mention race, I then asked questions explicitly, such as "How do you balance the racial demographics of the district in terms of reaching people via constituency service?" I often couched the initial discussion of reaching black constituents more broadly in terms of geographic, gender, partisan, or other demographic groups in the district (e.g., veterans and farmers). Finally, I asked numerous questions related to race, racial politics in the district, how the member interacts with black and white voters, whether specific efforts were made to reach black voters, and how much racial politics framed the decisions of the staff – but only after substantial rapport was established between myself and those being interviewed.

None of those questioned claimed that there was no racial dimension to the political contours of their districts. Some were initially hesitant to

---

[1] Also, most of the white legislators from black-influence districts have slightly smaller black populations than black legislators from black-influence districts. With the exception of white Republican Randy Forbes (elected from a district with a 39% black population) and black Democrat Sanford Bishop (also elected from a district with a 39% black population), white and black legislators do not always come from districts that are *precisely* comparable in terms of district black population. Thus, when comparing legislators from black-influence districts, we still have to be cognizant of these slight differences.

discuss these issues, though through persistence and follow-up, all were forthcoming. On occasion, some staffers asked that their names not be used with certain comments, though they gave me permission to report their comments. In most cases, however, the respondents were willing to talk and to allow me to report their comments fully.

Reaching Voters with Service: Race Trumps Geography and Party

Constituency service is based both on demand and supply. Much of serving constituents in district offices is based simply on dealing with requests, demands, and inquiries from constituents who walk into a congressional district office, write a letter, or make a phone call. All members of Congress will work with any constituent who requests help, regardless of the constituent's racial, partisan, or ethnic background – after all, each individual contact with a constituent can only help the legislator achieve reelection.

However, constituency service is not only based on demand. In most cases, members of Congress and their district staff proactively attempt to reach voters who may not even realize they needed assistance from their member of Congress. Where members open their district offices, where and how they hold mobile office hours, where district events are held, and where the events are scheduled for a member to attend are allocation and service decisions, many of which have a racial element to them in those districts with a significant proportion of black constituents.

For example, take a basic district allocation decision made by all members of Congress: where to locate the district office or offices. On its face, this does not seem to be racial. In fact, when I asked district directors in congressional offices why they chose to put offices where they did, often their initial responses were based on population and geography. Rose Auman, district director in white Democrat David Price's office, said they wanted offices in the main metro areas of the district that were "centrally located."

John Spratt, a white Democrat from South Carolina, has three district offices. The main office from which most of the staff operate is located in Rock Hill, the largest city in the district. Robert Hopkins, Spratt's district director, noted that the office "we are sitting in" had been the main congressional office for both congressional members who preceded Spratt, and thus he continued with the same office location: "In modern times, since World War II, Rock Hill has been the largest town in the district. It just makes sense."

Beyond the population of various towns and historical constraints based on previous legislators' office locations, political factors also play a role. Here, racial concerns were clearly part of the equation (and sometimes the primary part of the equation). To motivate this point, I will detail two cases: Randy Forbes (VA-4) and Earl Hilliard (AL-7).

Randy Forbes: "Big Shoes to Fill"

Dee Gilmore, district director for white Republican Virginia Representative Randy Forbes, declared that the decision to open three district offices was done in order to reach out to voters in his geographically sprawling district. The fourth district stretched from urban and suburban communities near Norfolk out to rural counties and towns in the western part of the district. Also in the district are suburban and urban communities south of Richmond (Petersburg and Colonial Heights being most prominent).

Norman Sisisky was a white Democrat who had represented the fourth district prior to Forbes. He died in March 2001, and a special election was held on June 19, 2001, to fill the vacancy. The district, which had a 39 percent black population and a 57 percent white population (according to 2000 census figures), was racially, politically, and geographically diverse. In the 2000 presidential election, 49 percent of the district voted for Bush and 49 percent voted for Gore.

The 2001 special election held to replace Sisisky pitted Forbes, a white Republican state senator from Chesapeake, against Louise Lucas, a black Democratic state senator from Portsmouth. Chesapeake and Portsmouth abut one another in the southwestern part of the district and are two of its largest cities. Portsmouth is a majority-black city (50.6 percent black in 2000) and Chesapeake is a majority-white city, with just a 28.5 percent African-American population. Interestingly, though, majority-white Chesapeake has elected a black mayor, who strongly supported Democrat Lucas in the special election. Driving near the border of the two cities, I immediately noticed a substantial change in the racial makeup of the two cities as I headed south across railroad tracks that divide the boundaries of each city. Portsmouth appeared more heavily African American, more manufacturing-based, and industrial. Chesapeake, or at least the portion where Forbes' district office was located, was a mostly white bedroom community of new housing developments with no central core.

In the 2001 special election, Forbes ended up squeaking out a victory of 52 to 48 percent. According to one of Forbes's staffers, precinct-level estimates of voting by race showed that only 2 percent of African-American voters in the district supported Forbes. Not surprisingly, he did well in his home base of Chesapeake and poorly in Portsmouth.

When the previous representative, Norman Sisisky, was in office, he was well known for his constituency service across the district. He had three district offices: one in Portsmouth (Louise Lucas's hometown), a second in Petersburg, and a third in Emporia. All three of these cities, according to 2000 census figures, were majority-black, and Sisisky relied heavily on African-American voters as part of his primary constituency (while appealing to enough rural, historically Democratic white voters to win reelection). When Forbes was elected, he faced a dilemma in terms of where to locate his congressional offices in the district.

His support came from white areas of the district, yet he was in some ways constrained by the past decisions of Sisisky. Gilmore, Forbes's district director, said they decided to move the main district office from Portsmouth to Chesapeake because their supporters, mostly white, were there: "Chesapeake is the key to his election. People here worked their butts off to elect him." Similarly, they moved another office from majority-black Petersburg to overwhelmingly white Colonial Heights: "We got 18 percent of the vote in Petersburg. Colonial Heights voted 85 percent with us.... You want something that reflects your base, where you're close to the people [who supported you]." With Forbes, his base, especially in his initial election, was overwhelmingly white. See Table 4.2 to see the population by race of these cities and the location of offices in the fourth district under both Sisisky and Forbes.

Forbes did stick with one office in Emporia, a small black-majority town (total population: 5,665) in the rural western part of the district. The rationale behind retaining this office was clearly to work to expand his reelection constituency to rural Democrats, especially rural farmers who lived in the district: "It was a no-brainer. It gives us a touchstone in the rural part of the district." In most of the rural areas in which Forbes traveled after winning the special election, he found farmers repeating the mantra that he had "big shoes to fill" in terms of replacing Sisisky. The staff for Forbes found this ironic, as Sisisky was often sick in his latter terms in office, which prevented him from regularly visiting with rural white voters who had often supported him. In fact, they suggested that Forbes's extensive presence in the district was slowly winning over rural white constituents who were very much tied to Sisisky. Thus, Sisisky's office in Emporia remained open, staffed by one person whose focus was on agricultural issues and who had also worked for Sisisky. Significantly, the staffer in Emporia, a small black-majority town, was white and had

TABLE 4.2. *Congressional District Office Locations in Virginia's Fourth District: Sisisky versus Forbes*

City	Sisisky Located Office There?	Forbes Located Office There?	Population of City by Race, 2000 Census	City's Total Population, 2000 Census
Portsmouth	Yes	No	46,096 white (45.8%) 50,899 black (50.6%)	100,565
Chesapeake	No	Yes	133,193 white (66.9%) 56,823 black (28.5%)	199,184
Petersburg	Yes	No	6,249 white (18.5%) 26,643 black (79.0%)	33,740
Colonial Heights	No	Yes	15,052 white (89.1%) 1,059 black (6.3%)	16,897
Emporia	Yes	Yes	2,405 white (42.5%) 3,181 black (56.2%)	5,665

strong connections in that part of the district's rural communities that staffer Gilmore described as "Mayberry" kinds of places.

All of this is not to say that Forbes was neglecting black constituents. In fact, it was clear that the staff were concerned about how to expand support for Forbes to African Americans in the district. Forbes and his overwhelmingly white staff were concerned about a possible challenge from a strong Democrat in future elections, especially in a district that was 39 percent African American. Gilmore, without being queried, suggested that Forbes had attempted to reach black voters in the district but appeared exasperated that black voters were so overwhelmingly Democratic: "It really is our job to represent *everybody* in the district." I later asked her how Forbes has attempted to reach the African-American community in the district, and she responded as follows: "Everybody's labelled. ...When you get to see him [Forbes] as a person, ... they just understand he's helping, whether you voted for him or not. ...[The racial and partisan lines are] breaking down one by one."

She expressed hope that Forbes would be able to use his conservative religiosity and positions on social issues such as abortion to reach black voters in the future (as she said this, she pointed to an immense Bible on her desk). She then pessimistically countered by noting that black constituents' policy preferences on economic issues were contrary to Forbes's voting record.

However, there was some evidence that Forbes was actually making at least a small attempt to be responsive to African Americans in the district. The office had recently hired Paul Gillis, a former president of the Virginia NAACP (who was also the only black staffer in the entire district). However, Gillis was not assigned to any specific district office and also seemed estranged from the mainstream black community in the district and the state (perhaps in part to his connections to Republican candidates and legislators). His official job title was "senior advisor" and another of Forbes's staffers told me that Gillis was responsible for "putting out fires" that occasionally sprang up in the district between Forbes and black constituents. In sum, unlike white representatives like Representative Jack Flynt (see Fenno 2000) in southern congressional districts circa 1970s or 1980s who may have outright ignored black constituents in a similar district, Forbes was extremely cognizant of his district's substantial black population – and was making attempts via constituency service to reach this constituency. However, as black voters clearly were outside his reelection constituency, this focus came only after his primary constituents (white suburbanites in Chesapeake and Colonial Heights) and his reelection constituents (rural whites) were already accommodated. His district was redrawn for 2002 with a slightly smaller proportion of black voters, which Forbes was likely happy with given his base of electoral support. Also, given the relative electoral insecurity that Forbes faced, his constituency service operation in his district offices was amazingly efficient – and clearly was effective in terms of reaching constituents of any racial background.

Earl Hilliard: "He Was Elected to Represent the People *Here*"

In contrast to Forbes, Earl Hilliard represented an overwhelmingly African-American (67%) district in Alabama (the seventh district). Very much like Forbes, though, his office allocation decisions mirrored attempts to first reach his primary constituency, but also with considerations on reaching beyond to his reelection constituency and possibly to those outside of his electoral coalition.

Hilliard was initially elected to Congress in 1992 in a newly created African-American supermajority district. He was the first black member of Congress from Alabama since Reconstruction. After a bruising 1992 primary election, Hilliard was electorally safe until 2002, particularly relying on a strong base of support among lower-income African Americans in the district.

The expectations among African-American constituents in Alabama following his initial 1992 victory were high, having finally achieved descriptive representation at the congressional level. Hilliard was cognizant of this and sought to open district offices in areas that were predominately African American. When I visited in 2002, he had four district offices. The primary office was located in Birmingham, the largest city in the district, whereas the other offices were located in Montgomery, Selma, and Tuscaloosa.

The Birmingham office was initially located in Hilliard's law office, though this caused him some ethical problems as his law firm was charging rent on his congressional office (he was eventually investigated by the House Ethics committee). Thus, it was alleged that Hilliard's firm was profiting from the federal government's payment for his district office space in Birmingham. Once local and Washington media raised this potential scandal and the House Ethics committee began an investigation, Hilliard wisely moved his main office a couple blocks down the street, though it remained in the same neighborhood, which is the most relevant point to this study.

The neighborhood in which Hilliard's Birmingham office was located was in the heart of historic black Birmingham. His second Birmingham office was located in a building that was adjacent to Kelly Ingram Park and the Sixteenth Street Baptist Church. Any student of contemporary American history would note the prominence of these locations as central battlefields of the Civil Rights Movement in the 1960s. Kelly Ingram Park was where Sheriff Bull Connor released dogs and water hoses on civil rights protestors, and the park is now a memorial to those protesters. The Sixteenth Street Baptist Church was infamously bombed on September 15, 1963, killing four African-American children.

The neighborhood is not simply of historical import but is also a contemporary locus of Birmingham's African-American community. Across the street from Hilliard's office was the Birmingham Civil Rights Institute, a museum and educational center devoted to chronicling the pre-civil rights and civil rights eras. Numerous black neighborhood development associations, nonprofits, and small businesses are just blocks away. As one of Hilliard's staffers noted, "the fact we are located in the black business district is significant." The building itself that housed the primary Birmingham office also housed the headquarters of the Southwestern Athletic Conference (SWAC), which is composed of historically black colleges and universities (such as Alabama A&M and Grambling State). This office location clearly signaled an attempt by Hilliard to reach his primary constituency, which was primarily African American.

In contrast, the previous member of Congress who represented Birmingham in the 1980s, white Democrat Ben Erdreich, had located his office in the federal building in Birmingham. A number of other legislators with district offices that I visited also chose to locate offices in federal buildings in their districts. I asked one of Hilliard's staffers if Birmingham's federal building was in his district and, if so, why they chose the black business and historical district of Birmingham, and not the federal building downtown, for their office location. Her response was as follows: "The federal building's in our district. But we wanted to be here, in this neighborhood, so the people can reach us. He was elected to represent the people here." Like Hilliard, Erdreich also relied heavily on black voters for electoral support. However, the racial demography of the district and the extent to which black voters were part of Erdreich's versus Hilliard's reelection constituencies differed.

In addition to and following the pattern seen in Birmingham, Hilliard's Selma office was located adjacent to the city's National Voting Rights Museum and Institute, which documents the history of voting rights struggles in Alabama and in the United States. The day I visited the Selma office (in spring 2000), I dropped into the museum, and Hilliard was there preparing for the arrival of then President Bill Clinton, who was in town to give a speech marking the anniversary of the civil rights march from the Edmund Pettus Bridge in Selma to the capital city of Montgomery.

I also visited Hilliard's office in Tuscaloosa. Unlike his other offices, the Tuscaloosa office was located in a federal building in what appeared to be a predominately white neighborhood (relative to his other office locations). Kay Presley, the one staffer working in this office, was white. She had also worked previously for Congressman Claude Harris, a white Democrat who served Tuscaloosa and surrounding rural areas in the 1980s. This office location indicated that Hilliard did attempt to reach white constituents as well, though his primary focus was clearly not white voters. Just as Randy Forbes hired one black staffer to be a touchstone in the black community of the fourth district of Virginia, Hilliard hired one white staffer to be a touchstone in the white community of the seventh district of Alabama.

What is noteworthy about both the Birmingham and Selma office locations were that they were dramatic, symbolic indications of an attempt by Hilliard to reach African-American constituents in these cities. Hilliard's opening of district offices in neighborhoods that had traditionally not been the primary focus of past white legislators also had a substantive effect on constituency service to black constituents. While I was in his Birmingham office, for example, the "foot traffic" by constituents came only from African-American constituents, which is what one might expect given the racial makeup of the neighborhood. In addition to the office location, the staff detailed events that Hilliard had recently attended in predominately black areas of the district: "The congressman visits schools and communities that previous congressmen had never visited. Young people are excited when they see him, and he tells them he's an example that anything is in reach."

To further demonstrate Hilliard's commitment to his primary constituency of black constituents in the Birmingham area, the staff in Hilliard's office bragged that they were sending out a newsletter to constituents that focused on African-American issues and concerns. Unlike newsletters that I examined in most offices of white legislators, Hilliard's newsletter had a particularly strong racial appeal in most of its articles. For example, he explained how he had been assisting black farmers and delivering grants to an HBCU in the district (C.A. Fredd Technical College at Shelton Community College). These are clearly small substantive efforts at constituency service.

Interestingly, the staff members were unusually proud of their newsletter, something that struck me as a bit odd because it is commonplace for congressional offices to send out newsletters to constituents (Grose and Middlemass 2010; Middlemass and Grose 2007). I asked if they had copies of other newsletters, to which they responded that this was only the second newsletter they had ever sent district-wide before. This surprised me as Hilliard was first elected in 1992, and I was visiting his office in 2002. They had never really done newsletters in the past, but they were facing a likely redistricting that would reduce the black population of the district by approximately five percentage points. Thus, they wanted to increase communications to constituents. Undoubtedly, the Ethics committee investigation and the announcement that African-American candidate Artur Davis would oppose Hilliard in the 2002 Democratic primary may have caused Hilliard and his staff to perceive that his continued tenure in office was more tenuous, and they began to crank up their service operation.

This anecdote about the paucity of previous newsletters indicated a broader point, however. Prior to the redistricting for 2002, Hilliard's voting record was very pro-civil rights and generally liberal. Thus, he had substantively represented his black constituents who also had relatively liberal views on civil rights and some other issues. His constituency service operation, while clearly geared primarily toward black constituents, was not as professional as the operations I had observed in other offices. The fact they bragged about their second newsletter ever in their fifth term in office indicated to me that the quality of his constituency service was lacking. This was especially in contrast to the offices I visited of black legislators who represented white-majority districts (Sanford Bishop, Corrine Brown, and Mel Watt). These offices were run extremely well, and a strong constituency service operation to white and black constituents alike was the norm. Perhaps unsurprisingly, Hilliard lost a close primary election to Artur Davis in 2002. Relevant to the topic of district office locations, Davis also opened district offices in predominately black neighborhoods upon his election to the House. In 2010, Davis chose to run for the Senate but lost the Democratic primary to a white opponent in part due to lack of support from some black voters who had more strongly supported Hilliard in 2002.

In conclusion, the quality of Hilliard's constituency service operation was not as high as the quality of the operations in other black legislators' offices from black-influence districts. However, service allocation decisions such as the location of district offices reflected a desire to reach his primary constituents – almost all of whom were African American. Basically, most of his district office location decisions reached voters within his primary constituency. Also, his office in Tuscaloosa was an attempt to reach white voters that likely were nominally inside or perhaps outside his reelection constituency. These district allocation decisions in some ways mirrored the decisions that Randy Forbes made in his own district, but their primary and reelection constituencies were clearly different.

Congressional Offices in Black Neighborhoods?

To see if the patterns observed in these two districts held generally, I visited twenty-seven district offices in the seventeen congressional districts in the sample. Again, all the caveats previously noted regarding small

samples continue to hold. I coded these districts as being located in predominately white neighborhoods, predominately black neighborhoods,
or in neighborhoods that were both black and white. With the exception
of two district offices (Mike McIntyre's Lumberton, NC, office and Mel
Watt's Charlotte, NC, office), there were no substantial Latino, Native
American, or other minority populations in the cities where offices were
located. These categorizations were based on the staffers' claims combined with my own observations of the immediate geographic areas by
the offices. The "both black and white" neighborhood category could
be racially integrated neighborhoods or offices located on the "border"
between two segregated neighborhoods. An example of this is black
Democrat Sanford Bishop's Albany, Georgia, office.

The location of this office demonstrates Bishop's attempt to balance a
39 percent black population and a majority-white constituency. The office
itself is located along a set of railroad tracks near downtown Albany. The
south side of the tracks is mostly black, whereas the other side is mainly
white. Hobby Stripling, Bishop's district director, commented to me that
the office was located there as a symbol that Bishop is reaching to both
black and white constituents: "We're right on the fringe. Like most southern cities, Albany is pretty divided black and white. ...We [also] try to put
campaign offices where it's neutral. I guess that's the best way to describe
it. ... We try to put it in a place where all of our constituency can feel
comfortable." Mel Watt, another black legislator from a black-influence
district, also located his main office in Charlotte, North Carolina, on the
"border" of a predominately black and Latino area of Charlotte and a
whiter section of downtown. This was done in order to appear accessible
to various segments of Watt's constituency.

Which explanatory factors – the race of the legislator, the district black
population, the party of the legislator, or racial trust – predict the location of district offices? In Table 4.3, I detail the offices that were visited
in the seventeen congressional districts, breaking down the racial background of the neighborhood by the variables of interest.

The race of the legislator is clearly the most important factor. Among
black legislators, only one office was located in a predominately white
neighborhood (Hilliard's Tuscaloosa office), and seven offices were
located in predominately black neighborhoods. Even black legislators
from majority-white, black-influence districts still located their offices in
either mostly black neighborhoods or those that were both black and
white. Black Democrat Corrine Brown, for example, representing a 47
percent black district, opened her main district office in Jacksonville,

TABLE 4.3. *District Office Locations and Predominant Racial Composition of Neighborhood of Office*

	Districts with a Black Population of 25% or Less	Districts with a 26–49% Black Population	Black-Majority Districts, 50% Black Population or Higher	Total
Black Democrats	–	• Sanford Bishop: Albany, GA: Black and white; Dawson, GA: Black • Corrine Brown: Jacksonville, FL: Black • Mel Watt: Charlotte, NC: Black and white; Greensboro, NC: Black	• Harold Ford, Jr.: Memphis, TN: Black • Earl Hilliard: Birmingham, AL: Black; Selma, AL: Black; Tuscaloosa, AL: White • Bill Jefferson: New Orleans, LA: Black	1 white neighborhood; 7 black neighborhoods; 2 black & white neighborhoods (n = 10)
White Democrats	• Allen Boyd: Tallahassee, FL: White • Mike McIntyre: Fayetteville, NC: Black and white; Lumberton, NC: Black and white • David Price: Raleigh, NC: White; Durham, NC: Black; Chapel Hill, NC: White	• Bob Etheridge: Raleigh, NC: White • John Spratt: Rock Hill, SC: White	–	5 white; 1 black; 2 black & white (n = 8)
White Republicans	• JoAnn Davis: Yorktown, VA: White; Fredericksburg, VA: White • Virgil Goode: Charlottesville, VA: White • Mark Sanford: North Charleston, SC: White	• Randy Forbes: Chesapeake, VA: White; Colonial Hts., VA: White • Jack Kingston: Savannah, GA: White; Brunswick, GA: Black • Robin Hayes: Concord, NC: White	–	8 white; 1 black; 0 black & white (n = 9)
Total	7 white; 2 black and white (n = 10 offices)	6 white; 4 black; 2 black and white (n = 12 offices)	1 white; 4 black; 0 black and white (n = 5 offices)	14 white; 9 black; 4 black and white (n = 27 offices)

Florida, in the same building as the city's oldest black-owned insurance company. Brown was initially elected in a majority-black district, and then her district was redrawn to be majority-white in 1996 following a Supreme Court decision. Interestingly, this office was opened up after her district became majority-white and thus is not an artifact of inertia based on the original office location when the district was black-majority. This is also the case for Mel Watt and Sanford Bishop, the other two black legislators in the qualitative sample whose districts were redrawn. Most of the offices examined here in Watt's and Bishop's districts were also opened after their majority-white districts were created.

The black population of the district, though, is also important. Those in majority-black districts overwhelmingly located their district offices in black neighborhoods. The more white a district is, the less likely that a district office is located in a predominately black neighborhood. However, this may be explained mostly by the intervening effect of the race of the legislator.

Party may also play a role, though any party results seem driven mostly by the presence of black Democrats. In total, Democrats located six offices in predominately white areas, eight in predominately black areas, and four in neighborhoods that were both black and white. Republicans, in contrast, only located one office in a black neighborhood and thirteen in white neighborhoods. However, only one white Democrat (David Price) located an office in a predominately black neighborhood. One other white Democrat (Mike McIntyre) had two offices in racially diverse areas. All other Democrats who located offices in African-American or racially diverse areas were black legislators. I asked Billy Barker, a staff member for white Democrat Mike McIntyre, how McIntyre kept a coalition of white Democratic voters, black voters, and Native American voters together. He glanced to the sky and simply said, "Divine intervention. He's got something that works for all of 'em." It was not clear if Barker implied "He" to be McIntyre or God, but Barker continued to explain that McIntyre makes explicit efforts to balance the interests of all racial groups in his district.

Jack Kingston was the only Republican to locate an office in a predominately black neighborhood. Kingston, while voting very conservatively, has regularly worked to reach African-American voters via constituency service. Many of his district staff are African American, and he has worked to provide federal funding for black historical sites in his (at the time of my visit) 31 percent black district. Since Price, McIntyre, and Kingston are the only white legislators to open offices (four total offices) in areas that are not mostly white, there does appear to be a slight party effect in terms of office locations, though not a very substantial one when the race of the legislator is considered (comparing white and black Democrats).

Racial trust does seem to also have a small impact on district office locations. Among black legislators, offices were generally and consistently located in neighborhoods with a black population presence, regardless of black population levels. However, black members of Congress in black-influence districts were surprisingly more willing to open up offices in black neighborhoods or "black and white" areas than were white members of Congress from black-influence districts.

In sum, the key finding regarding district office locations is that the race of the legislator matters. Black legislators are most likely to locate offices in predominately African-American neighborhoods, consistent with my argument that a legislator's race is likely to drive representational decisions beyond roll-call voting. One explanation for why race matters in the distribution of district offices could be based on the nature of the legislator's core constituencies. Black legislators like Earl Hilliard or Corrine Brown may place offices in or near predominately black neighborhoods or in symbolically meaningful locations because their primary constituencies or key subconstituencies (Bishin 2000, 2009; Fenno 1978) are African American. White Republicans, in contrast, place offices in white neighborhoods because they know from experience that they have little chance of attracting more than 10 to 20 percent of black voter support. White Democrats in the sample also leaned heavily toward placing offices in predominately white areas, even though these white Democrats need to garner support from African-American constituents. Whereas these white Democrats are likely to attract overwhelming support from black voters, given the differential in black turnout when represented by a white versus black legislator (see Chapter 2), these white Democratic legislators are more reliant on white voters than are black Democratic legislators.[2] Thus, whereas the

---

[2] Additionally, whereas I am able to study black legislators in both black-majority districts and white-majority districts in this chapter, no white Democrats represented black-majority districts at the time of my visits to the congressional districts. Thus, some of the district allocation decisions that appear to be based on the legislator's race are likely also based on the district black population, given that all the white Democrats will need to garner more white voter support than many of the black Democrats studied here (e.g., John Spratt needs more white voter support to win reelection than does Sanford Bishop, as Bishop has just slightly fewer white voters than does Spratt).

location of district offices is associated with the race of the legislator in the twenty-seven district offices studied here, the legislator's race may also be interacting with the nature of the core and reelection constituencies that exist for these legislators.

To see if these patterns hold for other measures of constituency service, in the next chapter I will also look at the effect of the racial representation variables on the hiring of district staffers that are African American.

5

Constituency Service in the District

Connecting Black Legislators, Black Staff, and Black Voters

> "You can't help anyone if you cannot relate."
> —An African-American staffer in Congressman
> Earl Hilliard's office, explaining why she thinks
> it is important to have African-American staff
> in congressional district offices.

Is there a link between descriptive representation at the staff level and substantive representation at the congressional district level? What proportion of district staff are African American, white, or from other racial/ ethnic backgrounds? Are these staff in the district working to reach black constituents? This chapter picks up where Chapter 4 left off, continuing to examine constituency service – a substantive, tangible good – delivered to African Americans. In this chapter, I argue that descriptive representation (the election of African-American legislators) is a key predictor of the hiring of black staff in congressional districts. Further, black staff are more likely than white staff to self-identify as being able to "relate" to African-American constituents.

Whereas members of Congress personally engage in constituency service, most of the day-to-day work dealing with casework and other services falls to the congressional staff, and most often to the congressional staff in the district. When a constituent requests assistance from their representative, typically the request goes through a staff member in one of the district offices. Legislative observers have long noted the importance of staff in assisting the representational activities of members of Congress, particularly constituency service activities.

African-American Staff and Substantive Congressional Representation

Having examined district office locations in the previous chapter, a second measure of constituency service to African-American constituents can be estimated by examining the extent to which black staff are hired in district congressional offices and how connected these staffers are to the black community in the congressional district relative to nonblack staffers. Providing black constituents with a measure of descriptive representation (hiring black staff) in the district office demonstrates a public attempt on the part of the legislator to reach out to that constituency – thus, in this case, descriptive representation at the staff level can be construed as substantive representation as well in terms of constituency service. Carol Swain (1995, 105) concurs, noting the following: "Having people of different racial backgrounds on hand to receive and relay information can lead to better representation of the district, and it shows a sensitivity to minority interests."

Critics may suggest that simply hiring any black staffer does not always imply substantive representation in terms of constituency service. As Lani Guinier (1994) has noted, "authentic" black representation is needed for the link between descriptive and substantive representation (as I have conceived it in regard to staff) to exist. Black staffers with roots and connections to the black community would need to be hired in this case, though it is clearly impossible to empirically determine the extent to which black staff are substantively connected to black constituents in a broad sample of districts. Thus, based on the analysis presented later in this chapter, I will assume that descriptive representation at the district staff level generally equals "authentic" black representation in congressional district offices (substantive representation on constituency service).

David Canon (1999) cites three reasons why the racial makeup of the congressional staff is critical – and why this also provides a clue as to whether legislators attempt to substantively represent black constituents. One is that it indicates the significance of race in a member's representational presentation to the district. A member with a racially homogenous district, one with little variation in its racial makeup, is unlikely to give much attention to the demographic diversity (or lack of diversity) of his or her staff. However, a member who represents a diverse district might do well to prove to his or her constituents that race is a concern and to show he or she is attuned to the racial breakdown of the district. If that member does not have a staff roughly reflective of the district, it may signal to his or her constituents, particularly those in the racial minority, that race is not a matter of concern to the member or that he or she is not in touch with that portion of the district.

Second, according to Canon, a staff that is racially heterogeneous will have a different effect on the member than a racially homogenous staff. Based on the premise that people of different races have different experiences in life, it is likely that the more diverse staff will provide the member with different viewpoints, provide different types of information, or emphasize certain aspects of politics than a less diverse staff. The end result may be that the member will represent his or her district differently.

Lastly, the staff's racial composition is important because constituents' contact with their legislator is more likely to be indirect, that is, by first encountering members of the staff (Canon 1999). Constituents may feel more at ease dealing with staffers who share their racial background and, therefore, believe they are being well served by the member. Claudine Gay (2002) has shown that black constituents trust black legislators more than legislators of other races, and this finding may be due to black legislators hiring a large percentage of black staff, as staff are most likely to be the conduit between representative and constituent on service matters.

These ideas are demonstrated in qualitative interviews conducted. Once again, black Democrat Earl Hilliard's office serves as a useful motivating example. As mentioned in the opening quotation of this chapter, an African-American staff member in the district of Earl Hilliard's office noted that having staff with a descriptive connection could help Hilliard reach his minority constituents (Hilliard, an African-American Democratic legislator, served from 1992–2002 in Alabama's seventh district). It is not that white staff cannot help black constituents, because they certainly have the incentive to assist any constituent as this assistance may help the legislator achieve reelection. However, the choice of hiring a black staffer or a staffer of another racial background makes a difference in terms of reaching out to black constituents on service issues – a substantive outcome. Many black staffers suggested that the racial background of district staffers did matter, simply because they had different contacts in the community and thus were able to drum up constituent requests for assistance from different segments of the community. Some of Hilliard's black staff, for instance, had degrees from area HBCUs (historically black colleges and universities), whereas white staff in his office and neighboring districts graduated from predominately white institutions. A black staffer in Hilliard's office noted that many African-American constituents from adjacent districts would call her because of her connections with Delta Sigma Theta, a predominately black sorority. Due to congressional courtesy, she would suggest they first seek assistance with their own member of Congress, though mimicking these outside-the-district requests, she said, "They say, 'Bachus can't help me' or 'I already have his number'," implying that the requestors did not have the connection between either Spencer Bachus (a neighboring white representative) or his staff. She said often it came down to the fact that many of these black Alabamians from outside of the district simply did not know any of the white staff in Bachus's office, but they did know Hilliard's black staffers – or had heard that Hilliard's staff could help (also see Swain 1995, 218 and Canon 1999, 55).

Another black staffer in the Memphis, Tennessee, office of Harold Ford Jr. said, "They [black constituents] would be more comfortable culturally with someone like them," pointing out that any demographic connection, but especially race, helps constituents trust the staff in the district. She quickly and adamantly followed up to point out that she was not suggesting that Ford's office turns down requests based on race or that the office favors black constituents, but simply that a connection does exist: "If you happen to be a white male, we can also help. White, black, or Asian or whatever ... We will help." However, it was clear that she also agreed that the higher the number of black staff, the more likely that black constituents would be "better" served substantively. These same patterns emerged among black staff in offices of other black legislators such as Mel Watt, Corrine Brown, Bill Jefferson, and Sanford Bishop.

These findings are not limited to staff only from black legislators' offices. David Price, a white Democrat representing the Research Triangle area of North Carolina, had three black staff members working in his Durham office. Of the major cities in the district, Durham is the one with the largest black population, and it has historically been home to a politically mobilized and active black community (Grose 2007). A political interest group called the Durham Committee on the Affairs of Black People endorses candidates every election, and their endorsement often leads to a Democratic primary victory and a general election victory.[1]

Durham had not always been in Price's district, but the black population of his district in the 1990s had always hovered around 20 percent.

---

[1] For more detail on Durham's African-American political activity, see Grose (2007), Kousser (1999), and Swain (1995, 160).

Price is a political scientist by training and had initially been elected to Congress in 1986, when his district included nearby Raleigh and Chapel Hill, but not Durham. Before his time in Congress, he was a Duke University professor and had served as chair of the state Democratic Party (Price 2004). Thus, his primary bases of support had traditionally been liberal academics and party activists – and most of these were white. However, he had always garnered substantial support from black voters in his runs for Congress before Durham was in his district.

In 1994, he faced one of his most difficult electoral battles, ultimately losing his seat by just 1,215 votes in the Republican wave of that year's election. Postmortems on his defeat concluded that black turnout in the district was lower than expected and thus was clearly one factor in the outcome. Had a few more African-American voters been mobilized, he may not have lost in 1994. At this time, remember that the politically active black community in Durham was not in his district but in the neighboring black-majority twelfth district represented by Mel Watt.

In 1996, Price ran for reelection, defeating the man who had beaten him just two years earlier, Republican Fred Heineman. Heineman's loss was credited primarily to a *faux pas* he committed during an interview with the *Raleigh News and Observer*. In the interview, Heineman claimed that he considered himself to be "lower middle-class," even though his congressional salary and pensions placed his income at around $180,000 per year.

Contrary to this conventional wisdom, other explanations for Price's 1996 victory include his efforts following his surprise 1994 loss to reconnect with Democratic constituencies in the district that he may have taken for granted while he served in Washington prior to 1994. During this period, he regularly met with black leaders and attended black church services in south Raleigh, the primary population center of black constituents in his district at that time.

Price's reconnection to the district's African-American constituents coincided somewhat with the addition of Durham to his district. Before the 1998 elections, the courts struck down North Carolina's infamous black-majority twelfth congressional district represented by Mel Watt. Thus, surrounding white-majority districts were redrawn, including Price's. He picked up all of Durham and its politically active African-American constituency, though the overall black population of the district remained constant at 20 percent. At this time, Price also hired Tracey Lovett, an African-American staffer who previously had worked for black Democrat Mel Watt. I spoke with her in the context of working for both

Price and Watt, and the conversation illuminates the importance of the presence of black staff, particularly in the offices of white members of Congress:

Q: Were black voters that had been represented by Watt unhappy or confused when they were redrawn into Price's district?

A: There was a little hesitancy with the [Durham] Committee and some black voters at first. We [Price] kept Mel's phone number for the Durham office, and I would take calls, and I'd hear "Well, I thought I called Mel Watt's office." ... Ultimately, though, they just want constituency service, no matter who it's from. And since David hired me when he picked up Durham, that could only help [Lovett had cut her political teeth by working for the Durham Committee on the Affairs of Black People].

Q: Do you see a difference in terms of working for Mel Watt and David Price?

A: Not a huge difference, except on issues of importance to Durham. [With these], Watt knew and didn't have to ask [me]. David had to ask.

By this last comment, Lovett implied that Watt was immediately in touch with the needs of black constituents in the Durham area, whereas Price was not personally connected to this racial-geographic constituency group. Over time, though, by communicating with his African-American staffers intimately involved in the Durham black community, Price was able to substantively represent these voters based on advice from his staff.

This account of David Price and his work with black staff suggests that a legislator's race may be independently important in terms of substantive outcomes for black constituents, but that having black staff in congressional offices who communicate the needs of black constituents directly to the legislator may be important as well. However, what about those districts with few or no black staff? What if the race of the legislator predicts the proportion of black staff?

White Staff and Substantive Representation via Constituency Service

In contrast to the cases detailed previously, many white staff in district offices of white legislators were clearly not enmeshed in the black community of their districts. Thus, substantive representation was less likely in those district offices that were highly populated with white staff members. In all offices where I spoke with district directors (the top job in district offices), all white legislators had hired white district directors. In the case of black legislators, all district directors that I spoke with were also black with the exception of Sanford Bishop's district director, who was white.

These hiring decisions by black and white legislators and the connections that district directors had with black constituents had serious
implications in terms of constituency service and the presentation of the
legislator to black constituents. For an example of where the lack of a
significant presence of black staff in a district office could negatively
affect the substantive representation of black constituents via service, I
point to the case of white Republican JoAnn Davis. A conversation I had
with Butch Downey, a white staffer for Virginia Congresswoman Davis,
indicates an unrealistic and disconnected view that white staff may sometimes have of their district's African-American constituents. Just for some
background, Davis was a white Republican who represented a 20 percent
black district (at the time of my visit) that stretches from the outskirts of
northern Virginia to the Yorktown/Williamsburg area. She represented
the district from 2000 to 2007, until she died of cancer. I asked Downey
about Davis's ability to reach out to black constituents, and the exchange
was as follows:

Q: Does Davis speak to African-American or women's groups in the district?
A: Yes.... When she goes out to speak to them, she speaks as a mother and a
   wife, as a woman. She don't pull punches. She tells it like it is.
Q: Seeing as how she did not get much support from African-Americans, how
   often and why does she address black constituent groups?
A: I think the blacks are trending away from Democrats.... But she ran against a
   black minister in 2000, and I don't know how much support she got from the
   blacks.... She has been out to several black churches [though]. I've even had
   some of the blacks who say I wish I lived in her district.... But historically the
   blacks do like the Democrats.

His responses were illuminating in multiple ways. First, it indicated,
somewhat surprisingly given the hypothesis related to party, that Davis
had made occasional visits to African-American churches and constituency organizations in her district. On the other hand, Downey con-
tinually referred to African-American constituents in Davis's district as
"the blacks," indicating a view of black constituents as monolithic and
unknown to him. The contrast to black staffers' knowledge and connections to black constituents in the district detailed earlier is stark.
Interestingly, Davis's district staff was entirely white.

Similar patterns were found with other white staff, and not just those
who worked for Republicans. Jerry Smithwick, a white district director
in the office of white Democrat Allen Boyd (representative of Florida's
second district) also demonstrates this lack of connection to black constituents, though in a more benignly misguided way. The following is an

excerpt from a conversation I had with Smithwick regarding scheduling in the district:

Q: Do you play a role in choosing which events Boyd attends when he is home in the district?

A: Well, what I was going to do this afternoon, until I got the call from you to sit down and talk to you, was go through this list of requests [pointing at a huge stack of letters on his desk]. I'll weed out ones we can't do.... [In weeding], I have to try to balance it as best I can so that I don't wake up one morning and say, by God, we haven't been to Bay County in five months.

Q: Is this similar with events with black constituents? Do you try to keep track of how often you have events with African-American groups?

A: I do, but I don't. Well, I'll tell you I do not. This is not a political statement. When I look at an event, I don't see it as a black event or a white event, but something he should do.... But, alright, do we do a black event every five events? No. You're just not going to have as many events out of the black community as you will from events that are district wide.

Q: So you don't consider race at all in choosing events?

A: Well, alright, it might get preferential treatment if the event request were the, oh, what do you call it? The Gadsden, oh, the 100 men ...? The black men of ...? Oh, what is it called? This group out of Gadsden County. Oh hell, I can't remember.... Well, I've got to balance that group as best I can: black, white, Gilchrist County, Bay County ...

Smithwick's answer suggests two points. First, after some hemming and hawing, he clearly indicated that he sometimes takes the racial background of a constituency group into account when determining whether Boyd should attend a specific district event. Second, it appears from his response that Smithwick is not intimately involved in the black community of Florida's second district to the point that many black staff I interviewed in other offices were in their respective districts. In trying to point out that Boyd attends events sponsored by African-American constituents, he failed to recall the name of the exact group he was using as an example of how they attempt to reach African-American constituents. The group whose name he was attempting to recall was an African-American men's group called the 100 Black Men of Gadsden County, a local community group affiliated with 100 Black Men of America, Inc. This group, among other things, works to expand educational opportunities among African-American youth. Whereas Boyd is apparently trying to reach black constituents, he is hindered by white staff members whose primary roots are in other parts of the district unconnected to African-American constituents.

A number of other white staffers I spoke with who worked in white legislators' offices suggested that I contact the neighboring black representative when I began my initial queries about how their offices reach black constituents. For example, I asked Kathy Worthington in white Republican Mark Sanford's office how Sanford attempts to reach black constituents. She claimed that, "They pulled all the blacks out [of the old pre-1992 district] for Clyburn [the neighboring black legislator who was elected in a black-majority district]. You should go talk to their office." This assertion belied the fact that Sanford's district did have a relatively sizable 20 percent black population, though it also indicated that Sanford was primarily serving his reelection constituency, which was overwhelmingly white. As a side note, Sanford chose not to run for reelection to the House in 2002 and went on to successfully run for South Carolina governor the same year. Most infamously, in 2010 Sanford went missing as governor and claimed to be hiking on the Appalachian Trail. Soon after, it was revealed that Sanford was in Argentina visiting a mistress. He was term limited from seeking reelection as governor in 2010.

Yet another example of the importance of African-American staff in the district office comes from Robin Hayes, a white Republican legislator from North Carolina. Hayes represents the eighth district of North Carolina, which during the 107th Congress (2001–02, when I visited the district) had a 26 percent black population based on the 2000 census. James Glaser (2005), in his case study of Hayes's 2002 reelection race, described Hayes as having a "conservative bent" and a "traditional approach to cultural issues" that is sometimes "masked" by "[h]is folksy person-to-person style" (141, 146–57). Hayes's district staff, when first elected, was all white, though Hayes quickly realized this was a problem in terms of reaching the district's black voters. Thus, he hired Sharon Banner, a black staff member who had worked for the white Democrat who represented the district before Hayes. I asked a former staffer of the previous Democratic incumbent why Hayes hired Banner, and she jokingly claimed, "She's the only black person Robin knows!" However, once Banner was hired, she connected white Republican Hayes to African-American constituents that she had cultivated during her service with the previous Democratic representative. Even though Hayes's voting record was generally antagonistic to the substantive needs and wants of his black constituents, he worked with Banner in particular to serve black neighborhoods of the district that he had previously not focused on. For example, he worked to redevelop parks in some African-American neighborhoods in the district. In the 2000 election, a staffer claimed that Hayes's black support was higher than one might expect for a white Republican, and the black turnout in these precincts was generally lower than in prior elections. In this case, the presence of a black staff member contributed to the substantive representation of black constituents in terms of service allocations. Hayes lost reelection in 2008 to white Democrat Larry Kissell.

These findings thus far are qualitative and based on conversations I had in just seventeen congressional districts in the South. Also, it is important to point out that I am not suggesting that only black staff can work with black constituents or that only white staff can work with white constituents – of course, this is not the case. However, a clear pattern does seem to emerge. Black legislators generally hired black staff that had connections to the black community of their districts in greater numbers than did white legislators. Occasionally, white legislators (such as David Price and Robin Hayes) did the same. These decisions allow a greater entrée into the black communities of these legislators' congressional districts and can only ease the delivery of constituency service to black constituents.

However, many white legislators typically hired a token black staff member. Similarly, white staff in these district offices ranged from forgetful to ignorant in regard to the needs of and the diversity within the black community in the their congressional districts. Thus, descriptive representation at the district staff level does appear to have a relationship with substantive representation in terms of the delivery of constituency service. If an office is filled primarily with white staff, it is less likely that black constituents are regularly contacting that office for help. Similarly, offices with black staff or especially predominately black staff are likely to deliver better constituency service to African-American constituents. Based on my visits to these districts, it appears that the race of the legislator and perhaps the district black population (more than other factors) are the primary predictors of the hiring of black district staff.

The Racial Backgrounds of Congressional District Staff Across the United States

To test these constituency service findings regarding staff more broadly, I gathered data on the race of district staff in offices across the country – in order to determine the proportion of black staff working in district offices. Clearly, it is not feasible to contact district offices for all 435 members of Congress, so the first step was to limit the data collection to only those districts that were 15 percent black or higher (in this case, for the 107th Congress).

Second, I attempted to contact (first by phone, then with a follow-up letter in some cases) all districts with a 15 percent black population or higher based on the 2000 census. This data collection was done at various points over the course of the 107th Congress (2001–02) in order to match the national findings with the visits to districts I conducted during the same time period. There were 105 districts with a black population of 15 percent or greater in the 107th Congress, and I was able to garner data on the racial background of district staffers for 41 of them (39 percent). Of those that responded, 58 percent were from the South and 42 percent were from districts outside of the South. Given the sensitivity of the subject matter, this is a relatively good response rate. In many cases, the staffers contacted were unwilling to divulge the information regarding race. For example, one staff member kept asking whether I was working for their opponent's current congressional campaign and then abruptly ended the phone interview without providing the data. In other cases, I simply was unable to convince the staffers to assist me as I was from outside the district. The office of Barbara Lee (D-CA), for example, sent a nice but perfunctory follow-up note saying that congressional courtesy requires that I contact my own representative for the information requested (of course knowing that my own legislator would not be familiar with the racial makeup of her Oakland-based district staff).[2]

Due to the delicate subject matter, I embedded questions about the race of district staff within a series of less controversial questions. I opened each phone conversation by indicating that I was a researcher conducting a study about constituency service and then asked questions regarding office locations, constituency service requests, and so on before leading into the questions about the racial backgrounds of staffers. In a few instances, I followed up with letters and questions by mail.

As mentioned previously, the sample of respondents is forty-one legislative districts. All legislators who responded are either black or white. Twelve are black Democrats, thirteen are white Democrats, and twelve are white Republicans. Although clearly not a large or perfectly random sample, these results are illuminating and support the qualitative material

---

[2] This suggests that there may be selection bias in these results. Because of this possibility, a selection model – with the percentage of African-American district staff as the dependent variable and party, race, and district black population as the independent variables in the outcome equation – was also estimated (though not presented here; see Grose, Mangum, and Martin 2007). Even when controlling for selection effects, the results presented in this chapter still held.

previously presented. Further, the sample size here is as large or larger than similar analyses conducted by David Canon (1999).

First, I examine the difference in hiring patterns at the district level by party, race, and the black population of the district.[3] To examine the effect of a legislator's political party, I look at the difference in the mean proportion of black district staff hired by Republicans and by Democrats. To examine the impact of the race of the legislator, I look at the difference in the mean proportion of black district staff hired by black and white legislators (all legislators in the sample are either black or white). I also examine the effect of the black population of the district by comparing the proportion of black staff of legislators in black-majority districts and districts without a black majority. I consider these three predictors of black staff hiring separately by region as well. The fourth explanation regarding racial trust is considered by examining a simple graph of the proportion of black district staff, the black population of the district, and the race of the legislator.

Second, I also revisit David Canon's (1999) finding that black legislators that promote a "politics of commonality" are most likely to hire black staffers in the closest proportion to the black population of their district. That is, if a legislator represents a district that is 50 percent black, then the staff will be approximately 50 percent black as well. I do this by examining the mean of the following: the percent of the district staff that is black minus the percent of the district that is black. I also use this measure with the aforementioned difference of means' tests for party, race, and black population of the district. This measure is taken directly from Canon (1999, Ch. 5), though he examined *the percent of Washington staff*. My contention is that Canon's finding that "difference" members hire many more black staff is not borne out at the district level, as the legislator's race and the black population of the district are the key factors.

---

[3] Typically, quantitative-oriented political scientists have grown accustomed to using the most advanced statistical techniques, even when a simpler technique may be more appropriate. Given the small sample size, the multicollinearity between the four independent variables of interest (party of legislator, race of legislator, black population of the district, and racial trust) is extremely high. Without increasing the sample size, it is difficult to estimate one model incorporating these four variables without the standard errors being overly inflated. As a result, I am likely to underestimate the statistical impact of these variables if considered together in a multivariate model predicting the proportion of black district staff in each congressional office. However, as noted in the previous footnote, I did also estimate a selection model that yielded similar results to the cross-tabular results presented here.

Which Members of Congress Disproportionately Hire African-American Staff?

I first considered the effect of party on the hiring of black district staff. In Table 5.1, the mean percentages of the district staff that are black for the sample of Republican legislators (n = 12) and the sample of Democratic legislators (n = 29) are listed. The mean percentage of black staff in Democratic offices was significantly higher than in Republican legislative offices (45.5% as compared to 13.4%). Also as shown in Table 5.1, this result was found when looking at southern and nonsouthern districts separately. In southern districts represented by Democrats, African Americans made up 43.1 percent of district staff, whereas only 11.1 percent of staff were African American in GOP southern districts. In the non-South, these numbers were 48.1 percent and 20.4 percent, respectively. However, to best interpret these results, we should also control for the black population of the district.

Thus, in the top part of Table 5.2, I computed the following for each sample (Republicans and Democrats in all districts, South, and non-South): the percentage of the district staff that is black minus the black population of the congressional district (%). We can get an idea as to if Republican legislators "underhire" black staff proportionate to the black population of their district and whether Democratic legislators "overhire" black staff. This appears to be the case: Republican members of Congress, on average, hired fewer black staff than the black population of their congressional districts (12.2 percentage points less), whereas Democrats, on average, hired more black staff than would be expected based on the district black population (9.9 percentage points more). Thus, the expectations regarding the effect of political party are confirmed.

However, these results regarding party are driven by region as can also be seen in Table 5.2. Interestingly, outside of the South, both Republican and Democratic legislators overhire black staff relative to the African-American district population percentage. In the South, though, there is a large gap between parties as Republicans underhire black staff relative to the district's black population by 17 percentage points. In contrast, southern Democrats hire about 10 percentage points more black staff than would be expected based on the district black population.

As shown in Table 5.1, I also examine the effect of the presence of a black legislator in a district on hiring black staff. As expected, black legislators hire more black staff. Without controlling for the district black population and simply looking at the mean percentage of the district

TABLE 5.1. *Party, Race, and the Hiring of Black Staff in District Offices*

Political Party and Black Staff in District Offices

	Mean % of District Staff that are Black, all Districts	Mean % of District Staff that are Black, South	Mean % of District Staff that are Black, Non-South
Republican legislators (n = 12)	13.4%	11.1%	20.4%
Democratic legislators (n = 29)	45.5%	43.1%	48.1%

Note: These are statistically significant difference of means (significant at .01 level).

Legislator's Race and Black Staff in District Offices

	Mean % of District Staff that are Black, All Districts	Mean % of District Staff that are Black, South	Mean % of District Staff that are Black, Non-South
White legislators (n = 29)	23.9%	21.1%	29.2%
Black legislators (n = 12)	65.6%	69.1%	63.2%

Note: These are statistically significant difference of means (significant at .01 level).

Black-Majority Districts and Black Staff in District Offices

	Mean % of District Staff that are Black, All Districts	Mean % of District Staff that are Black, South	Mean % of District Staff that are Black, Non-South
Black-majority districts (n = 8)	71.3%	78.0%	67.3%
Black-influence districts and other districts (15–49% black) (n = 33)	27.6%	24.4%	33.1%

Note: These are statistically significant difference of means (significant at .01 level).

TABLE 5.2. *Comparing the Hiring of Black Staff in District Offices to the District's Black Population*

Political Party and Black Staff in District Offices

	Mean of (% District Staff that is Black) – (% Black Constituents in District), all Districts	Mean of (% District Staff that is Black) – (% Black Constituents in District), South	Mean of (% District Staff that is Black) – (% Black Constituents in District), Non-South
Republican legislators (n = 12)	–12.2%	–17.5%	3.7%
Democratic legislators (n = 29)	9.9%	10.8%	8.8%

Note: The non-South difference of means is not statistically significant. The others (all districts and South) are statistically significant differences of means (significant at .01 level).

Legislator's Race and Black Staff in District Offices

	Mean of (% District Staff that is Black) – (% Black Constituents in District), all Districts	Mean of (% District Staff that is Black) – (% Black Constituents in District), South	Mean of (% District Staff that is Black) – (% Black Constituents in District), Non-South
White legislators (n = 29)	0.5%	–4.1%	9.1%
Black legislators (n = 12)	10.6%	16.7%	6.2%

Note: The non-South difference of means is not statistically significant. The others (all districts and South) are statistically significant differences of means (significant at .01 level).

Black-Majority Districts and Black Staff in District Offices

	Mean of (% District Staff that is Black) – (% Black Constituents in District), all Districts	Mean of (% District Staff that is Black) – (% Black Constituents in District), South	Mean of (% District Staff that is Black) – (% Black Constituents in District), Non-South
Black-majority districts (n = 8)	9.6%	18.6%	4.1%
Black-influence districts and other districts (15–49% black) (n = 33)	1.9%	–2.4%	9.5%

Note: The non-South difference of means is not statistically significant. The others (all districts and South) are statistically significant differences of means (significant at .01 level).

staff that are black, on average, 65.6 percent of black legislators' district staffs are also black. The mean for white legislators is only 23.9 percent. These results are the same regardless of whether the member represents a southern or nonsouthern district, as can be seen in the last two columns of the race of legislator results in Table 5.1.

These results, like the party results, could be driven in part by the black population of the district. So I also computed the mean difference of the percent of the staff that is African American and the percent African American in the congressional district (see the middle part of Table 5.2). Here, the results are interesting and suggest that electing black legislators is important for increasing black political empowerment through the hiring of black congressional district staff. Nationally in all districts, white legislators just slightly overhire black staff when compared to the mean proportion of their districts (+0.5 percentage points). Essentially, this number demonstrates that, on average, white legislators are hiring black staff approximately proportionate to the black population in congressional districts. However, black legislators clearly overhire black staff above and beyond their districts' mean black district populations (+10.6 percentage points). There are important regional differences to this finding, though. In the South, the difference between the mean percentage of black staff and the mean district black population is +16.7 percentage points in districts with African-American representatives, whereas this gap is −4.1 in white legislators' districts. However, in nonsouthern districts, there is no significant difference between white and black legislators when it comes to hiring black staff relative to the baseline black population of their districts.

The aggregate implications of these results suggest that electing black representatives in the South, which has traditionally occurred in black-majority and black-influence districts, is crucial for increasing the hiring of black staff. However, in congressional districts outside of the South, both black and white legislators are hiring black staff more than what might be expected based on a proportionality criterion (though given the very small samples, we should be cognizant of the limitations of these data). Following the earlier discussion showing that black staff generally had stronger connections to their districts' black communities than did white staff, this implies that the election of black legislators results in better constituency service (a substantive outcome) for African Americans in the South. However, descriptive representation plays a much smaller role outside of the South (based on the results in Table 5.2; though it does play a role based on the results in Table 5.1). This result is interesting as

Swain (1995) found few differences between black and white legislators in their hiring of staff in her examination of thirteen legislators, contrary to my findings here regarding the South. One reason my results may differ is because some of her sample came from outside of the South.

Finally, I examine the type of district. Again at the bottom of Table 5.1, the hiring of staff by type of district (black-majority districts compared to districts without a black majority) is considered. As would be expected, legislators from black-majority districts have a much higher mean proportion of black staff than legislators from other districts (71.3% to 27.6%). Interestingly, there are not major differences between southern and nonsouthern districts, though legislators from nonsouthern black-minority districts hire slightly more African-American staff than legislators in southern districts without a black majority.

The bottom of Table 5.2 examines hiring by the type of district (black-majority or black-minority) given the baseline of the district black population percentage. In districts without a black-majority, these legislators are generally hiring black staff proportionate to their district populations (a mean of +1.9 percentage points more black staff than black constituents in the national sample of all districts). The legislators representing black-majority districts hired a mean of +9.6 percentage points more black district staff than black constituents. When we look at nonsouthern versus southern districts, it appears this empirical pattern is regional. There is no significant difference between black-majority and non-black-majority districts outside of the South, as northern legislators overhire black staff relative to their underlying district black populations. Legislators from black-majority districts in the South overhire black staff to a large degree (+18.6 percentage points), whereas legislators from black-minority districts in the South do not. They just barely underhire black staff relative to the district black population (though at -2.4%, it is more or less proportionate to the district black population).

This clearly suggests that, even in the aggregate, the drawing of black-majority districts enhances constituency service to African Americans. In the north, if all types of districts are hiring black staff slightly more than the proportion expected based on the underlying district black population, there is no dilutive effect in drawing black-majority districts in those surrounding districts that have smaller black populations. In the South, because districts without a majority of black constituents are hiring black staff approximately proportionate to the population levels in their districts and legislators from black-majority districts are hiring significantly more black staff than their district black populations would suggest, the aggregate result would be more black district staff hired in all congressional districts under districting plans that maximize the number of black-majority districts. Given the small samples examined here, an important caveat should be noted regarding these results. The findings may apply only to this particular sample of districts for which staffers were willing to share the data with us. Nevertheless, the patterns revealed by this analysis are generally consistent with the evidence presented elsewhere in the book. Even with the small samples examined here, the small sample sizes are much larger than those used by Swain (1995) and Canon (1999) when they examined staff (also see Meier et al. [2005] who finds that descriptive representation on school boards yields the hiring of more minority teachers with a much larger sample than examined by me, by Swain, or by Canon).

Commonality versus Difference: No Difference

As this section clearly builds from David Canon's (1999) work, it is also worth examining his conception of black legislators as falling into one of two categories ("difference" members and "commonality" members) and the implications for constituency service. Canon presented a well-reasoned theory that the racial makeup of candidates in a primary election in black-majority and black-influence districts will predict the style of the candidate who wins the primary. If black candidates run against white candidates in a primary election to a black-majority or black-influence district, then Canon shows that the black candidate who wins will normally engage in what he terms "the politics of difference." That is, this type of legislator will have won office by appealing primarily to black voters, and thus the "presentation of self" to voters will reflect this. Specifically, these "difference" members are more likely to present themselves in an overtly racial way, primarily appealing only to black voters.

The other category of black legislators is "commonality" members. These legislators tend to have initially won election to office in primaries with only black candidates. Thus, they won by appealing to a subset of black voters and also white voters in the primary. The style of this type of black legislator, according to Canon, is one that engages in biracial appeals, perhaps focusing on race but in a way that is not exclusive to only one racial group. Thus, the presentation to the constituency for a "commonality" member would be less focused on directly racial issues and would instead make decisions that would appeal to both black and white voters in the district.

I coded the twelve black legislators in the national staff sample as either "difference" members or "commonality" members. Seven of the members in this sample were also in Canon's sample, and thus were coded the same as Canon's coding suggested (1999, chapter 3). There were five black members in my sample, though, that I had to determine independently from Canon's coding scheme, as he did not include them in his sample. I did this by examining newspaper and other accounts of their first primary campaigns to see whether they presented themselves to appeal to a biracial group of voters or if they appealed via "difference" with only black voters. Again, with the very small samples, any inferences based on the evidence is limited.

For example, black Democrat Harold Ford Jr. (D-TN) was in my sample but not Canon's. Thus, having examined how Ford campaigned and his "presentation of self" in newspaper accounts during his initial election, he clearly struck a tone to reach both his district's black constituents (which are a majority) and white constituents. Thus, he was coded as a "politics of commonality" member.

Canon argues that commonality members are more likely to engage in legislative outcomes that are directed toward black *and* white constituents, whereas difference members will focus primarily on black constituents. His analysis in regard to the hiring of staff, however, is problematic because he measures substantive representation via constituency service by tallying the proportion of black staff who work in Washington offices, when most constituency service occurs in the district.

An example of why his analysis is problematic is the case of Ford (a commonality member). In May of 2002, I visited his only district office in Memphis, Tennessee, and learned that six of the seven staff there were African American. However, at the same time, in his Washington office, he employed four white staff and four black staff. His district in the 107th Congress, centered around Memphis, was 59 percent black. The staffers there indicated, however, that more than 59 percent of the requests from constituents generally came from black constituents. So, Ford's staff is much whiter in Washington, as he ambitiously sought to move to other positions beyond his House seat. He has unsuccessfully run for House Democratic leader and lost a close race for the U.S. Senate in Tennessee in 2006. By having a more racially diverse and whiter staff in his Washington office, he has a better chance of putting forward a more moderate, biracial "presentation of self" to the Washington community. However, the political and demographic needs of his district predict that he will hire a large proportion of black staff

TABLE 5.3. *Commonality versus Difference: No Difference?*

	Canon (1999, 208) Results: % Washington Staff that is Black) – (% Black Constituents in District)	Results Based on District Staff, 107th Congress: Mean of (% District Staff That is Black) – (% Black Constituents in District)
Commonality members	4.51% (n = 8)	13.7% (n = 8)
Difference members	19.07% (n = 6)	4.3% (n = 4)
t statistic, difference of means	2.53*	1.03

Note: Canon reports that his results based on Washington staff (the second column) are statistically significant at the 0.05 level, but my replicated results based on district staff (the third column) are not statistically different.

in the Memphis office, and his presentation in Memphis is different than in Washington.

To test this more broadly, I again compare means of staff, this time for black legislators who are difference members and for black legislators who are commonality members in Table 5.3. In the second column in Table 5.3 are Canon's findings based on Washington staff (the mean of [the percentage of a legislator's Washington staff that is black minus the percentage of the district's black population]) In the third column I present my results based on district staff (the mean of [the percentage of a legislator's district staff that is black minus the percentage of the district's black population]). I do not consider regional differences between southern and nonsouthern districts given the small sample sizes. Somewhat surprisingly, I find that commonality members actually overrepresent black district staff proportionally to the black populations of their districts (a mean of 13.7 percentage points more), whereas difference members only slightly overrepresent. This is in stark contrast to Canon's findings, which are exactly the opposite.

It is important to note that the difference of means test for my sample is not significant, and this simply indicates that there is not a statistically significant difference between commonality and difference members in regard to the number of black district staff. Thus, whereas this difference versus commonality categorization may be useful for other measures of black representation that Canon details, in regard to staff it may not be. The key factors that explain the hiring of black staff in districts, and thus the delivery of constituency service to black constituents, are the race of the legislator, party, and possibly the black population of the district.

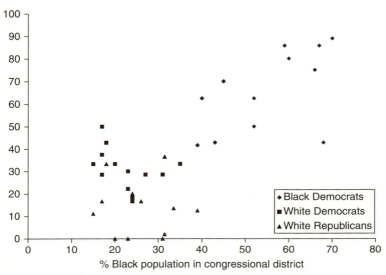

FIGURE 5.1. Black Democrats, white Democrats, and white Republicans: Hiring patterns of African-American staff in congressional district offices.

Just to summarize the findings in regard to these three explanations (legislator's party, legislator's race, and district black population) and having dispatched with the commonality/difference explanation, in Figure 5.1, I have plotted the proportion of black staffers hired for white Republicans, white Democrats, and black Democrats based on the black population of their districts. The vertical axis in the figure is simply the number of black staff divided by the total number of staff (multiplied by one hundred), whereas the horizontal axis is the black population (%) of the district. There appears to be a pattern based on all three factors. The proportion of black staff generally increases as the district black population increases. Black legislators hire more black staff than do white legislators in most cases, though surprisingly not in all. Also, many Republicans do not hire black staff proportionate to their district's population.

Finally, the racial trust hypothesis can also be examined by looking at Figure 5.1 as well. Do black legislators respond differently than white legislators to the size of the black population? This appears to be the case. African-American members of Congress, designated by the diamond symbol in the figure, hire a larger proportion of black district staff as the size of the district's black population increases. There is not as clear or discernible of a pattern for white legislators, which are designated by squares and triangles in the figure. Thus, it appears that there is a difference in the allocation of African-American district staff based on the interaction of the black population of the district and the race of the legislator.

Conclusion: Race and the Quality of Constituency Service to Black Constituents

Quite a bit of evidence was presented in this chapter and in Chapter 4 regarding constituency service; so in conclusion, I would like to synthesize and summarize the findings. In addition to summary, I would also like to suggest a few implications related to the quality of constituency service to African-American constituents that are slightly more subjective than the objective evidence presented throughout the chapter.

Fredrick Harris, Valeria Sinclair-Chapman, and Brian McKenzie (2006, 8) state that "newly elected black officials in the South noted how their electoral wins raised hopes for improving services ... in black communities." I find that these expectations are demonstrated through constituency service. First, the race of the legislator clearly affected the substantive representation of black constituents in terms of constituency service allocations. In most cases, white legislators simply did not work as closely with black constituents as did black legislators – as measured by district office locations or by the proportion of black staff in the district. Contrary to Carol Swain's (1995) findings in this regard (and based on a larger sample of white legislators than Swain's), I did not find consistent evidence of white legislators working to reach black constituents at a comparable level as most black legislators (there were of course exceptions, such as David Price, but these were notable because they were unusual). This may be caused by the fact that the white legislators Swain examined hailed from black-majority districts or districts with black populations nearing 50 percent. As noted earlier, there were hardly any districts with these black population levels represented by white legislators during the time period I examine.

Second, there was variation in terms of the quality of constituency service to black constituents based on the black population of the district and its effect on just the subset of black legislators, which suggests racial trust may also play a role. Consistent with Carol Swain's suggestions for enhancing the substantive representation of black constituents, I did find that black legislators from white-majority districts did a much better job in terms of all-around constituency service – and also constituency service geared toward black constituents – than did their black colleagues

form black-majority districts. Perhaps because of their relatively tenuous holds on white-majority districts, black legislators Sanford Bishop
and Mel Watt particularly (who had the lowest black population of all
black legislators in the districts I visited, 39% and 45% respectively) had
extremely efficient constituency service operations in place. Bishop and
Watt were also better than comparable white legislators at delivering
constituency service to black constituents.

Earl Hilliard, in contrast, the black legislator hailing from the district
with the largest black population (67%), clearly did not have as an effective constituency service operation. Similarly, Harold Ford Jr., also representing a black-majority district (59%) seemed focused on activities and
events beyond his district, which may have inhibited his ability to strongly
serve his black constituents in his congressional district. Ford's ambitions
for statewide office were demonstrated as staffers in his office told me
that his typical weekend "home" often included stops in Nashville or
Knoxville, cities far afield of his Memphis-based congressional district.
Ford went on to run unsuccessfully for the U.S. Senate from Tennessee in
2006, losing to white Republican Bob Corker by 51 to 48 percent. Even
though losing in a racially charged contest, Ford won a significant percentage of white voter support. The same year that Ford lost to Corker,
white Democrat Steve Cohen won election to replace Ford in the black-
majority ninth district of Tennessee. In 2010, Ford toyed with the idea
of challenging incumbent Senator Kirstin Gillibrand (D-NY), but he
ultimately chose not to run.

Like Swain's finding regarding "historically black" districts, Hilliard's
case and Ford's case indicate that districts that are overwhelmingly
black can become so safe for black incumbents that this safety may
be a detriment to African-American constituents. Was Hilliard a better
representative than comparably white legislators that may have served
previously? This is likely – as detailed earlier, his office locations and his
staff were connected to the black community of the district, reaching
voters that may have been less of a focus for white legislators. In contrast to these specific examples, though, Hilliard clearly used symbolic
politics to reach black voters, and his constituency service operation –
particularly to African Americans but also to white voters – suffered
relative to black legislators from black-influence districts. Hilliard, in
2002, lost a primary to black Democrat Artur Davis. Accounts suggest
that Davis was similar to Ford as he quickly began focusing on building
relationships for a statewide run for office (Ifill 2009). Representative

Davis failed in his quest for governor of Alabama in 2010, losing in the Democratic primary.[4]

Third, the black population of the district in general did play a role in constituency service outcomes, though not a very significant one when compared to the race of the legislator. There were some differences among black legislators in terms of the proportion black staff hired based on the black populations of their districts. Also, few of the white legislators from districts classified as low in black population (in the qualitative sample) focused much on the delivery of constituency service to black constituents. However, the most robust findings regarding constituency service to African Americans centered around the race of the legislator.

Finally, in the qualitative sample of the seventeen districts I visited, party did not appear to play a large role. In the quantitative sample of black district staff proportions, party was important, though its effect was perhaps overshadowed by the effect of the race of the legislator. Democrats hired a larger proportion of black district staff than did Republicans. However, black Democratic legislators did a much better job of reaching black constituents than did white Democratic legislators on both the office location and black staff measures. The qualitative evidence also indicated a willingness by some Republican legislators to reach out to black constituents, albeit sometimes in small or naïve ways (e.g., Randy Forbes and Robin Hayes).

---

[4] I want to note that these legislators (Ford, Hilliard, and even Davis) may not be entirely representative of all black members of Congress serving in black-majority districts due to the uniqueness of their cases (in Hilliard's case, some nonracial problems that arose during his representation of the district; and in Ford's and Davis's cases, their interests in statewide office may have yielded a bit less focus on responsiveness within their districts). Even if these cases are somewhat exceptional, I am not arguing that black legislators in black-majority districts are unresponsive to black constituents, but simply that they have greater leeway than do comparable black legislators from districts without a black majority to pursue a multitude of representational strategies and non-district-oriented pursuits. Black legislators from white-majority districts, at least initially when negotiating the representational relationship between member and constituents, may need to be more responsive to black constituents in their districts.

6

Bringing Home the Bacon

Delivering Federal "Pork" to African Americans

"Senator, do you think in our Congress we'll ever be able to get rid of the pork situation?"

–Unidentified Mississippi citizen,
questioning Sen. Trent Lott (R-MS) at
Square Books in Oxford, MS, Oct. 14, 2004

"Well, first of all, you have to define 'What is pork?' I have quite often defined it as federal spending north of Memphis. [laughter from audience] ... Do you know of any pork I brought to Mississippi? The funds I've gotten for Oxford, the funds I've gotten for DeSoto County, the highway money? Is that pork? The 100 million for the Greenville bridge? That, why that's not pork, is it? And of course, the story of how that happened was Richard Shelby from Alabama was chairman of the transportation appropriations subcommittee and he came over and said, Trent – I was majority leader then and you know I got to call up bills or not – and he said, you know, we've got about 300 million left here in our allocation and I was wondering what you thought we ought to do with it. I said, well let's be fair. You take a hundred, I'll take a hundred, and we'll let the rest of the country have the remaining hundred. And it seemed fair and that's what we did. [Laughter from audience]."

–Sen. Trent Lott (R-MS), responding to question[1]

When asked to rank the most important activity that members of Congress engage in, 47 percent of African Americans chose "making sure the district gets its fair share of government money and projects" (Tate 2003). In contrast, only 15 percent of all U.S. citizens think this is a representative's

---

[1] The author recorded these quotes from www.c-span.org, where a video of the event with Lott at Square Books is archived.

most important responsibility.[2] Given the value that African Americans place on the delivery of federal projects and funds to the district, we would expect that political scientists studying minority representation in Congress would have addressed this topic. However, most scholars have only addressed the effect of black representation on roll-call voting. In fact, to my knowledge, no scholar has examined the impact of racial representation on the distribution of "pork" projects to black constituents.

Pork projects are often derided by critics, such as the citizen quoted previously, as wasteful, inefficient spending by the government. However, pork projects, as Trent Lott pointed out, are not typically considered pork by the recipients. In fact, pork projects are sought after and happily accepted by constituents. As a result, legislators have an interest in delivering federal spending to their constituents in order to reward supporters and to reap the credit. Even more interestingly, something that a large percentage of African Americans think is a vital component of a representative's role is derided by others as "waste" and "pork." The fact that pork has been framed in this way given the differential in opinion on it by race is worthy of further inquiry.

In this chapter, I answer three interrelated questions that by now should be familiar to the reader: (1) Do representatives elected from majority-black districts allocate more federal projects to black constituents than representatives from other districts? (2) Do black representatives allocate more projects to black constituents than white representatives? (3) Do Democratic representatives allocate more projects to black constituents than Republican representatives? I also consider how racial trust (the interaction of the race of the legislator and the black population of the legislator's district) affects the allocation of pork projects to black constituents as well. In answering these questions, I will continue to test the theory offered in Chapter 2.

The four primary findings of this chapter are as follows. First, the election of black legislators enhances the substantive representation of black interests: Black representatives are more likely than white representatives to allocate projects to black constituents, all else being equal. Black legislators allocate more projects and federal funding to African-American constituents. The election of African Americans results in millions of dollars more allocated per Congress to African-American citizens, a significant and substantive result. Further, I also argue that there

---

[2] This result for all U.S. citizens is from Cain, Ferejohn, and Fiorina (1987, 38). The question was the same in the Cain, Ferejohn, and Fiorina study (NES) as the Tate study (NBES).

is a direct relationship between the election of African-American legislators and increased federal spending for traditionally African-American educational institutions. African-American members of Congress allocate more projects than white legislators to geographic areas that are heavily African American and to historically black colleges and universities (hereafter referred to as HBCUs).

Second, when examining only those districts *represented by black legislators*, black-majority districts do not always enhance the substantive representation of black interests: Black representatives elected from black-influence districts allocate more projects to black constituents than do black representatives from majority-black districts. Thus, in order to maximize the number of projects and federal dollars allocated to black constituents, black-decisive districts – influence districts where black candidates can win – may be the best prescription. Third, racial trust is a key predictor of project delivery. White representatives are somewhat responsive to different levels of district black population, and black legislators also differentially respond to varying levels of the district black populations of their districts. These findings lend support to the broader idea that representatives allocate projects in order to appeal to and appease subsets of constituencies within their districts – and that legislators rationally respond to electoral incentives in their districts.

Fourth, and perhaps most surprisingly, white Republicans can sometimes substantively represent black interests: White Republicans are slightly more likely to allocate projects to historically black colleges and universities than are white Democrats. Thus, the election of both Republicans *and* black Democrats leads to more federal money diverted to African Americans. This suggests that districting plans that result in the election of both black Democrats and Republicans are not problematic for the substantive representation of black interests, when these interests are measured as federal goods delivered to African-American constituents.

In fact, some of these findings, most notably the ones about white Republicans and black representatives of white-majority districts, suggest that the relationships between race, party, and constituency size are not as clear-cut as the conventional wisdom might suggest. When examining project allocations, a legislative activity beyond roll-call voting, the traditional expectations do not always hold as representatives will engage in allocations in order to both appease their core supporters (black Democratic legislators in white-majority districts) and reach out to voters beyond their electoral coalitions (white Republican legislators).

This chapter continues to address the questions posed earlier in the book. If we are interested in questions about American democracy and concerned about how best to enhance minority representation, is it important to elect black representatives? What arrangement of black and nonblack voters in a district maximizes the representation of black interests via public policy? Do black legislators or legislators from black-majority districts allocate more federal projects and spending to African Americans? As detailed in Chapter 1, scholars have not given a clear answer. Further, I again rely on the districts in the mid- to late-1990s so we can assess the effects of African-American legislators separate from the effects of black-majority districts.

Results from this chapter can best be interpreted within the context of the entire book. They suggest a more nuanced view of the policy effects of electing black representatives and drawing black-majority districts. Based just on the results in Chapter 3, the clear conclusion is that voting records changed little in the aggregate with the drawing of black-majority districts. Further, party is the key predictor of the substantive representation of black interests in Congress when examining roll-call voting, and racial factors (the race of the legislator, the district black population, and racial trust) are not as important. However, as will be demonstrated in this chapter, these conclusions regarding substantive representation based only on roll-call voting are not consistently demonstrated with other congressional activities. Voting is not the only way policy gets made in Washington. The delivery of pork projects, also called distributive public policy, is a critical policy activity that members of Congress have substantial individual control over.

This chapter's findings, however, are not just applicable to research on minority representation; they also shed light on broader questions of legislative representation. How does the descriptive connection between legislator and constituent affect the allocation of projects to constituents? The results pertaining to African-American constituents are potentially applicable to other constituency groups as well: Constituency groups that are core components of elected officials' coalitions may receive pork (Cox and McCubbins 1986). Further, constituency groups will receive more projects from representatives if these constituency groups are large enough to affect the potential electoral outcome but not such a large majority in the district as to be taken for granted. Similarly, the electoral coalitions of legislators and levels of trust between representative and constituents affect the delivery of projects to constituency groups.

Pork *Is* Substantive Representation

As detailed in Chapters 1 and 2, the study of roll-call voting has been the bread-and-butter of scholars of both Congress and minority representation. However, few observers of race and Congress have examined activities beyond roll-call voting, and none have examined pork project allocation, perhaps the most substantively significant form of public policy decision making in terms of the direct benefits to African Americans. The amount of money spent per year on federal grants and projects delivered to congressional districts is astounding, and the share of this federal pie allocated to African Americans is highly contingent on the types of congressional districts drawn and whether African-American legislators are elected.

In this chapter, I extend the study of substantive representation and racial redistricting in a new direction. I analyze the distribution of federal pork projects within congressional districts in order to capture manifestations of policy representation beyond roll-call voting. Pork projects are likely to be of importance to constituents in ways that voting on bills may not be. Tangible goods delivered to the district are important for legislators hoping to establish and expand personal connections within their districts.

Another advantage of studying the distribution of projects is that we are examining legislative policy outputs that are not as ideologically oriented as other policies. Distributive policy outputs (or pork projects) are much more likely to be passed than other more ideologically charged legislation that may be favored by black constituents, such as redistributive policies or social policies (e.g., affirmative action and civil rights). Unlike voting on ideological policy, legislators often form large coalitions spanning party and ideology when considering federal spending bills (Weingast 1979; Shepsle and Weingast 1981; Weingast, Shepsle, and Johnsen 1981). Thus, individual legislators have the ability to garner projects and give them to multiple constituencies, whereas with roll-call voting they must cast either "yea" or "nay." Every member of Congress has access to some federal projects and dollars, so the question becomes not whether they are successful at securing federal funds, but who in the district receives those federal funds. By charting the distribution of projects to particular constituents – in this case, African-American constituents – we can learn more about congressional behavior in general.

For example, congressional staff that I interviewed suggested that they have much greater control over their ability to deliver projects to constituents of their choosing than with roll-call voting. I asked all staff I spoke with whether their congressional office seeks out grants for constituents or whether they simply help with requests for applications. One staffer from Sanford Bishop's office, Hobby Stripling, said that a substantial portion (though not all) of his offices' assistance with project grants occurs based on a constituent's unsolicited requests: "We don't have to look for much business." Most other staffers, however, indicated that they seek out grant projects for a variety of constituents, especially their strongest supporters. Tracey Lovett, a staffer in David Price's district office said that "it's a little bit of both [responding to constituents' project requests and seeking out constituents to apply for grants]." An example she offered was Price's work to encourage the continuation of funding for a program called the "Saturday Academy" at North Carolina Central University, a historically black college in Durham, North Carolina. This program brings in African-American elementary and middle-school students to the university on the weekends for practice in taking standardized tests. Price was attending an event at the university one Saturday and learned about the program while visiting the campus. According to Lovett, he encouraged the program's administrators to apply for a federal grant for the program, saying he "would hate to see this fall through the cracks."

Thus, legislators encourage grant applications from constituents who may not be aware of federal opportunities for funding, while also assisting those constituents who come directly to them. Given this pattern, it is likely that factors such as the legislator's party and race may play a role in project allocation to black constituents.

Bringing Home the Bacon to Predominately Black Counties and Historically Black Colleges and Universities

My goal is to measure the distribution of federal projects to black constituents within congressional districts. However, it is impossible to chart the flow of individual projects to each individual recipient by race. There are numerous ways that legislators can direct federal spending to their districts. They can "earmark" spending for certain projects in spending bills, though the identity of the earmarker was not publicly revealed during the period studied. Legislators can further encourage applications within their districts for existing grant opportunities. Also, legislators can work extensively with the federal bureaucracy and lobby administrators directly to acquire projects. Unfortunately, direct data on the race of the recipient receiving the grant allocations do not exist. However, we do have extensive data available on the federal projects allocated to specific geographic units within a congressional district (e.g., heavily black counties) and to colleges and universities. Because of this, to examine federal project allocation to African Americans, I analyze the allocation of federal dollars and projects to heavily black counties and to historically black colleges. The examination of grant allocations to black counties and to historically black colleges is a subset of all potential grant allocations to African Americans, but they serve as useful proxy measures of the allocation of project grants to individual African-American constituents (because these data are not available). Past work on pork project allocation unrelated to race typically examines the geographic allocation of federal projects at higher levels of aggregation than to the individual constituent as well (e.g., Stein and Bickers 1995).

Predominately Black Counties
Due to residential and historical segregation in many parts of the United States, members of individual racial groups are highly concentrated in some geographical areas. In this chapter, I look at one of these geographical subunits, counties within congressional districts. Specifically, I look at counties with significant black populations in order to capture the flow of federal projects to black constituents. Although this is not a perfect surrogate measure of African-American constituents' receipt of projects, it does have appeal, given what we know about how members of Congress view and compartmentalize their own districts.

Many representatives regard counties as "building blocks" that make up their overall geographic constituency. Kathy Worthington, a staff member for former South Carolina Congressman (and Governor) Mark Sanford, explained how Sanford regarded his district when in Congress: She immediately divided up the district, county by county, detailing which county's residents were most likely to support Sanford. In fact, she mentioned one particular county that was visited less often than others when Sanford returned home on weekends and recesses. The explanations offered were that its population was small and that Sanford's support was particularly weak there, given the county's large proportion of black constituents. It was clear from this exchange that Republican Sanford (or at least his staffer) intertwined county-based geography and race when thinking about the district.

I will look at the distribution of projects within congressional districts to those counties that have very high levels of black population. Simply delivering projects to counties with large black populations, though, does not immediately imply that black constituents will receive these projects. As John Ferejohn (1974, 53) has noted, local projects can sometimes be opposed by a subset of constituents. In fact, just because a new bridge or road, for example, is placed in a community, this does not mean that it is necessarily beneficial to those who live there. For example, if a new, federally funded road physically divides a neighborhood, then those living there may not in fact want it.

However, I do not think this scenario is likely for most federal projects. Members of Congress will generally allocate projects to specific counties with large black populations in order to appeal to black voters. For example, see Table 6.1, which is a 2000 press release from John Spratt, another South Carolina representative. Spratt, a white Democrat, hailed from a 31 percent black district (when this press release was issued) and relied on black voter support for reelection. This particular press release is typical of those from his office and other offices. The press release announces that three *counties* in his thirteen-county district received a grant from the Department of Education. Two of the three counties that received grants, Dillon and Marlboro, are, respectively, 44 and 49 percent black in population. Although race is not explicitly mentioned, nine of the other counties in the district have substantially lower black populations. These projects, in all likelihood, will be beneficial to black constituents in these counties. Additionally, Spratt's press release points out that these counties were selected for their rural nature. His district has many whiter, rural counties, yet these three counties were singled out to receive the project. Even though race is not discussed explicitly in this or most other press releases, by sending projects to heavily black areas, legislators can avoid appearing to make decisions along racial lines even when, in fact, they are. Minority media sources may cover these grants whereas other news sources may not (Grose 2006), thus allowing a more surgical attempt by the legislator to reach out to black voters. This way, legislators can engage in the sometimes difficult task of appealing to black voters while not appearing to forsake white, Latino, or Asian-American voters.

Like the previous example, I assume that many of the projects allocated to counties with large black populations are both sought after by the black residents and are allocated by representatives with the intention of reaching out to black voters. Just to make sure I am actually measuring the receipt of projects by black constituents, as I discuss later, I extend the analysis and look at project distribution to historically black colleges and universities (black institutions that undoubtedly welcome projects). As we will see, the results from both the aggregate analysis of all projects to

TABLE 6.1. *John Spratt News Release*

U.S. Representative
John Spratt South Carolina – 5th District
News Release
September 18, 2000, For Immediate Release Contact: Chuck Fant,
   202–225–5501

Spratt Wins Major Grant for Schools in Darlington, Dillon, and Marlboro Counties

WASHINGTON – U.S. Rep. John Spratt (D-SC) announced today that schools in Darlington, Dillon, and Marlboro counties will benefit from a major Department of Education grant to fund online access to advanced placement courses.

"This is great news for the Pee Dee," said Spratt. "I was delighted to work with Inez Tenenbaum, our State Superintendent of Education, to help schools in South Carolina win this grant."

Spratt said the grant will fund a project known as "AP Nexus," an experimental effort to use new media – especially the Internet – to provide expanded access to Advanced Placement (AP) courses in rural schools.

The Pee Dee schools that will be participating in the program are Darlington High School and Mayo High School in Darlington County, Latta High School in Dillon County, and Marlboro County High School in Marlboro County.

Four other South Carolina schools will also participate: Mullins High School and Terrell's Bay High School in Marion County, Lockhart High School in Union County, and Kingstree High School in Williamsburg County.

South Carolina will share the $1.37 million grant, which covers the next three years, with the states of Georgia and Tennessee.

Spratt said the program will contract with Apex Learning, of Bellevue, Washington, for online courses. The company offers a broad selection of advanced placement courses, online instructor-led courses, and exam preparation. The online courses will help to supplement the existing AP programs at the participating schools.

"Many of these schools," said Spratt, "are able to offer only a small number of AP courses to their students. AP Nexus will provide access to far more AP courses, which will give these students a huge leg-up when they are applying for college."

1536 Longworth Building • Washington, DC 20515 • www.house.gov/spratt

---

Source: Primary document collected during field research.

heavily black counties and the results of project allocations to HBCUs are consistent and robust; therefore, we can feel confident that the distribution of projects to black constituents has appropriately been measured.

To capture the distribution of projects to black constituents, there are some obvious criteria to use when determining which counties to look at. Counties with numerically large black populations are clearly of interest.

Thus, I examine counties that are greater than or equal to 40 percent in black population and compare how much federal money and grants are sent to these counties when represented by different types of legislators.[3] Because of the mid-1990s court-ordered redistricting that caused a number of African-American legislators to represent white-majority districts, I examine all congressional districts from the 104th through 106th Congresses (1995–2000). Additionally, by looking at the county as the unit of analysis, there is substantial variation allowing us to assess the effect of black legislators, black-majority districts, and racial trust on project allocations at the same time.

One additional point needs to be made about the unit of analysis. Previously, I simply use the word "counties." However, in order to utilize more complete data, I also include those counties that are split into multiple congressional districts. Thus, the previous measures include both whole counties and portions of counties. When I refer to "counties" in this chapter, I also include county portions that are split between congressional districts. However, for the sake of parsimony, I typically refer to all as "counties" throughout the chapter.

For example, Clarke County, Alabama, was split in a district map established for the 1992 elections. The county was split between the state's first and seventh congressional districts. In the 106th Congress (1999–2000), the first district was represented by Sonny Callahan, a white Republican, and the seventh district was represented by Earl Hilliard, a black Democrat. The portion of Clarke County in Callahan's district has a 41.0 percent black population, whereas the portion in Hilliard's district has a 55.5 percent black population. Thus, both of these county portions are included as *separate observations* in the sample of counties that are 40 percent black or higher. Presumably, both Callahan and Hilliard will consider their respective portions of Clarke County when working to deliver projects to the district.

In sum, studying project allocations to heavily black counties (1) will allow us to assess the effects of black legislators versus black-majority districts on the substantive representation of African Americans; and (2) examine whether the billions of dollars in federal spending in a given year reach African Americans. Predominately black counties are those most

---

[3] Forty percent is a somewhat arbitrary cutoff indicating a county with a high black population. Though not presented here, I also examined project allocations to only counties with a black majority, and the results were substantively the same as those presented in this chapter.

likely to have been neglected prior to the extension of the Voting Rights Act. These counties are quite often (though not always) in the South, sometimes poorer, and often populated with citizens with lower educational levels than their fellow citizens from other counties. In fact, 90 percent of the counties with greater than 40 percent black population are from the South, so the conclusions drawn from this analysis are primarily limited to the South. Thus, these counties may lack the infrastructure of institutions (e.g., research hospitals and universities) or individuals (e.g., those familiar with grant application procedures who can apply without the assistance of a legislator) that can lead to access to federal largesse. Thus, the member of Congress that represents these counties may be one of the only opportunities for federal spending to reach predominately black counties. Further, by examining counties, the correlation between two of the key explanatory factors – black legislator and district black population – is reduced.

In order to test the unified theory of black representation specified in Chapter 2, I am interested in looking at the effect of the same four key variables from earlier chapters on project allocations to black constituents: (1) the congressional district's black population percentage; (2) the presence of a black representative; (3) racial trust (the interaction between the two other racial variables); and (4) the party of the representative. These four factors are likely to have an impact on the substantive representation of black constituents and next I briefly detail how we might expect these variables to affect project allocation to African-American constituents.

We know that the size of particular constituency groups within a district affects the representative's responsiveness to that group. In order to secure reelection, a member of Congress cannot neglect large groups of voters within the district. I showed earlier that the black population of a district leads to a legislator having a more pro-civil rights voting record in Congress. Taking this logic to the level of distributive policy projects, I expect that the larger the black constituency is in a district, the more likely that the district's representative will allocate projects to counties with substantial black populations.

Representatives who want to appeal broadly to black voters can do so by giving projects to counties that are predominately black. Jim Clyburn, who has represented South Carolina's black-majority district since 1992, serves as an example. Serving on the Transportation committee during the 105th Congress, he included many projects for his district in the committee's final authorization bill. Clyburn was asked about these pork projects by an interviewer, and his response is illuminating (Duncan and Nutting 1999, 1239): "[Black constituents in my district] have been historically neglected. ... I do not take kindly to efforts to improve their quality of life being labeled pork. ... These [small, black] counties don't have the numbers. They don't have the political clout."

Much like the Trent Lott anecdote at the opening of this chapter, Clyburn bristled at the label pork given by the interviewer. However, it is clear from his response that Clyburn both directed projects toward black constituents and that he conceived of his black constituency in political-geographic terms. The question remains whether Clyburn's actions are more generalizable to other legislators from districts with large black populations.

Alternatively, perhaps Clyburn was not motivated by the size of his black constituency as much as his own racial background. Clyburn is South Carolina's first black legislator since Reconstruction, and his presence in office may also predict his focus on the delivery of projects to black constituents, regardless of the demographics of the district.

Third, racial trust is also expected to predict project delivery to black constituents. The idea here is that white legislators may be more responsive than black legislators once the district black population becomes very large. That is, due to the lack of a shared racial background, trust of white legislators will be lower among black constituents compared to black legislators, and thus white legislators will need to engage in activity that indicates to black constituents that they care about black voters. Thus, the interaction of the race of the legislator and the district black population may also have an independent effect on project delivery outcomes.

Finally, it is expected that Republicans will be less likely to reward those who do not support them, and thus are likely to deliver fewer projects to heavily black counties than Democrats. Because black voters have historically been unlikely to support Republican congressional candidates, it is also unlikely that Republican legislators will work extensively to distribute projects to African-American constituents. Jay Dickey, a Republican who served the fourth district of Arkansas from 1993 to 2001, was caught admitting as much when speaking before a group of black farmers in his district. Dickey was asked why he did not secure more federal projects for black constituents in his district. His response was surprisingly blunt but may characterize what many congressional

Republicans are afraid to utter publicly: "You want us to take away from projects that serve our base and give it to people who not only don't vote for you but who work for your defeat? It's a miracle I can get anything done for them [black farmers]" (from George 2000, A1). This statement caused a subsequent firestorm, hurting Dickey more than he may have anticipated. After extensive media attention and criticism, Dickey finally made peace with the black farmers' group and even sponsored legislation to assist black farmers in the district. It is unlikely that he would have sponsored this legislation, though, had he not made such an embarrassing public statement. Dickey lost his 2000 reelection bid.

If Dickey's surprisingly blunt statement is applicable to other members of Congress, then we should expect Democrats to reward black voters with higher levels of projects, whereas Republicans will not, because black constituents are rarely part of their electoral coalitions. Alternatively, other Republican legislators may not be as hostile to black constituents as Dickey was, but given that black constituents are usually not part of Republican electoral coalitions, it is still likely that Republicans will allocate fewer projects to black constituents.

Historically Black Colleges and Universities

There are two reasons to study the distribution of projects to HBCUs. First, as mentioned earlier, by isolating specific projects in one issue area, the conclusions from the analysis of predominately black counties connecting racial representation and pork barreling will be more robust if the results from HBCUs are consistent.

Second, HBCUs serve as a proxy for project allocations to black constituents generally. In this chapter, I conceptualize responsiveness to black constituents by also looking at a key institution within the black community in many congressional districts – historically black colleges and universities. HBCUs have served an important role in the social, educational, economic, and political life of many black communities in the United States (Roebuck and Murty 1993; Stewart et al. 1989). Additionally, black institutions such as universities are key political forces in African-American lives. Marion Orr (1999, 12–13) claims that black colleges are part of a "dense network of African-American organizations" that are important in building social and political participation within the black community.

Politically, black colleges are significant. Of the thirty-seven black legislators serving in the most recent Congress examined in this chapter (the 106th Congress, 1999–2000), seventeen attended an HBCU, whereas only one nonblack legislator did (Wayne Gilchrest of Maryland). Similarly, William Gray, the first black member of Congress in history to serve as chief party whip, resigned from his Pennsylvania House seat in 1991 in order to become president of the United Negro College Fund (UNCF). Black colleges clearly are intertwined with the educational and professional life of many black legislators.

Black colleges have played an important historical role as well. Much of the student wing of the 1960s civil rights movement began on historically black campuses. These universities have also been important to the education of many black Americans. Before desegregation in the 1960s, HBCUs were often the only opportunity for most African Americans to garner a college education. Moreover, HBCUs have retained their significance to the education of many African Americans even today. Twenty-eight percent of black Americans graduating with a bachelor's degree obtained it from a historically black college or university, even though these colleges make up only 3 percent of the country's total universities (Rodrigues 1998). Although black colleges do not serve just black constituents, they are most strongly identified with the black community. For example, of the 115 historically black colleges and universities, only 3 have a white majority, and often the white students are commuter students (Levinson 1999). Similarly, 85.6 percent of all bachelor's degrees awarded by black colleges go to non-Hispanic blacks (U.S. Department of Education 1996, 10). Of course, an examination of allocations to HBCUs does not imply that I am measuring pork project allocations to all African Americans (as a majority of black college students receive their degrees from institutions other than HBCUs). However, it is a useful proxy measure in the absence of data on allocations to individual African-American constituents. Whereas the majority of HBCUs are located in the U.S. South, a significant minority of HBCUs are located outside of the South. Of the 203 congressional districts that have HBCUs in them during the time period studied, 34 percent are outside of the South. Given this, it is important to remember that these analyses are primarily of southern congressional districts, yet it is still a national sample of all districts with HBCUs.

More relevant to this book, the U.S. government has, at times, recognized the role of HBCUs and passed legislation to ease the delivery of federal projects to these schools. In 1965, Congress passed a law declaring that historically black universities serve the "unique role of educating black, educationally disadvantaged, and low-income students" and making more federal funding available for HBCUs. As president, Bill

Clinton established a federal organization whose explicit purpose was to aid the distribution of projects to HBCUs.[4]

Further, when I asked congressional staff about responding to black constituents, various House representatives and their staff members, regardless of race and party, have pointed to higher education projects. Legislators who represent districts with HBCUs claim to steer education funds to these universities, using both the federal programs directly targeting HBCUs as well as other programs. I look at the distribution of federal projects to historically black universities – unquestionably a key set of black institutions in the United States – in order to assess the effect of racial representation on the distribution of congressional pork projects. Studying the flow of projects to HBCUs will allow broader conclusions to be drawn about project distribution to black constituents and the substantive representation of black interests in general.

The same factors discussed in regard to predominately black counties are likely to affect project allocations to HBCUs. As theorized, the race of the legislator, black-majority districts, racial trust, and the party of the legislator are likely to impact HBCU project allocations. Black voters are more likely to be important to a representative when they are a substantial portion of a district's population. Glen Browder, a white Democrat from Alabama, represented a district from 1989 to 1997 that included Tuskegee University. Tuskegee University, founded by Booker T. Washington in 1881, and its surrounding community are both central to the black community of Browder's former district. Historically, Tuskegee has been strongly identified with the civil rights movement. For example, in 1960, black residents of the city of Tuskegee brought one of the first major racial gerrymandering cases before the U.S. Supreme Court, *Gomillion v. Lightfoot*. In fact, the plaintiff, Dr. Charles Gomillion, was a professor at Tuskegee Institute.

Browder, winning election with the support of most of his district's black Democratic voters and a portion of the district's conservative white Democratic voters, needed to appeal to both of these groups in order to

---

[4] Instead of just looking at projects to HBCUs, an alternative research design may compare project allocations to historically black colleges and other, predominately white, institutions. However, I chose to focus just on HBCUs given the specific programs that already exist to funnel projects to these universities. Direct comparisons between HBCUs and predominately white colleges are not as easy because many of the projects to each of these types of institutions originate in different programs, agencies, and so on. Project money is available for HBCUs; it is up to specific legislators to decide whether to access these funds.

continue winning reelection (Glaser 1996). On a variety of salient roll-call votes, Browder explained to me in an interview that he would appeal to his white supporters, who he referred to as his "basic constituency," by voting more conservatively. His "nonbasic constituency" was anyone in the district whom he felt he did not directly represent by his roll-call votes on these salient issues. Black voters, sometimes, would fall into this nonbasic constituency. As Browder detailed, "Roll-call voting was done to represent the basic constituency. I would try to help out my nonbasic constituency by getting grants. ... Every year, I'd ask for something for Tuskegee." Browder clearly viewed Tuskegee University as an institutional embodiment of his black supporters, and this anecdote exemplifies the importance of looking at project allocations to HBCUs more generally.

Pam Stubbs, a district staff member to Mel Watt, a black representative from North Carolina, claimed that black representatives like Watt were more likely to focus on the needs and concerns of historically black universities. I asked her whether black representatives were more likely to deliver pork projects to historically black colleges than their white counterparts. She felt that this was the case but also pointed out that the role of a black legislator may go even further:

Let me give you a different take on it. ... Mel had a meeting for all the presidents of HBCUs in the district. He brought in people from various agencies to explain what they're looking for [in grant applications]. In this office, we like to think out of the box, and this was the first time people from ... [these schools] were brought together.

Black representatives like Watt are interested in motivating their base of black voter support. Given the expectations related to racial trust, this is particularly true in Watt's case, because following the 1998 elections, he began representing a majority-white district. The allocation of projects to black constituents can help him mobilize black voters without turning off more conservative white voters. White voters, I presume, are less likely to be aware of project allocations to HBCUs. Robert Stein and Kenneth Bickers (1995) find that organized groups with interests in projects will be more aware of project allocations than the district as a whole (see also Lowry and Potoski 2004; Rundquist and Carsey 2002). Applying this logic to HBCU allocations, we can assume that black voters will be more aware of HBCU allocations than will voters from other racial groups.

Black Legislators Deliver More Projects
to African Americans

To examine the effect of the district black population, the race of the legislator, the party of the legislator, and racial trust on pork project delivery to predominately black counties and HBCUs, I estimated four statistical models. I estimated these statistical models so that I could consider the effect of the key variables of interest (e.g., district black population and race of legislator) at the same time, though also control for other explanations of pork project allocations. I will not present the details of these statistical models here, but they are available in Appendix 3. In this chapter, I instead present the predicted values of the number of pork projects delivered by each member of Congress given their race, their party, their district's demographics, and the interaction of the legislator's race and district black population. By focusing just on these predicted values, the casual reader will be able to assess the substantive results, whereas the interested reader can still examine the details in Appendix 3.

To examine federal project allocation broadly, I examine both (1) the *number of new project grants* that are allocated to African Americans by each legislator; and (2) the *dollar amounts of new project grants* allocated to African Americans by each legislator. I examine new project grants because these are the federal grants that legislators have the most control over. Further, I look at the 104th through 106th Congresses (1995–2000), as this time period provides the best variation between the race of legislator and district black population variables. All congressional districts in which there are counties greater than or equal to 40 percent black are included in one analysis, and all congressional districts with HBCUs are included in another analysis. As discussed in Appendix 3, the unit of analysis in the first set of statistical models is the county, whereas the unit of analysis in the second set of statistical models is the congressional district. There are a total of 729 counties or portions of counties during the 104th–106th Congresses (1995–2000) that have a black population greater than or equal to 40 percent. There are 203 congressional districts during the 104th–106th Congresses (1995–2000) with HBCUs.

I examine the number of grants and the dollar amounts because both are good measures of substantive policy outcomes. The larger number of grants to African Americans in one congressional district indicates that the House member has worked to reach a number of different African Americans and groups within the district. The amount of money spent, though, is also important to substantively assess the work of the House member in the district. If a legislator allocates fifty projects all worth $1,000, these fifty projects are substantively important because they are likely to affect a larger number of voters. However, arguably, twenty-five projects worth $2 million each may be substantively more important given the dollar amounts. Thus, I look at both the number of new projects and the amount spent total on all projects per district.

The results from the analyses of both project allocations to predominately black counties and to HBCUs are quite interesting. All else equal, black representatives allocate more projects than their white colleagues do. However, the district's black population affects the allocation levels of projects for both black and white representatives in different ways. These findings lend support to the theory of electoral coalitions and minority representation presented in Chapter 2.

Further, there is only a small difference by party: Somewhat surprisingly, white Republicans allocate just slightly more projects and dollars than do white Democrats. I will discuss these unusual findings regarding party in a moment, but I will first discuss the findings in regard to a legislator's race.

The Effect of a Legislator's Race on Project Allocations

Table 6.2 and Table 6.3 show the effect of a legislator's race and party on the number of new federal projects and the dollar amounts allocated. Black legislators allocate more projects and a substantially larger amount of federal money to African Americans than do their white colleagues. Without question, descriptive representation affects substantive representation. Table 6.2 displays the results for project allocations to predominately black counties. Numerically, black legislators representing heavily black counties are likely to allocate about thirty-seven pork projects per county. In contrast, white legislators representing heavily black counties – both Democrats and Republicans – only allocate around three federal projects to these heavily black counties (I do not consider black Democrats separately from black Republicans because the two black Republicans serving during the time period studied [1995–2000] did not represent heavily black counties or districts with HBCUs). Further, the gap in federal dollars is quite large: A heavily black county represented by a black legislator receives more than $37 million dollars, whereas the same county would only receive $7 million dollars from a white Democrat and about $12 million dollars from a white Republican (see Table 6.2). The effect of descriptive representation on project allocation to heavily

TABLE 6.2. *Bringing Home the Bacon: Black Democrats, White Democrats, and White Republicans and Projects Allocated to Heavily Black Counties*

	Number of Projects Allocated to Predominately Black Counties, per Legislator	Dollars Spent on Projects to Predominately Black Counties, per Legislator
Black representatives	37.12	$37,943,878
White Democratic representatives	2.78	$7,301,664
White Republican representatives	3.12	$11,983,664

Note: These figures are predicted values computed from two statistical models (one with the number of projects as the dependent variable and a second model with the dollars allocated as the dependent variable), where other factors such as district black population are controlled for by holding them at their means. See Appendix 3 for details.

TABLE 6.3. *Bringing Home the Bacon to Colleges: Black Democrats, White Democrats, and White Republicans and Projects Allocated to Historically Black Colleges and Universities*

	Number of Projects Allocated to HBCUs, per Legislator	Dollars Spent on Projects to HBCUs, per Legislator
Black representatives	53.27	$16,632,678
White Democratic representatives	10.58	$6,015,371
White Republican representatives	13.38	$6,553,621

Note: These figures are predicted values computed from two statistical models (one with the number of projects as the dependent variable and a second model with the dollars allocated as the dependent variable), where other factors such as district black population are controlled for by holding them at their means. See Appendix 3 for details.

black counties is quite meaningful. This result is important because I have controlled for the effect of district black population, and thus the effect of a legislator's race is clearly a significant predictor above and beyond the effect of the district's black population. Further, other demand-level predictors of projects such as county population, poverty, education, and so on are also controlled for (see Appendix 3).

In Table 6.3, we can see the effect of descriptive black representation on project delivery to HBCUs. Again, black legislators allocate more projects and more federal money to HBCUs. Black legislators in districts with HBCUs allocate about fifty-three projects to historically black colleges, whereas white legislators representing HBCUs allocate about forty fewer projects.[5] White Republicans allocate about thirteen projects to HBCUs, whereas white Democrats allocate a little more than ten projects to HBCUs. An examination of the amount of federal dollars allocated also shows similarly astounding gaps between white and black legislators (in Table 6.3). Black legislators bring home about $16 million in federal dollars to HBCUs, whereas white legislators bring home about $6 million per district. Again, these results consider the effect of race above and beyond the effect of other factors like district black population, whether a legislator is on the House Appropriations committee, and demand-level variables such as the number of faculty and students enrolled at HBCUs in each district.

The Effect of Party on Project Allocation to Black Constituents

When examining only white legislators, the party results are somewhat surprising: Republican representatives are more likely to allocate projects to both predominately black counties and HBCUs in their districts than are Democratic representatives, though the actual differential in number of projects is only slightly higher (see Tables 6.2 and 6.3). These results, although substantively small, are statistically significant (see the numeric projects analyses in Appendix 3).

Given previous work demonstrating the lack of importance of black voters to white Republican representatives, these findings are unusual. However, congressional Republicans in the latter half of the 1990s and 2000s have made an effort to be more of a "big tent" political party, though some of these attempts at outreach have been relatively small (Philpot 2008). Given the conservative voting records of most Republicans on civil rights, perhaps the best way to try to expand their support across racial lines is through non-ideological pork projects. The Republicans have used funding of HBCUs in particular in this effort to reach out specifically to black voters. In 2000, J.C. Watts was the only black Republican in the House. At that time, Watts unveiled a Republican-sponsored task force and summit to help deliver projects to HBCUs, even though his own district had no HBCUs: "Republicans need to have a sound understanding of the importance of the HBCU community to our nation" (Myers

[5] I use the term "white legislators" because all legislators representing counties 40 percent black or greater and representing districts with HBCUs are either white or African American except for one Latino legislator. For simplicity, when I refer to white legislators, this reference also includes the one Latino legislator in each sample.

2000).[6] Because the Republicans were in the majority of the House and Watts was a member of the GOP leadership, it is likely that these efforts to reach black voters explain the party results. Michael Lomax, president of historically black Dillard University stated: "It's fair to say Democrats have been outstanding advocates for these issues. Getting competition from Republicans is certainly something we find attractive."[7]

James Clyburn (D-SC), though, disagrees that the Republicans in general are doing anything for HBCUs: "It's hard to imagine that the 'summit' was little more than a photo opportunity for members who have absolutely no history of involvement and support for HBCUs and who in fact, have a track record of hostility toward these very institutions" (Hurd 2000). The results of this analysis indicate the opposite, however.

We should cautiously interpret the party results, as the difference in the number of projects between white Republican legislators and white Democratic legislators is small, and there is no statistically significant difference in the dollar amounts allocated by Democrats and Republicans (see Appendix 3). On the other hand, given expectations based on previous electoral coalitions, we would have expected white Republicans to have dramatically lower levels of project allocations. Perhaps white Republican legislators consider the interests of their black constituents, at least as measured by the number of project allocations to African Americans. Perhaps Republican legislators, less able to represent black voters via other means (roll-call voting) rely on the symbolism and substance associated with donating grants to black institutions such as HBCUs. By doing this, they are attempting to reach out to a set of constituents within their geographic constituency, though not likely to be in their reelection constituency. One alternative explanation for this finding may simply be geography. Heavily black counties and HBCUs are predominately located in the South, and the Republican Party is now heavily based in the South. As a result, there may simply be more opportunities for Republican legislators to provide federal projects to African-American constituents because of this geography.

Interestingly, though, Republicans are offering more projects numerically to HBCUs but not more money than Democratic representatives. This may be evidence of the GOP's attempt to engage in a more cosmetic

---

[6] Watts was not included in the county analyses; he did not represent any counties > 40 percent black.

[7] Popular press mentions of a Republican effort with HBCUs occurred as early as 1998. The data analyzed here are from the 104th to 106th Congresses (1995–2000).

outreach to black constituents. Increasing numbers of grants might be an attempt to garner some electoral favor and an improvement in the party's reputation on racial issues (Philpot 2008) with black constituents and moderate white constituents, but the fact that Republicans do not allocate more actual dollars (see Appendix 3) to HBCUs than Democrats suggests the extent of Republican substantive representation via project allocation is still somewhat small.

Racial Trust: The Interactive Effect of District Black Population and a Legislator's Race

Having assessed the impact of the race of legislator and party while keeping other variables constant, I now want to examine the effect of racial trust – both the race of the legislator and the district black population – on project allocations. Figure 6.1 visually displays the expected values of the number of projects allocated to predominately black counties while varying the race of the representative and the district black population for the sample of counties that are at least 40 percent black (holding other variables at their means). Figure 6.2 displays the number of projects allocated to HBCUs, also while varying the district black population and the race of the legislator.[8] The results imply that the effect of a large black population on project allocations to African-American constituents is contingent on the race of the legislator. In Figure 6.1, supporting the racial trust argument, counties receive substantially greater numbers of projects when represented by black representatives *in districts with a white majority*. Black representatives in black-majority districts allocate significantly fewer projects than their black colleagues from other districts.

For white representatives in the 40 percent county sample (Figure 6.1), though, the black population of their districts appears to have little effect on the number of projects allocated to black constituents. Remember, though, that only one black-majority district in the sample is represented by a white representative. Districts in this sample represented by black representatives vary from 37 to 74 percent black. Thus, in the range of districts in which black and white legislators overlap, black representatives always allocate more projects than do white representatives. Thus,

---

[8] In the interest of space, I simply discuss these results for the number of projects allocated, though the results were similar for the dollars allocated. See regression results in Appendix 3 for more details regarding the dollar amounts allocated and the interaction between race of legislator and district black population.

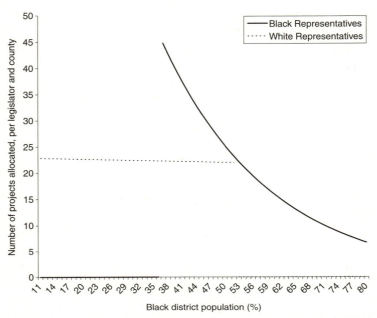

FIGURE 6.1. The number of projects allocated to predominantly black counties: The interactive effect of a legislator's race and district black population.
This figure is based on expected counts computed from a statistical model, where other factors are controlled for by holding them at their means. See Appendix 3 for details.

for this sample of counties, the expectation related to the race of the representative was correct, though the expectation that white representatives would be more responsive to differences in the district black population was mistaken. However, black legislators clearly respond to differences in district black populations.

Black representatives are most likely to give substantial numbers of projects to black constituents in districts without black majorities. In Figure 6.1, contrast the expected number of projects received when there is a black representative representing a 37 percent black district (37% is the district in the sample with the lowest black population yet still represented by a black legislator) and when there is a black representative representing a majority-black district. In a 37 percent black district, a black representative allocates approximately forty-five projects to counties with at least a 40 percent black population. A black legislator from a district with a 55 percent black population allocates less than half that number, only about twenty projects.

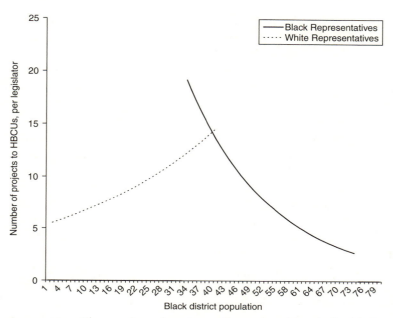

FIGURE 6.2. The number of projects allocated to historically black colleges and universities: The interactive effect of a legislator's race and district black population.

This figure is based on expected counts computed from a statistical model, where other factors are controlled for by holding them at their means. See Appendix 3 for details.

An analysis of allocations to HBCUs yields similar results to the analysis of allocations to counties. When examining the HBCU allocations (see Figure 6.2), the effect of an increasing district black population has a differential impact on white and black legislators. Racial trust – or the interaction of a legislator's race and district black population – suggests that white representatives are actually more positively responsive to increases in the district black population than black representatives.[9]

Clearly, black representatives allocate significantly more projects to HBCUs than white representatives in districts with large percentages of white voters. This is interesting, because the perceived scholarly wisdom is that black and white representatives respond to increases in black population levels in a similar manner – as the black population increases, the

---

[9] The analysis in Figure 6.2 was done by varying the values of district black population, the race of the legislator, and the interaction term of race of the legislator and district black population. Other variables were held at their means.

expectation is that both black and white representatives would become more responsive to black constituents.

However, black representatives allocate more projects to black constituents as the black population in their district *decreases*. These HBCU findings are consistent with the analysis of federal projects to heavily black populated counties. The explanation is clearer if we think about the sample of districts and about the theory established in Chapter 2. In this sample of districts with HBCUs, black representatives represent districts ranging from 34 to 74 percent black, whereas white representatives represent districts ranging from 2 to 41 percent black. Interestingly, at around 40 percent black, the differences in the number of grants allocated by the race of the legislator are negligible. Thus, it appears that white legislators from black-influence districts allocate approximately the same or slightly more than black legislators from districts more than 40 percent black. Unfortunately, there are very few cases of white legislators representing districts with HBCUs in this range (a 41% black district population is the maximum for white legislators) and few cases of black legislators from 34 to 40 percent black; thus, any conclusions should be tempered by these data limitations. However, the results suggest that black-influence districts – when represented particularly by black legislators but also by white legislators – result in higher project allocations to historically black colleges.

These findings suggest that supermajority-black districts may actually be a bane to the representation of black interests in Congress when considering the distribution of federal dollars and projects to African Americans. Jim Clyburn, chair of the Congressional Black Caucus during the 106th Congress, concurs when discussing his own supermajority-black district: "This district is 62 percent black. ... It's one thing to create opportunity districts. It's something else to create guaranteed districts. We ought not be doing that" (Piacente 2001). These results also suggest that black and white legislators rationally and differentially respond to different electoral incentives contingent on the type of district they represent: Electoral concerns at least partially explain these results or else there would be no variation among African-American members of Congress based on their districts' black populations.

In sum, these results demonstrate that racial representation affects the allocation of projects to black constituents. In both the analysis of predominately black counties and the analysis of districts with HBCUs, black representatives always allocate more projects than white representatives regardless of the district black population. Thus, a conclusion based on this evidence is that black legislators seem to view their role as being responsive to black constituents in general. African-American constituents benefit substantially from descriptive representation as African-American legislators "bring home the bacon" much more than their white colleagues.

Pork Delivery, Electoral Coalitions, and Racial Representation

The results from these analyses are important for three reasons. First, to my knowledge, never before has a scholar undertaken an examination of the effect of racial representation on pork projects. Second, the findings suggest that descriptive representation affects the substantive representation of black constituents, rebutting some scholars' claims. Third, the relationships between the black population of a district, the presence of a black representative, and policy outcomes are not always in the direction initially thought by most scholars. Fourth, surprisingly, white Republicans allocate more projects than do white Democrats, even though the difference is somewhat small.

Clearly, black representatives allocate more projects to black constituents. Although enough data do not exist to test what would occur when white legislators represent majority-black constituencies, these results at least suggest that black representatives in the 104th, 105th, and 106th Congresses allocated more projects to black constituents than did their white counterparts. However, in isolation of constituency and electoral factors, this conclusion is too simplistic. To really understand the results, we have to consider the electoral coalitions of both white and black legislators, racial trust, the court-ordered redistricting that occurred in many southern states in the 1990s, and roll-call voting patterns gleaned from Chapter 3.

All black legislators in this analysis are Democrats, and presumably these legislators rely on black voters in their districts as part of their "primary constituency." James Glaser (1996, chapter 5) shows that in majority-black districts, black legislators primarily need black votes to win general elections. Especially in supermajority-black districts in which the constituency is "packed" with black constituents, the need for white voter support is likely to be minimal for black representatives.

Given the racial demography of these districts with a large percentage of black constituents, black legislators do not need a large turnout of black voters on election day in order to secure reelection. In fact, based on the results presented at the end of Chapter 3, it is likely that just on ideological grounds, black Democratic legislators in majority-black districts have "substantively represented" the interests of their primary black constituents, and this may be sufficient to motivate a majority of their districts' voters to the polls.

On the other hand, consider black representatives from black-minority constituencies. These representatives are divided into two categories: those with substantial populations of other minorities (usually Latino voters) and those with white majorities. Most of the black legislators representing constituencies without black majorities in the samples studied here fall into this latter category. Thanks to court-ordered redistricting in six southern states throughout the mid-1990s, black representatives initially elected in black-majority districts were forced to run again in substantially redrawn districts with reduced levels of black voters.

These representatives were initially elected in black-majority districts mostly with the support of black voters (see Chapter 2 of this book and Voss and Lublin 2001 for evidence of this). These black representatives from districts without black majorities have more conservative voting records than black representatives from districts with large black populations. Having once represented majority-black districts with more liberal constituencies, redistricted black representatives now had to appeal to a biracial coalition (or in some cases a triracial or triethnic coalition) of voters. To do this, these black representatives from white-majority districts voted more conservatively than their counterparts from black-majority districts – and more conservatively than they had in previous congressional sessions (see Grose 2001 and LeVeaux and Garand 2003 for evidence of this in terms of redistricting).

However, even with changed districts, these black legislators could not neglect black voters, their primary constituency (as well as a substantial minority of voters in these new districts). Pork projects are a perfect way to appeal to black constituents in the hopes of increasing black turnout. Partisan black voters who did not like the conservative tilt of some black representatives' roll-call votes could find solace in the fact that these black representatives were delivering projects.

These black representatives not only worried about spurring black turnout in general elections, but they also relied on their black voter base of support in primary elections. Even though these districts were redrawn to be majority-white, they were still Democratic districts. Most black incumbents faced with new districts in 1996 or 1998 also faced white primary challengers. However, the racial dynamics of Democratic primaries

TABLE 6.4. *Shifts in Roll-Call Voting Among African-American House Democrats*

	Mean ADA Score, 1994	Mean ADA Score, 2000	Percent Increase in Conservatism
African-American House Democrats redistricted into districts without a black majority during mid-90s	90.71	76.43	+18.69%
African-American House Democrats not redistricted into black-minority districts in mid-90s	90.74	89.1	+1.84%

in these districts are distinct from the dynamics of general elections in which a much larger (and whiter) group of voters participate. Here, by continuing to appeal to black voters through the distribution of projects, black incumbent representatives could work toward a primary victory against white Democratic opponents.

For example, Sanford Bishop, a black Democrat, was initially elected to Georgia's second district in 1992. At the time, the second district had a 57 percent black population. Although Bishop had a reputation as a moderate even then, he became decidedly more conservative once his district took on a whiter hue. In the 103rd Congress, representing a black-majority district, he voted with the liberal interest group Americans for Democratic Action (ADA) 75 percent of the time (in 1994). For a Democrat, this is a relatively low score, though this is a pretty liberal voting record for a south Georgia congressman. For the 1996 elections, following the Supreme Court's decision in *Miller v. Johnson*, his district was redrawn with a 39 percent black population. By the 106th Congress, after his district changed, Bishop's vote agreement score with the ADA in 2000 dropped to 50 percent. This score is much more conservative than the scores of his colleagues from districts with black-majority constituencies for the same Congresses. Without question, Bishop altered his ideological voting as the district took on more white constituents and the views of the majority of voters changed on some issues. This pattern of increased conservatism was not limited to Bishop. Table 6.4 displays the ADA scores in 1994 (the final year of the 103rd Congress) and in 2000 (the final year of the 106th Congress) for all African-American House Democrats, comparing those black legislators (like Bishop) that were redistricted into a district without a black majority to the black legislators who were not redistricted into a district without a black majority. As can be seen in Table 6.4, Bishop is no anomaly. Those black legislators in redrawn districts that were no longer black-majority became more conservative, as the mean ADA score declined from a liberalism score of just above 90 to a liberalism score of only about 75 (an increase of nearly 20% in conservatism). In contrast, other black Democratic legislators exhibited nearly no change in ADA scores, going from a mean of just over 90 to a mean of just over 89 during the same time period.

Hobby Stripling, Bishop's district director, indicated that Bishop often catches flak from black constituents for voting too conservatively. According to Stripling, though, Bishop has a lot more leeway with black constituents thanks to the trust that exists based on shared racial background. He really had to work, especially initially in the redrawn majority-white district, with some whites who felt he was a little too liberal and voted with Democrats too much. The impression I received from talking with Stripling is that if an issue divides white and black constituents, then Bishop likely may vote with white constituents or at least try to avoid taking a stance altogether, as the African-American population will cut Bishop more slack than will white voters. Stripling said the typical response to a constituent who is unhappy with how Bishop voted on the bill is to say, "After reviewing the bill entirely and looking at his *whole* district, he supports or opposes it." Most white constituents, on the other hand, do not have this trust, and he really has to demonstrate that he is taking conservative stances (Hancock 2004, 110).

An example of this was the issue of the Georgia state flag. The flag of Georgia prominently contained the confederate flag when Bishop served in Congress. Roy Barnes, the white Democratic governor of the state from 1999–2003, proposed changing (and eventually did change) Georgia's state flag. This was overwhelmingly favored by most African-American Georgians and strongly opposed by many white Georgians, especially whites in the southern part of the state that Bishop represents. For Bishop, this issue was toxic, as a substantial part of Bishop's reelection constituency could be offended by any position he took on the issue. As Stripling detailed: "During the flag issue, there were some people who tried to bring him into it. He refused to be brought into it. He said, 'Whatever the state flag is, I'm going to fly it.'" He essentially sidestepped taking a stance by pointing out that this was an issue for the state legislature and governor, not a member of Congress. In a black-majority district, it is unlikely he would have taken this nonposition and instead probably would have supported a new flag (Bullock and Hood 2005). However, there was a concern that taking a position on the flag would lead to a loss in important white voter support, even if black voters were angry at Bishop.

However, to secure victory in both the general and primary elections, Bishop still needed to retain and mobilize his voter base of black constituents. Thus, his representational strategy was, not only about appealing to a numerical majority of white voters, but also keeping African-American voters in the fold and enthusiastic. In the 1996 Democratic primary in his new white-majority district, Bishop faced two white challengers, W.T. Gamble III and Walter Lewis. Bishop was able to get enough white voter support through his conservative voting record but was also able to rely on nearly unanimous support from the black voters in his district (Bullock and Dunn 1999).

One way that Bishop appealed to his black constituents was to increase the number of projects distributed to counties with large black populations. To provide evidence of this, it is useful to compare counties with the highest black population in Bishop's district with the counties in his district that received the most projects. Both his first district (which he represented from 1993 to 1996 following the 1992 election) and his second district (which he represented from 1997 to 2002) had more than thirty counties or portions of counties. Both of these districts can be seen in Figure 2.1 in Chapter 2. The first version of Bishop's district had a black majority, whereas the second version had a white majority. When he represented the black-majority district (i.e., based on data in 1996), only two of the ten counties with the highest black population were *also* two of the top ten counties to receive the most projects in the district, controlling for overall county population.[10] Clearly, the counties with the greatest black population did not receive most of the projects when Bishop represented a black-majority district. Only two of the ten most heavily black counties, Stewart and Talbot, were in the group of ten counties that received the most projects.

Contrast this data point with Bishop's new, white-majority district drawn for the 105th Congress. With a much whiter constituency, five of the top ten project recipient counties were also in the group of heavily black counties (based on data from 1998). Now representing a district with a majority of whites, Bishop allocated numerically more pork projects to black constituents than he did when the district was black-majority. With a more conservative voting record, Bishop needed

---

[10] To control for overall population, an index of the ten counties with the highest number of projects divided by the overall population of the county was created.

to utilize the other perquisites of office to reach black voters. Stripling, Bishop's district director, indicated that they were much more concerned about reaching black voters once the district was reshaped to become white-majority: "We wanted, er, we were very, very aware that we needed to attract white voters, [but] we really made an effort to reach the black vote." One way Bishop was able to reach out to black voters was via project delivery. Also, as was demonstrated in the last two chapters, constituency service to black constituents was also a more important focus in Bishop's white-majority district.

As evidenced here, Bishop delivered fewer projects to heavily black counties prior to the remap. However, following the general pattern seen in the aggregate analyses of all congressional districts, once he took on a white-majority district and a more conservative voting record, he increased his project allocations to counties with large black populations.

This example helps explain the general results found for black representatives. Electoral coalitions differ for black representatives from black-majority districts and those from white-majority districts. For white representatives, though, we see a slightly different outcome. For the analysis of projects allocated, white representatives were somewhat more responsive in districts that had a larger black population (for HBCUs, but not to predominately black counties). Unlike black representatives, white representatives have considerably less leeway with black constituents. Claudine Gay (2002) demonstrates that black constituents distrust white representatives more. As a result, white representatives representing districts with substantial black populations need to reach out to black voters in ways that black representatives do not. This helps explain the result that black constituents receive more projects from white representatives in districts with large black populations compared to white legislators from low-black districts (e.g., in Figure 6.2, there is an increase in the slope of the line indicating project allocations for white legislators).

The electoral coalitions of white representatives also help explain patterns of project allocations. In districts with fewer black residents, white representatives (especially Republicans) do not need to focus on responding to black constituents (either via roll-call voting or with projects). However, in racially heterogeneous constituencies, even with white majorities, white representatives need to form biracial coalitions (if they are Democrats) or at least not antagonize black constituents (if they are Republicans).

White representatives from black-influence districts distribute more project grants to HBCUs than white colleagues from districts with fewer black residents, supporting a racial trust explanation of distributive policy allocations. This result may also be driven in part by the court-ordered redistricting that placed more black voters in white representatives' districts. Because white representatives were not appealing to black voters as much via roll-call voting, then projects become a good way to appeal to black constituents in districts that are larger in black population.

Conclusion and Discussion

The analysis in this chapter has focused on the distribution of federal pork projects to black constituents – as measured by projects allocated to predominately black counties and to historically black colleges and universities. This chapter is significant, as never before has a connection been found between racial representation and distributive policy outcomes in Congress. Numerous studies have looked at the effect on other policies, but the allocation of projects to black constituents is an important way to measure substantive representation.

The primary findings pertaining to minority representation presented in this chapter are as follows. First, the race of the representative – descriptive representation – causes an increase in the number of project allocations to black constituents (thereby enhancing substantive representation). Millions of dollars more per district are allocated to African-American constituents when the district is represented by an African-American legislator. Second, the black population of a district affects project allocations, but this differs depending on the race of the legislator representing the district. Black representatives representing majority-white districts will allocate more projects to African Americans than black representatives in black-majority districts, and thus racial trust impacts project allocations to black constituents. White representatives respond to increases in their districts' black populations. Finally, white Republicans will allocate slightly more projects than white Democrats to predominately black counties and to black colleges.

The results here find that the presence of black representatives, majority-black districts, *and* racial trust lead to increased project allocations to African Americans. Ironically, though, the "best" district for increasing the number of project allocations to African Americans may be a black-influence district represented by a black legislator or perhaps a white Republican. These results raise serious questions about the somewhat simplistic assumptions underlying most studies of majority-minority districting and racial representation. The results suggest that proponents of drawing districts in order to elect black representatives are not in error, because black representatives allocate more projects to black colleges than their white colleagues. However, proponents of black-influence districts, districts with substantial black minorities not above the 50 percent line, are also not in error, as black representatives are even more responsive in terms of project allocations to black constituents when elected from white-majority districts.

Following the results presented in this chapter and preceding chapters, a pattern has emerged. On high-profile behavior (like roll-call voting) in which the individual legislator has little control over the agenda, representatives' general ideological behavior is primarily targeted to those voters in the reelection constituency but not in the primary constituency. On project allocation and constituency service, representatives attempt to appeal to subsets of voters within their constituency. These appeals are dependent on the racial heterogeneity of the district. In some cases, as evidenced here, legislators will allocate projects to constituents who are unlikely to even vote for them (e.g., white Republican legislators allocating to African-American constituents). Alternatively, in other cases legislators will allocate projects to constituents in their primary constituency (e.g., black legislators from black-influence districts). In the next and final chapter, I will assess these broad patterns and what policy implications they have for racial redistricting, voting rights, and the substantive representation of African Americans.

7

The Future of Racial Redistricting

Black-Decisive Districts

"North Carolina should have 7 women, 3.5 African-Americans in the House based on the numbers. All are taxpayers, but you don't get the services. You get tired of it."

— Tawana Wilson-Allen, staffer to Representative Mel Watt, also quoted at the opening of Chapter 1, arguing why her state needs descriptive representation in Congress.

Race matters in Congress. The descriptive representation of African Americans in Congress leads to substantive legislative outcomes favoring black constituents. The outcomes in which descriptive representation matters, though, are not those that have typically been examined by scholars of African-American legislative representation. Based on this research, a number of policy implications and other questions now present themselves. In the remainder of this book, I will examine a few of these. First, I will detail how this research fits in specifically with the major works in the research area of minority congressional representation detailed in both Chapters 1 and 2, focusing particularly on Carol Swain (1995), David Canon (1999), Katherine Tate (2003), and Kenny Whitby (1997) as they have also examined congressional behavior other than roll-call voting. Second, I will consider the aggregate implications of these findings, offering possible advice for the "best" districting arrangement for maximizing the substantive representation of black constituents. These aggregate implications include my recommendation to the courts and policy makers to draw *black-decisive districts*. Black-decisive districts are (1) districts that are electorally competitive; (2) districts in which black voters are likely to be decisive in electing the winner; and (3) districts that are likely to elect African-American legislators.

Race, Legislative Representation, and the Importance of Elections

David Canon (1999) concludes that black-majority districts enhance democracy (1) by increasing substantive representation of African Americans; and (2) by causing biracial electoral coalitions between white and black voters to sometimes occur. Katherine Tate (2003) and Kenny Whitby (1997), in contrast, conclude that electing African Americans enhances democracy by increasing substantive representation. However, these scholars are unable to appropriately disentangle both of these explanations in their analyses due to the sample of districts they study (Canon: 103rd Congress; Tate: mostly the 103rd and 104th Congresses; Whitby: mostly prior to the 104th Congress).

Although I find some support for Canon's contentions, his findings are not entirely supported. The presence of a black legislator in office certainly has positive effects for black constituents; however, black-majority districts do not have as positive an effect as black-influence districts. Further, within the subset of black legislators, I find that black-majority districts have a negative effect on the substantive representation of black constituents – at least when compared to black-influence districts.[1] Like Tate and Whitby, I argue that descriptive representation is important for substantive representation. However, unlike Tate, I show that the effect of a legislator's race on congressional outcomes is also highly contingent on the racial makeup of the legislator's district. The conclusion that a legislator's race affects congressional outcomes is dependent on what activity is studied and what type of district the legislator hails from.

Canon, in contrast, examining just districts from the 103rd Congress, generally finds that variation in the district black population has no real impact on black legislators' decisions. His main finding is that "commonality" or "difference" black members of Congress (more than the racial demographics of their districts) affect legislative outcomes by African-American

---

[1] I draw this conclusion because the findings in Chapter 3 showed that the race of the legislator was a key predictor for increased roll-call voting outcomes favoring African Americans at the individual district level (but less than the district black population) *and* the results in Chapters 4–6 showed that in districts represented by black legislators, black-minority districts resulted in a greater allocation of substantive outcomes to African-American constituents. However, if one is only interested in increasing substantive representation at the individual district level as measured by roll-call voting within the subset of black legislators (and ignoring other measures of substantive representation such as project and constituency service allocations, and also ignoring the aggregate results of districting on roll-call voting in the House), higher substantive representation at the individual district level results from districts with larger black populations.

legislators. Commonality members are generally portrayed as "better" for both black and white constituents, but these members are no more or less likely to come from "high" or "low" black populated districts.

My findings rebut some of Canon's findings in his book though also concur with others (just as with Tate's book). In most of the cases where Canon finds commonality from certain black legislators, I see legislators representing districts that are not heavily black-majority. In supermajority-black districts, members of Congress are generally very safe – especially in the general election. Black turnout in these districts is generally low, but so is white turnout. Legislators from these districts generally vote in favor of civil rights and thus substantively represent the needs and interests of the black majorities of their districts. These safe legislators also engage primarily in symbolic measures (as Katherine Tate notes), and the delivery of service and projects is less important to these legislators as they are already substantively representing black constituents (the majority of constituents in their districts) with roll-call voting. Further, black-majority districts in the aggregate do not have much effect on the location of the decisive legislator on civil rights roll-call outcomes.

African-American legislators from heavily black districts are substantively representing black voters through their behavior on the floor of the House. However, as David Canon (1999) finds with his "difference" members (most of whom are elected in heavily black districts) and Carol Swain (1995) finds in her "historically black" districts, these black legislators from supermajority-black districts are not as engaged with service allocations in their districts.

Thus, another broad conclusion to take from this book for those interested in questions beyond race and congressional behavior is that the importance of competition in democratic elections cannot be understated. Electoral institutions and systems that enhance safety may lead to complacence from elected officials in terms of reaching out to groups of voters in any minority (racial, numerical, or otherwise).

In the case of racial districting and competitiveness, black voters cannot be ignored when the district is competitive and when the black population is relatively large. Much like Griffin (2006) has found that electoral competition leads to responsiveness by legislators in roll-call voting, I also find that competitive districts lead to greater responsiveness when it comes to constituency service and project allocations to constituents. This holds true even when a district is represented by a legislator who does not have African Americans within his or her electoral coalition (e.g., Republicans in black-influence districts).

Constituency service and the delivery of government projects, two important and often overlooked aspects of congressional representation, are more likely to reach minority constituents if the legislator needs to balance an electoral coalition in order to reach these voters. In a safe, majority-black district, the legislator simply votes with the preferences of his or her black constituents and does not need to focus as much on the delivery of goods and services to these same black constituents. Similarly, white representatives hailing from districts that are overwhelmingly white do not need to balance the concerns of black constituents with projects or service either. Thus, when crafting districts to enhance black representation, it is important to draw districts that are not overwhelmingly black yet still provide the opportunity to elect black representatives. Future redistricters should maximize these districts, which I call black-decisive districts.

In some ways, Carol Swain's (1995) analysis is supported by this work. She suggests that future strategies to enhance black representation should come from working to elect black legislators from districts that are not overwhelmingly black-majority. Like her, I find that black legislators from districts that are overwhelmingly African-American are less likely to be effective representatives of black interests than are their African-American counterparts from districts without a black majority. In part due to the safety of their seats, these black legislators substantively represent black legislators with roll-call voting but little else. In terms of constituency service, these black legislators from heavily black districts resort to symbolic efforts to reach African Americans (see also Sinclair-Chapman 2002 and Tate 2003). What is interesting about the findings presented here compared to Swain's is that I have more broadly tested some of the controversial propositions raised in her book. She based many of her claims about black legislators from overwhelmingly black districts on a small sample of congressional districts, mostly outside of the South. I have found evidence to bolster her claims broadly when looking at project distribution to black constituents and more narrowly when looking at constituency service in southern congressional districts.

Swain, however, also concludes that white legislators may in fact be as good at representing black interests as black legislators. Here, I differ with her findings (and concur with Kenny Whitby 1997). On every measure, black legislators (even when controlling for other factors including the black population of the district) are better substantive representatives of black interests. Whereas black legislators from overwhelmingly black districts are not as substantively "good" for black interests as their black colleagues from districts without black majorities, this does not suggest that these black legislators from black-majority districts are worse than their white colleagues.

It is important to note that very few white Democratic representatives in the Congresses that I studied hailed from districts greater than 40 percent black. Thus, Swain's conclusions regarding white Democrats (two of whom represented majority-black districts, and two of whom represented black-influence districts with a substantial black minority) may be constrained by the sample she examined. Of course, my conclusions are constrained by the sample I examined as well.

Another insight is that once the black population is high enough in a district, both white Democrats and Republicans will work to reach out to black constituents with constituency service and projects. The idea that Republicans completely neglect black constituents is not accurate. However, this is clearly not to say that Republican legislators are the "best" representatives of black interests. On roll-call voting and civil rights policy agenda setting, Republican legislators do not substantively represent black constituents. With project allocation, there is some evidence that Republicans do work to give federal projects to African Americans within their districts. In terms of constituency service, if Republicans hail from districts with sizable black populations, near at least 30 percent or higher, they sometimes appear to work to reach out to African Americans within their districts, though not always. The Republicans who attempt to reach black voters also seem to do so in somewhat naïve ways.

White Democrats, in contrast, tend to vote in the interests of African-American constituents. However, with regard to constituency service, they engage in a sort of semiproportionate tokenism. Black constituents are taken into account with regard to constituency service, but white Democratic legislators' service decisions are not as focused on black constituents as service decisions by black legislators in comparable districts. Black Democratic legislators, on the other hand, in almost all cases, work to reach black constituents more than their white Democratic colleagues – and in many cases to the point of overemphasizing black constituents given the demographic baselines of their districts. White Democrats are generally safer in black-influence districts than are black Democrats, and this may explain the differential in efforts on service and project allocations to black constituents. Service and project delivery may be needed more to reach voters when a member is less electorally safe.

Competitive elections, according to Morris Fiorina (1974), can lead to policy representation from a member of Congress that does not necessarily reflect the broad views of a district's constituents. Often, the member needs to respond to specific constituencies within a heterogeneous district so that roll-call voting does not necessarily appeal to the median of the district. It is suggested from Fiorina's work that competition in congressional elections is not "good" in the sense of reflecting a district's constituency (see also Buchler 2005; Brunell 2008; and Gulati 2004; but see Griffin 2006). However, in terms of racial representation and the results of this research, competition appears to be very important for constituency service and project allocation. Those legislators who face competitive threats are more likely to reach black voters with these particularistic activities. The implications of this analysis more broadly is that competition in heterogeneous districts may lead to unrepresentative roll-call outcomes (according to Fiorina), but those groups of voters who are not fully represented with roll calls are represented with service and project delivery.

These findings and conclusions regarding electoral safety and the interactive effect of a legislator's race and district black population raise broader implications regarding the rationality of black legislators. Scholars such as Mary Hawkesworth (2003) have, in my view, incorrectly interpreted that behavioral and rational choice theories cannot explain differences in outcomes in Congress based on race. If she were correct, then I would not have found different behavior among black legislators dependent on the district black population. Further, the electoral underpinnings of racial differences (and similarities) in congressional outcomes (votes, service, and project allocations) are clear – or else black legislators would uniformly behave the same regardless of the type of congressional district elected from. Further, an understanding of these electoral incentives of legislators is important when suggesting policy implications for drawing congressional districts to maximize black interests.

The Need for Black-Decisive Districts: Policy Implications for the Future of Majority-Minority Districts and Representation

So, in conclusion, what is the "best" districting arrangement for enhancing black interests in Congress? Much has been written, by both scholars and judges, about the best districting arrangement to enhance the substantive representation of black voters. Those focusing on roll-call voting outcomes have suggested that black-majority districts are not needed, and perhaps may be a detriment to the best aggregate representation of black interests in the legislature (e.g., Lublin 1997; Swain 1995; Whitby

1997). However, given that the number of black-majority districts did not have a dilutive effect on median civil rights preferences on the floor of the U.S. House, these concerns are less warranted. Instead, to assess racial redistricting plans, a greater focus should be on delivering district-oriented benefits.

Morgan Kousser (1999, 270) states that "[r]edistricting cannot be race-unconscious until the country ceases to be." I concur and suggest that those interested in maximizing African-American interests in districting plans should be able to balance the competing goals of "race-unconscious"-ness with the creation of congressional districts that value electoral competition yet also consider the racial population of the district. In terms of service and project allocation, an arrangement that allows for the election of the most black representatives in black-influence districts or perhaps districts that are just barely black-minority or black-majority seems to be the best. This way, black legislators can win in districts that are not overwhelmingly black, yet surrounding districts will not be diluted so substantially that white representatives can ignore black constituents or take them for granted. Whereas the Supreme Court initially ruled in *Miller v. Johnson* (1995) that districting schemes should be "color-blind" (see Kousser 1999), following the Congress's 2006 "fix" to *Georgia v. Ashcroft* (2003), it appears that race can be taken into account. However, the state of voting rights law and whether black-influence or black-majority districts are likely to be drawn is constantly in a state of flux. Thus, I offer a number of policy prescriptions regarding what I perceive as the best redistricting plans that maximize black substantive outcomes with less regard to the current state of the law and more with an eye toward the findings drawn from the evidence in this book. I leave it to the courts and policy makers to determine how and whether my policy prescriptions are politically or legally viable.

The best districting arrangement would clearly be a districting plan that maximizes black-decisive districts, which are competitive districts likely to elect black legislators. Depending on the local context, black-decisive districts will sometimes be black-majority and sometimes be black-influence districts. The best plans would maximize the election of black legislators from black-influence districts when possible (one form of black-decisive districts), while leaving surrounding districts represented by white legislators with significant black populations as well. In the case of project allocations, black legislators (regardless of black population) allocated more projects and federal dollars to African Americans than did white legislators. In black-influence districts, however, black legislators allocated even greater numbers of projects to black constituents. With constituency service, similar results held. For example, black legislators overhired black staff relative to the population of their districts, whereas white legislators did not. In the aggregate, then, maximizing black legislators while not "diluting" surrounding districts clearly seems to be the best policy prescription for the maximization of substantive representation in regard to these activities.

This policy prescription should also consider the role of region. Much of my analyses have been focused specifically on the South, and thus my policy prescriptions regarding racial redistricting are perhaps likely to apply to the South more than to the entire United States. Furthermore, in some of my findings in which I examined a national sample, the effect of the race of the legislator was much greater in the South than outside of the South. The results on constituency service suggest that some southern districts were more likely to underhire African-American staff, thus providing less political empowerment and substantive representation. Districts represented by white legislators and Republican legislators in the South did not hire as many African-American staff as one would expect based on the percentage of black constituents in the district. Furthermore, in the qualitative analysis of only southern districts in Chapters 4 and 5, only black legislators delivered the most constituency service directed toward African Americans.

This policy suggestion of black-decisive district maximization that is reliant primarily on drawing more black-influence districts may be easier said than done, however. First, in 2006, Congress extended the Voting Rights Act, and in so doing included a "fix" that essentially overruled the Supreme Court's endorsement of black-influence districts. Based on the 2006 extension, districts that are black-majority are now more likely to be drawn than they were prior to the act's extension. Yet the Supreme Court, in its limited 2009 *Bartlett v. Strickland* and *NAMUDNO v. Holder* decisions strongly implied the 2006 voting rights extensions, including the *Ashcroft* "fix," may not hold constitutional muster in future court decisions. I would encourage Congress to especially rework Section 5 of the Voting Rights Act to allow for the drawing, not of black-influence districts, but black-decisive districts (in which the black population is closer to 45–50% but not maximized above 50% in most districts).

Second, it is not clear that many congressional districts and localities are willing to vote for black candidates in white-majority districts. The cases analyzed here of black legislators from districts without a black majority are only very recent phenomena. It is not clear whether white voters with histories of racially polarized voting are ready to elect black legislators in open-seat elections. Other than Obama's election for president in 2008, there are few instances of a substantial number of white voters voting for a black candidate for federal office. Many analysts have been quick to point to Obama's victory as evidence that black candidates can win anywhere in the United States. However, the reality is that it is still quite unlikely for black candidates to win federal office in many white-majority areas of the country (Lublin et al. 2009). The cases of black legislators representing white-majority districts studied here are almost entirely those who were forced to run in white-majority districts as incumbents once the courts ruled their districts unconstitutional. Would Mel Watt, Corrine Brown, or even Sanford Bishop have been able to win in their court-ordered white-majority districts had they not been incumbents? Staff that I spoke with who worked for black legislators as well as surrounding white legislators all unanimously concluded that it would have been unlikely. When I asked Hobby Stripling, Sanford Bishop's district director, whether he thought Bishop would have won in his white-majority (39% black) district without having initially been elected in a black-majority district, he remarked as follows: "Without having the name recognition and providing the services, no. Quite frankly because he's black. I wish it weren't true." Similarly, even in multiethnic settings in which no racial or ethnic group is the majority, African-American mayoral candidates performed better when running as incumbents (Stein, Ulbig, and Post 2005).

A number of black politicians are beginning to test this proposition by running in white-majority settings (Ifill 2009). President Obama, based on a coalition of African Americans, Latinos, and a numerical (though quite large) minority of white voters is obviously the best example of black success in a white-majority setting (both in his 2004 U.S. Senate race and in the 2008 presidential election). Yet Obama is in many ways an anomaly, as very few black candidates have, even recently, been successful in their pursuit of federal office in white-majority settings. African-American Democrat Harold Ford Jr. ran for the U.S. Senate in Tennessee in 2006, winning a significant fraction of the white vote but ultimately losing to white Republican Bob Corker. Following Obama's election in 2008, no U.S. Senate seat was held by an African American who was elected to the office. In the U.S. House, black candidates profiled here such as Mel Watt continue to win reelection in their districts. However, following the 2000 census, many of the black Democratic House representatives I have profiled in this book have run for reelection in districts that are once

TABLE 7.1. *Black Electoral Success in General Elections for the U.S. House,
Incumbents in 2000, 2004, and 2008*

	> 50% Black Districts	< 50% Black, But Majority-Minority Districts[a]	> 50% White[b]	Total Districts with at Least One Black Candidate
Successful incumbent black candidates	69	30	11	110 (99%)
Unsuccessful incumbent black candidates	1	0	0	1 (0%)
Total incumbent black candidates	70 (63%)	30 (27%)	11 (10%)	111 (100%)

[a] Majority-minority districts are those that have a combined black, Hispanic, and/or Asian population higher than 50 percent.
[b] Non-Hispanic white.
Source: Racial population data of districts are from *Politics in America*.

again majority-black or majority-minority with few additional gains for black candidates in House districts that are white-majority. Whereas Obama's historic election as the first African-American president is a major advance in racial politics in the United States, the statistical fact remains that very few black candidates for federal office who have run in open-seat elections succeed in white-majority electorates.

Few black members of Congress have been elected in districts that are white-majority, and most that have were initially elected in districts with a black majority. To examine the opportunity for African-American candidates to be elected in Congress, see Tables 7.1 and 7.2. Table 7.1 charts the number and percentage of African-American congressional incumbents who were elected in 2000, 2004, and 2008, whereas Table 7.2 shows the number and percentage of successful African-American challengers who ran against nonblack incumbents or who ran in open seats in 2000, 2004, and 2008 (complete data on racial backgrounds of candidates for 2002 and 2006 were unavailable, so I only discuss 2000, 2004, and 2008).[2] As Table 7.1 shows, in these three election years, 111 black incumbents ran for reelection, and all but 1 (scandal-tainted Bill Jefferson, D-LA) were successful. Eleven of these were elected in white-majority districts, and 30 were elected in districts with a black minority

[2] Source: Joint Center for Political and Economic Studies.

TABLE 7.2. *Black Electoral Success in General Elections for the U.S. House, Challengers Running Against Nonblack Incumbents and Open Seats in 2000, 2004, and 2008*

	> 50% Black Districts	< 50% Black, but Majority-Minority Districts[a]	> 50% White[b]	Total Districts with at Least One Black Candidate
Successful nonincumbent black candidates	3	1	2	6 (18%)
Unsuccessful nonincumbent black candidates	0	4	23[c]	27 (89%)
Total nonincumbent black candidates	3 (9%)	5 (15%)	25 (76%)	33 (100%)

[a] Majority-minority districts are those that have a combined black, Hispanic, and/or Asian population higher than 50 percent.
[b] Non-Hispanic white.
[c] Includes 2001 special open-seat election between Louise Lucas and Randy Forbes.
Source: Racial population data of districts are from *Politics in America.*

but a majority of African-American, Asian-American, and/or Latino constituents (Casellas 2009b and Lublin 1997 have found that African Americans are likely to win election in districts with high percentages of black and Latino constituents).

However, as seen in Table 7.2, nonincumbent black candidates running against nonblack opponents clearly did not fare as well in 2000, 2004, and 2008. Of thirty-three black candidates who ran in open seats or against incumbents, six were victorious. In 2000, only one nonincumbent won: Lacy Clay, running in an open seat in a black-majority district. In 2004, Cynthia McKinney (D-GA), Al Green (D-TX), Gwen Moore (D-WI), and Emanuel Cleaver (D-MO) were all nonincumbents who won in open seats (McKinney had served in Congress, was defeated in 2002, and successfully reclaimed her seat in an open-seat race in 2004). Most importantly, though, only two of these five candidates in 2000 or 2004 won in districts with an outright white majority (Moore and Cleaver).[3] These two candidates are breaking barriers, much like Obama. Yet, the

[3] Keith Ellison (D-MN) is an African American that won in 2006 in an overwhelmingly white-majority district, but he is not included in this list because the data used for Table 7.2 were only available for 2000, 2004, and 2008.

likelihood of additional black candidate successes in white-majority settings remains to be seen. With the election of Moore, Cleaver, and Obama,
I am optimistic for continued black success in white-majority settings. It
is possible that the advances we have seen in municipal elections that
have yielded increased white support for black candidates (Hajnal 2007)
could continue in the realm of congressional elections. Yet I also temper
this optimism with the reality that few black candidates have won open
seats that are not in majority-minority districts (Crayton 2007; Lublin
et al. 2009). In 2008, the same year that Obama won the presidency, no
black candidates won in white-majority districts when running against
incumbents or in open seats.

All other African-American candidates, some of whom included low-
er-level elected officials and some of whom included inexperienced candidates, lost when running for open seats or against incumbents in districts
that did not have a black-majority population. Four lost in majority-
minority districts without a black majority and twenty-three lost in
white-majority districts. Success in white-majority settings is still limited
for nonincumbents; thus, prospects for many more black members of
Congress appear fairly bleak given these trends.

Yet some black legislators have succeeded in winning in white-
majority settings. Julia Carson, who represented the Indianapolis-based
tenth district of Indiana until 2007, initially won an open-seat election
in 1996 in a district with a 30 percent black population. Her grandson
won election to the seat following her death. Further, in 2004, Gwen
Moore (D-WI) surprised some observers by defeating a white candidate
in the Democratic primary and the general election in a district based
in Milwaukee, Wisconsin (a city that in the same year voted for a white
candidate over the appointed acting mayor, who was black). Whereas
clearly a boon for both descriptive and substantive representation of
black constituents, these examples may be rare occurrences.

Criteria for Drawing Districting Plans Maximizing
Black-Decisive Districts

Black-decisive districts are a good idea as they maximize African-
American substantive representation. This is particularly the case if the
substantive outcomes one cares about include activities like project allocation and constituency service. If one is only concerned about these
substantive outcomes, then there is no trade-off between drawing black-
decisive districts and the surrounding districts that are likely to elect

white legislators. The maximization of the election of black legislators is the best option for those wanting to enhance voting rights and black substantive representation.

However, as Tables 7.1 and 7.2 show, electing black legislators in districts without a black majority (and especially those with a white majority) is not very easy. I offer four criteria that policy makers and judges charged with crafting redistricting plans can use to maximize black-decisive districts – and thus maximize black substantive representation without diluting it in surrounding districts.

(1) Assess Local Conditions When Drawing Black-Decisive Districts
First, black-influence districts will not work in all geographic areas – if the result is almost certain to be the election of a white candidate, then the district is not a black-decisive district. In order to craft districting plans with black-decisive districts, those highly likely to elect African-American legislators, local conditions should be examined when determining whether black legislators can succeed in garnering some nonblack voter support. What is different between Indianapolis, where Julia Carson was able to win, than, say Cincinnati? Indiana's tenth district, Carson's district, is a compact district taking in most of Indianapolis and some surrounding areas. Ohio's first district is also compact, taking in most of Cincinnati and some surrounding areas of Hamilton County. Nationally, both cities are considered conservative for urban areas, though Cincinnati is arguably more Democratic than Indianapolis. The racial and ethnic demographics are virtually the same in each district. In both Indiana's tenth and Ohio's first, the black population is just under 30 percent and the white population makes up about two-thirds of the population in each district. Both cities have rich African-American histories and heritages. Also, outlying areas of the cities are somewhat affluent and give the areas a Republican bent. Yet, the first district of Ohio was represented by white Republican Steve Chabot until 2008, when Chabot was defeated by white Democrat Steve Driehaus. In contrast, black Democrat Julia Carson represented the Indiana tenth district until her death in late 2007 (she was replaced by her grandson Andre Carson, also a black Democrat, in a 2008 special election). Future researchers should in more detail examine the preconditions that may allow for black candidates to win in white-majority settings to determine what causes these differences in outcomes by candidates such as Carson, Chabot, and Driehaus (see Grofman and Handley 1989 and Lublin 1997 for a discussion of the districts most likely to elect black legislators).

Policy makers charged with drawing districts should simply examine local conditions to assess whether white-majority districts that are able to elect black members of Congress are feasible in certain areas. Voting rights advocates interested in revising Section 5 coverage of the Voting Rights Act (in the wake of the Supreme Court's sharply worded encouragement to do so in their 2009 *NAMUDNO v. Holder* case) should examine the extent of racially polarized voting in localities, including the extent that whites were willing to vote for Obama for president. Obama's election does not obviate the need for voting rights protections and the drawing of districts that enhance African-American influence in Congress. However, it does suggest that past election results in states and localities can and should be considered in revising voting rights act protections and drawing legislative district lines. For instance, based on 2008 election results, a state like Alabama (which had high levels of racially polarized voting) likely will require drawing a 50 percent black-decisive congressional district, whereas other states with less racially polarized voting like North Carolina may only require 40 to 45 percent black-decisive districts.

(2) Draw Districts that are Just Under or Equal to 50 Percent Black
Second, beyond assessing local conditions, a general strategy for increasing the number of black legislators from white-majority districts is to draw black-decisive districts that are just barely black-minority. Because black legislators enhance black representation, districts that are almost 50 percent black or exactly 50 percent black may be needed. In these districts, black legislators should be able to mobilize African-American voters in primary elections (Branton 2009) so that a black candidate is able to win the primary. Moreover, if the district is just slightly black minority, then it is also likely that at least a handful of nonblack voters can be found to cross over and support a black Democrat in the general election. Yet, these districts will be competitive enough to cause the winning legislator to aggressively deliver goods and services to African Americans in the districts. These sorts of districts are those whose black voters will clearly be decisive to the victory of the legislator (along with a handful of white voters) because no candidate can win without at least some black voter support.

(3) In Some Geographic Areas, Black-Decisive Districts May Have to be Black-Majority
In some instances, black-majority districts will be needed for black voters to be decisive to the outcome. If there is a recent history of low black

voter turnout or participation, a black-majority district may be needed for a district to be considered a black-decisive district. In regions such as parts of the rural South with longer histories of racial discrimination (Kousser 1999) or with histories of voter discrimination as identified by Section 5 of the Voting Rights Act (Hajnal 2009), black-decisive districts likely need to be black-majority. However, these districts should only have a small black majority of just over 50 percent in order to remain electorally competitive.

Some have suggested that black-majority districts should only be drawn in areas where the result does not dilute Democratic voting strength in surrounding districts. I do not agree with this contention given that aggregate voting floor preferences changed minimally with different redistricting schemes. Further, black legislators in southern states are better at delivering constituency service to black constituents than are their white colleagues. White representatives, both Democrat and Republican, simply did not match the efforts from black legislators. The same can be said for project grants: African-American legislators clearly delivered more projects and federal dollars to black constituents than did white colleagues. Thus, even in southern states and other states with conservative white populations, if we are concerned about constituency service and project delivery to African-American constituents, then it still may be useful to draw black-majority districts (resulting in greater substantive representation for black constituents beyond roll-call voting) – if these are the only districts that will allow black voters to decisively determine the winner. Black-decisive districts are critically important for enhancing black substantive representation even if the result is that nearby districts are likely to elect Republicans.

Critics of black-majority districts who argue that black-majority districts dilute surrounding districts by causing the other districts to elect Republicans may take issue with my policy prescription to draw competitive, black-decisive districts. These critics would likely argue that if the black population has been concentrated in districts (even black-decisive districts of only 40–50% black), then neighboring districts may have so few African-American residents that the white legislators (be they Democrat or Republican) likely to win in these districts have little inducement to provide benefits to the few African-American constituents living in these neighboring districts.

My response to these critics is twofold. First, the evidence from Chapter 3 on roll-call voting suggests that whereas racial gerrymandering may cause ideological shifts *within* state delegations that are not favorable to substantive black policy outcomes, drawing supermajority-black districts did not shift the median voter on the floor of the House in the aggregate. Given this, it is highly unlikely that drawing black-decisive districts with just under 50 percent of black voters would cause a dramatic shift in the floor outcomes in the U.S. House. Second, as seen in both the 1994 and 2006 elections, a multiplicity of factors often can lead to a change in partisan control in the U.S. House. Whereas racial gerrymandering may have a small impact, there are often bigger, macro-level factors (such as the shift of the South toward the Republican party separate from racial redistricting in 1994; and the unpopularity of the Iraq war in 2006) at work in partisan shifts in the U.S. congressional elections. I concede that racial gerrymandering can have an impact on partisan control of the legislature, but its impact is relatively small. If the maximization of substantive outcomes for African Americans is conceived as project allocation, the delivery of federal dollars to African Americans, and access to effective constituency service, then there is no trade-off in drawing black-decisive districts even if the surrounding districts are supermajority-white districts. However, if the maximization of substantive outcomes by individual members of Congress on roll-call votes is the goal, then there very well may be a trade-off.

(4) Increase Black-Minority Districts with a Majority of Minorities

Another type of black-decisive district that can lead to more black legislators from districts without a black majority, and thus increase substantive representation, is to create more majority-minority districts with a black plurality. Black legislators can more easily win in districts that have a black and Latino majority, though with only a black minority. Also, a district with Asian-American, black, and/or Latino voters together may be more likely to elect a minority legislator (Casellas 2009b; Lublin 1999; Saito 1993), though the evidence on the extent that Asian-American voters would be likely to cross over and vote for a black candidate is more limited.

Whereas drawing majority-minority districts with black pluralities in order to elect black legislators may enhance the substantive representation of black interests, it is not clear what impact this will have on other racial and ethnic minorities. Are Latino voters substantively represented? Or might Latino voters receive less attention from African-American and other non-Latino legislators? This may especially be the case when Latino voter registration rates are significantly lower than black voter registration rates or because Latino turnout is often lower unless Latinos are activated to participate by certain political issues (Pantoja, Ramirez, and Segura

2001). Nonvoters – such as Latinos in some congressional districts – tend not to have their preferences represented by elected officials (Griffin and Newman 2005). Thus, a black-plurality district in terms of population may result in the election of a black legislator, providing enhanced substantive representation for African Americans but perhaps not for Latino constituents. Furthermore, these districts with African-American pluralities but significant Latino populations may inhibit Latino descriptive representation, as Latino descriptive representation has not been increasing even as the Latino population grows (Casellas 2009a). This question of Latino substantive representation by non-Anglo, non-Latino representatives deserves further study, as do other questions of race, ethnicity, and representation that are raised in this book. The findings uncovered here as applied to African-American representation should be extended to the study of Latino representation, a now burgeoning field of research (Fraga et al. 2006).

A Los Angeles-area congressional district is an example of this. During the 1990s, Maxine Waters, a black Democratic congresswoman, represented a 43 percent black and 43 percent Latino congressional district. Her district in the 2000s was only 34 percent black and 47 percent Latino. However, her representational style is very focused on black constituents (Carter 2001), and this appears to be her most important "subconstituency" (Bishin 2009). Are Latino constituents receiving less substantive representation from black legislators like Waters who focus on black constituents? This is a question also left for future research. However, we know that black-decisive districts with a majority of minority voters enhance the likelihood of electing black legislators, especially when turnout differentials between black and nonblack constituencies are likely. Thus, to maximize the substantive representation of black interests, drawing more black-decisive districts like Waters's may be a useful strategy.

Conclusion and Closing Thoughts

Having laid out criteria policy makers and judges can use to draw and assess black-decisive districts, I want to conclude with a summary of the book's general findings. On legislative activity beyond roll-call voting, the presence of a black legislator clearly has an impact on the substantive representation of black constituents. This finding is robust across legislative activities, as black legislators allocate more federal projects and more constituency service to black constituents than do white legislators. The

TABLE 7.3. *Summary of Findings*

Measures of Substantive Representation	Roll-Call Voting	Project Allocations	Constituency Service
Race of MC	Small effect	Significant effect	Significant effect
District black population	Significant effect	Sometimes significant effect	Sometimes significant effect
Racial trust	No effect	Significant effect	Sometimes significant effect
Party of MC	Significant and greatest effect: Democrats	Significant effect: Republicans	Occasionally significant effect: Democrats

finding is also robust when considering other hypothesized factors such as the party of the legislator, the district black population, and racial trust. Thus, contrary to the conventional wisdom established by much of the first generation of scholarship on this topic, I have found a link between descriptive and substantive representation, even when considering the separate impact of a district's black population. Also, contrary to the arguments put forward by scholars such as David Canon (1999), Kerry Haynie (2001), Katherine Tate (2003), and Kenny Whitby (1997), I have shown that the race of the legislator plays a smaller role in roll-call vote outcomes in both the aggregate legislature and at the individual level of the legislator.

Consistent with the theory presented in Chapters 1 and 2, the racial background of the legislator is not the only significant predictor of substantive non-roll-call voting outcomes in Congress. However, it is the only explanation that is always a significant predictor. In Table 7.3, I briefly summarize the results of this book, focusing on the four explanatory factors that were hypothesized to affect the substantive representation of black interests – both for roll-call voting and for activities beyond the vote.

I theorized in Chapter 2 that the party of the legislator would be most likely to affect substantive representation when measured as roll-call voting – and that other factors would be more likely to affect substantive representation beyond the vote. This proved to be the case, as the party of the legislator was shown to have the biggest impact on roll-call voting at the end of Chapter 3. The race of the legislator and the district black population also had significant effects, though the magnitude of their effects was smaller than that of party. Further, for roll-call voting outcomes, the aggregate implications are clear. In terms of civil rights preferences on the floor of the U.S. House, neither black-majority districts nor African-American legislators are particularly important. Even the change in party control of the U.S. House between the 103rd (1993–94) and 104th Congresses (1995–96) did not alter the location of the decisive legislator on civil rights policies.

Also in Table 7.3, I summarize the findings for activities beyond roll-call voting. I examined constituency service to black constituents in Chapters 4 and 5, whereas I examined project allocations to black constituents in Chapter 6. I found that the race of the legislator was a strong predictor of substantive outcomes when measured as constituency service. African-American legislators are more likely to open district offices, hire staff connected to their districts' black communities, and hire a larger proportion of black district staff in general. The other three factors (district black population, racial trust, and party) also had an impact on the delivery of constituency service to black constituents, though the findings were less robust than those of the race of the legislator.

With regard to project allocations, the presence of a black legislator and racial trust always lead to greater substantive representation for black constituents. These two factors always have an impact on project allocations to black constituents. The party of the legislator and the district black population also had an effect on project allocations, though the effect of these factors was smaller. Interestingly and somewhat surprisingly, Republicans were slightly more likely to allocate projects than were Democrats, all else equal.

Clearly, though, racial trust had an impact on constituency service and project allocations. For districts represented by black legislators, there is consistent evidence that districts with smaller black populations are more likely to produce representatives that will deliver more substantive goods for black constituents. With regard to white legislators (with constituency service at least), districts with larger black populations are likely to result in greater substantive representation for black constituents.

These results are unique for a variety of reasons. This is the only study that measures substantive representation in so many different ways while also including all four relevant racial representation variables. Unlike past scholars, I have not been forced to exclude a relevant variable or variables in most of the analyses. Methodologically, this work is an advance as I have generally been able to avoid problems of observational equivalence that have plagued previous scholars. This was done by using new data on post-*Miller v. Johnson* districts and also by increasing the sample size to more than what previous researchers have considered.

Substantively, also, this work is a key advance. So much of what goes on in a legislature is more than simply voting on the floor. Thus, by examining activities that are more likely to impact specific constituents back home in the districts, we have learned more about the nature of representation in Congress. African-American constituents are substantively better off by having African-American legislators as representatives, and thus black-decisive districts should be strongly encouraged by advocates of African-American interests.

Appendix 1 (for Chapter 3)

Methods Used to Measure the Civil Rights Issue Space

The civil rights issue space in Chapter 3 was estimated using Bayesian Markov Chain Monte Carlo (MCMC) methods (see Clinton, Jackman, and Rivers 2004; Martin and Quinn 2002). I assume there is a unidimensional civil rights policy space over the time period from 1969 to 2004 (the 91st to 108th Congresses). I then estimate House members' ideal points on this civil rights issue space.

The estimation is based on the civil rights votes of House members during these Congresses. These civil rights ideal point estimates – similar to ideological positions – are comparable across time periods and vary over time for legislators who serve over multiple Congresses. I estimate all legislators' positions on a scale on which negative indicates more liberal positions on civil rights and positive numbers indicate more conservative positions on civil rights. Enelow and Hinich (1984) posit that a roll-call vote is a choice between a position along a (unidimensional, in this instance) policy space consistent with a "yea" vote (φ_j) in favor of the proposal and that with a "nay" vote (γ_j) against it. The unidimensional civil rights policy space, X, a subset of the real line, is a continuum of policies ranging from extremely pro-civil rights on the left (negative values) to extremely anti-civil rights on the right (positive values). Ideological predilections along the civil rights space may be *induced* by preferences and other various factors, but that is beyond the scope of this research.[1] However, others have examined whether partisan, constituency, racial,

---

[1] Induced preferences denote expected utility preferences over some large policy space, portions of which are unobservable. The unobserved preferences induce preferences over observable elements of the policy space, and the latter do not generally constitute expected utility preferences (Kreps and Porteus 1979).

or other inducements affected votes on civil rights (e.g., Canon 1999; Hutchings 1998; Lublin 1997; Swain 1995; Whitby 1997; Whitby and Krause 2001).

Formally, House member *i*'s utility from "yea" and "nay" outcomes can be specified respectively by the following random utility functions:

$$u_i(\varphi_j) = -d(\hat{x}_i - \varphi_j) + \varepsilon_{ij} \qquad u_i(\gamma_j) = -d(\hat{x}_i - \gamma_j) + \eta_{ij}$$

where $d(\cdot)$ represents the squared Euclidean norm. In this notation, $\hat{x}_i$ is the ideal point of House member *i*, φ_j indicates a "yea" position by House member *i* on roll-call vote *j* and γ_j indicates a "nay" position by House member *i* on roll-call vote *j*. The House member votes "yea" if $u_i(\varphi_j) > u_i(\gamma_j)$ and vice versa. The specification assumes random errors, ε_{ij} and η_{ij}. Following Clinton et al. (2004, 356, 367), this difference in utility values yields a linear probability model, $y_{ij}^* = u_i(\varphi_j) - u_i(\gamma_j)$, where y_{ij}^* is the *latent* trait that drives House member *i*'s vote choice. Thus, we can stipulate that observing $y_{ij} = 1$ means that the latent $y_{ij}^* > 0$, whereas observing $y_{ij} = 0$ suggests that $y_{ij}^* \le 0$. Assuming that the difference $(\varepsilon_{ij} - \eta_{ij})$ is identically and independently distributed standard normal, then we can write:

$$y_{ij}^* = d(\varphi_j - \hat{x}_i) - d(\gamma_j - \hat{x}_i) + (\varepsilon_{ij} - \eta_{ij})$$

By allowing $\beta_j = 2(\varphi_j - \gamma_j)$ and $\alpha_j = \gamma_j' \gamma_{j} - \varphi_j' \varphi_j$, we have a two-parameter item response model:

$$\Pr(y_{ij} = 1) = \phi(\beta_j x_i - \alpha_j)$$

where ϕ represents the normal cumulative density function, β_j is the item discrimination parameter, and α_j is the item difficulty parameter (Clinton et al. 2004, 356).

I use a matrix of roll-call votes in which each legislator has voted yea, nay, or (in some instances) has abstained. In the case of abstention, I do not impute. In total, between the 91st and 108th Congresses, 232 nonunanimous votes on civil rights were cast by 7,501 House members (in total over the entire time period). In addition to the 7,501 House members, I also include positions that the Leadership Conference on Civil Rights (LCCR) took on roll calls during this entire time period and estimate the LCCR as a "legislator" in the matrix of roll-call votes. This allows the LCCR to be used as a reference point to estimate the other legislators and identifies this actor (the LCCR) that has a constant ideal point over the entire time period (1969–2004). As I note later, the LCCR's ideal point and one House member's ideal point are fixed over this entire time period. Including the LCCR as a "legislator" with the other 7,501 House members results in a data matrix of dimension 7,502 legislators x 232 roll calls. I estimate the spatial location of all House members on one civil rights dimension.

Priors

This approach is Bayesian, permitting the analyst to include prior information about the distribution of the latent ideal points when estimating the statistical model.[2] I fixed the position of two actors. Recall that the LCCR is treated as a "legislator" in the matrix. To identify the direction and scale of the recovered unidimensional space, I imposed "spike" priors on the latent ideal point parameter for two actors – the LCCR at strongly pro-civil rights and Rep. Phil Crane (R-IL) as strongly anti-civil rights during the entire time period. The position of the LCCR is assumed to be fixed over the entire time period at -1. I also fixed the position of Rep. Phil Crane (R-IL) at +1 over the entire time period. Crane is one of the only legislators serving this entire time period. Throughout his tenure in Congress, he regularly and consistently voted against civil rights (or at least the civil rights positions as indicated by the LCCR). All other legislators during this time period are estimated based on the scale established with the LCCR at −1 and Crane at +1. These other legislators' ideal point estimates are not fixed across time. They are able to move from one Congress to another.

This does *not* imply that the LCCR's and Crane's ideal point estimates will lie on the polar left or right of the civil rights dimension, but only that the remaining 7,500 House members' ideal points are estimated based on the information that Crane and the LCCR take extreme positions on civil rights.[3] Indeed, this is similar to identification restrictions employed

---

[2] Clinton et al. (2004) argue that these methods are better than maximum likelihood methods such as W-NOMINATE when such a small number of roll-call votes are being scaled. Given the small number of votes, I choose the Bayesian procedure for greater reliability.

[3] To facilitate this, the "precision" for the LCCR and Crane was set at an arbitrarily large number, $1+e^{12}$. The "precision" is the inverse of the variance (Jackman 2003, 6). This effectively constrains estimates of the latent traits for the LCCR and Crane to lie at −1 and 1 respectively. Starting values for $\hat{x}_i$ were obtained by sampling uniformly on a $[-1,1]$ interval and allowing the Gibbs sampler to run to a very large number of iterations. Initial values for α_j and β_j were set at zero. Given the small number of votes, computational time is not overwhelming but was fairly extensive. The estimates are based on as much or more information about the posterior distribution than typically recommended by Clinton et al.

in the non-Bayesian NOMINATE procedures. All other legislators' ideal points were given uninformed priors – the prior distributions for their latent ideal point parameters in the estimation are $N(0,1)$. This is a commonly used uninformative prior that, in combination with the spike priors described previously, identifies a rotation and scale that resembles the estimates made popular by Poole and Rosenthal (1997).

In addition to priors for the ideal point parameters, I also used informative priors for the bill parameters. Given that the LCCR only takes positions on approximately twenty roll calls or less in each Congress, for identification purposes, I chose to place priors on the bill parameters as well. This strategy is used by others faced with a small number of roll calls (e.g., Clinton and Meirowitz 2004). Given the number of "votes" the LCCR takes in a given Congress, I used a prior mean of -1 and a prior variance of 0.10 for all bills for which the LCCR professed support (equivalent to a "yea" vote). I did not use informative bill priors for votes for which the LCCR professed opposition (equivalent to a "no" vote). In the cases of LCCR "no" positions, I used vague $N(0,100)$ priors for the mean and variance of the bill parameters. I used informative priors only on bills that the LCCR took an affirmative position on because we know that these bills are pro-civil rights. I did not constrain LCCR opposition positions with tight bill priors because the LCCR may oppose legislation, not because a no vote is the strongest civil rights position, but because the opposition to the bill may occur for a variety of reasons.

Estimation Procedure

I employed Jackman's (2003) IDEAL routine to perform the estimation. The routine employs a Gibbs sampling algorithm (see Clinton et al. 2004 for technical details). The estimates are based on 500,000 iterations of the Gibbs sampler, discarding the first 100,000 iterations as "burn-in." I thinned the estimation and only recorded every 500th iteration after the burn-in.[4] Thus, the civil rights ideal point estimates are simply the posterior means of the 800 total draws (400,000 divided by 500 = 800).

(2004, 368): "For simple unidimensional fits, we usually let the sampler run for anywhere between 50,000 and 500,000 iterations and then thin the output (storing the output of every 100th to every 1,000th iteration) so as to produce a reasonable number of approximately independent samples from the posterior for inference (say, between 250 and 1,000 samples)."

[4] Burn-in refers to the initial iterations discarded in order to remove data generated when the sampler may be far off the mean and has not yet converged. Thinning of the chain reduces the computational burden.

Why Use Only Civil Rights Votes to Construct the Ideal Point Estimates?

As mentioned previously, a matrix of all roll-call votes for which the LCCR took a position over this time period was constructed. The LCCR has frequently been used as a measure of civil rights voting records (Canon 1999; Grose 2005; Hutchings 1998; Hutchings, McClerking, and Charles 2004; Whitby 1997). Also, Canon (1999), Swain (1995), and Tate (2003) note that civil rights issues are one of the only issue areas in which African Americans have distinct policy preferences from citizens of other racial backgrounds. Given that civil rights votes may be the only policy dimension in which African Americans have cohesive policy preferences – and the LCCR is the best existing measure of these civil rights preferences in Congress – I employ this measure. However, using the MCMC ideal point estimation procedure instead of simply using the raw LCCR scores allows me to get around scale comparability problems that exist with the raw LCCR scores. Further, Hutchings (1998) points out that the LCCR embeds salient and nonsalient votes in its scale, and thus some votes may win easily, whereas others may provide more useful cutpoints between legislators. Thus, my method of ideal point estimation accounts for this problem but still utilizes all votes – and thus these new civil rights measures will prove to be useful to research questions beyond the scope of this manuscript. Furthermore, by using this scaling method, we find that some legislators are actually to the left of the LCCR. Mel Watt (D-NC), for instance, had a voting record to the left of the LCCR during the 104th Congress. This would not have been picked up in the existing LCCR scores, which are bounded at 0 and 100. Thus, the civil rights ideal point estimates presented here, which are based on existing LCCR scores, are better measures of the civil rights policy space than existing LCCR scores.

Appendix 2 (for Chapters 4 and 5)

Methods for Qualitative Research

In Chapters 4 and 5, the dependent variable is constituency service allocations to African-American constituents. Most of the analyses in Chapters 4 and 5 come from a qualitative sample of districts. I interviewed twenty-seven district staff members of legislators in seventeen districts during the 106th and 107th Congresses (visiting twenty-seven total district offices). Interviews in three of these districts were conducted jointly with political scientists Maurice Mangum and Christopher Martin. Through interviews and participant observation during these visits, I have gathered data and qualitative evidence on these district offices and these seventeen members of Congress. See Table 4.1 in Chapter 4 for a list of members whose district offices I visited, broken down by relevant independent variables (this qualitative sample was selected based on variation in the independent variables; see King, Keohane, and Verba 1994). The selection of these districts was not random, but was done scientifically in order to vary the independent variables of interest. More on this subject is detailed later. I rely on this field research to illuminate the results throughout the book as well.

Methodological issues are not just the realm of quantitative research. Whereas issues plaguing quantitative research are different from those in qualitative small-n research, the issues in qualitative research are often stickier and deal with more fundamental questions of research design. Through small sample studies, we can learn much more about the context of representation in the district. Dick Fenno (1978, 2000, 2003) is the most prominent example of one who uses this sort of research in Congress, if not all of political science in general. Carol Swain (1995) and James Glaser (1996, 2005) also use qualitative research in order to address questions of race in Congress. Fenno (1978) examined eighteen congressional districts, Fenno (2000) examined two congressional districts, Fenno (2003) examined four congressional districts, Glaser (1996) examined six congressional districts, Glaser (2005) examined five congressional districts, and Swain (1995) looked at thirteen districts. The seventeen districts that I chose to examine were done in order to vary the independent variables of interest and were chosen without knowledge of the outcome of the dependent variable (and thus I did not select on the dependent variable). Also, I examine only southern districts in order to reduce the likelihood of regional explanations in the outcomes regarding constituency service and in order to lower the costs of travel between districts.[1]

In my analysis of constituency service, I measured the dependent variable as: (1) the location of district offices in black, racially mixed, or white neighborhoods; (2) the race of staffers in congressional districts; and (3) the general perception from staff that black voters were important members of the district's constituency. Given the potentially controversial nature of the subject matter (race), I faced a few obstacles in my research.

First, some offices were more cooperative than others. After an initial contact in most offices, they were willing to sit down and meet with me. In a few cases, however, I had difficulty garnering an appointment. Instead of dropping these cases from the analysis, which could cause selection bias, I arrived at the district office anyway and simply requested an opportunity to meet with a staff member. In all but one case in which an initial interview was not scheduled, after having learned that I had flown and driven many miles to talk to them, I was treated to a lengthy interview. In the one case without a lengthy interview, a short interview was conducted followed by a longer phone interview. In a few other cases with in-person interviews, follow-up phone calls were also conducted to garner additional information or to verify certain data.

Second, the race of the interviewer can certainly have an effect on responses and what is observed. In phone interviews, black respondents are often not as likely to speak as openly about race when the perceived race of the interviewer is white (Davis 1997; Gurin, Hatchett, and Jackson 1989). In personal interview situations, this effect is likely to be

---

[1] This, of course, limits the generalizability of the sample to the South. However, the results from the quantitative national analyses in Chapters 4, 5, and 6 generally support the findings from the qualitative analysis.

exacerbated, and Canon (1999) and Swain (1995) detail these possible effects during qualitative research. I am white, and this had the potential for limiting the full amount of information that I could garner in the offices of black members of Congress. As a result, as mentioned earlier, for three of the six black legislators in the sample, African-American colleagues (Maurice Mangum and Christopher Martin) conducted the interviews with me. Hopefully, this reduced the likelihood of negative race-of-interviewer effects.

In other cases, my racial background worked in my favor. In many white legislative offices, the staff spoke more freely about the realities of race in their districts (and occasionally made some rather unguarded comments about their black and white constituents). Also, in all offices, whether represented by white or black legislators, I developed a strong rapport and trust with the staff members that I interviewed, especially by the end of the lengthier interviews (most interviews lasted approximately one and a half to two hours). For example, an interview in a North Carolina congressman's office went so well that a staffer encouraged me to run for Congress in a neighboring district and suggested that I pick up the congressman from the airport later that night as he was coming home from Washington. A number of staffers invited me back for follow-up visits with the legislator and often continued talking with me well after the office had closed for the day.

Appendix 3 (for Chapter 6)

Data, Methods, and Models for Project Allocations to African Americans

The analyses in Chapter 6 of project allocations to predominately black counties and to historically black colleges and universities (HBCUs) are based on four regression models. The figures displayed and discussed in Chapter 6 are predicted values based on varying the key independent variables of interest while holding the other "control" variables at their means. This appendix presents the details of these four statistical models in more depth than in Chapter 6. I examine four regression models, with four different dependent variables, all measuring either the number or dollar amounts allocated to either predominately black counties or HBCUs. The data used in Chapter 6 for the dependent variables are from the Federal Awards Assistance Data System (FAADS), which is discussed in detail in Stein and Bickers (1995). Other details regarding the unit of analysis were given in the text of the chapter.

The FAADS data are available from the U.S. census bureau as a list of every project allocated with associated geographic information. For Chapter 6's analyses of project allocations to predominately black counties and to HBCUs, I excluded all types of federal assistance other than project grants – formula-based grants, loans, contingent financial aid, and so on were not included. Project grants, and not these other forms of assistance, are the most likely to be particularistic to constituencies. Next, for the black counties analyses, I aggregated these data to each county so that the *total number of new projects* allocated and the *total amount of federal spending on new project grants to each county* was known. Finally, I collected independent variables associated with each of these counties, their congressional districts, and the districts' representatives. For the HBCU analyses, I aggregated data on *total number of new projects* and *total amount of federal spending on new projects at the level of the congressional district.* I will discuss the county models first, and then detail the HBCU models later in this appendix.

Models for Predominately Black Counties

I only look at the final year of each session (1996, 1998, and 2000) for two reasons. First, pork projects may have a greater effect during election years (Anagnoson 1982). Second, there may be some lag between the time when a project is actually approved by Congress and when it is processed. It is difficult to determine whether project data in early 1999, for example, are a result of maneuverings of the representative elected to the district in November 1996 or of the representative elected in November 1998. Thus, just election year data are analyzed.

A Methodological Advance

There are three reasons this study is an advance over prior ones. First, substantively, it is the first time that distributive policy allocations have been looked at through the lens of minority representation. Second, the data and research design of Chapter 6 allow for inferences to be drawn about the effects of the race of representatives, the black populations of districts, and racial trust in the same statistical model. Third, this study is a methodological advance over prior studies of project allocations, as I use a more appropriate negative binomial regression analysis when examining the number of projects allocated by each legislator. The first and second advances are discussed elsewhere in the book, but I further address the latter two here.

Minority representation scholars have had difficulty distinguishing between the effects of (1) electing black representatives; and (2) the overall black population of districts on the substantive representation of black constituents due to multicollinearity. As we know from Chapter 2, by examining legislators in the 104th to 106th Congresses (1995–2000), a substantial number of black legislators from districts without a black majority are analyzed in order to reduce this multicollinearity. Beyond this greater variation in black legislators, I also overcome this multicollinearity problem in Chapter 6's analysis of predominately black counties by examining counties. King, Keohane, and Verba (1994) argue that looking at lower levels of aggregation with larger sample sizes can solve these statistical inference problems.

TABLE A.1. *Incidence of Counties Represented by Black and Nonblack Representatives by Black Population of Congressional District, 104th to 106th Congresses (1995–2000)*

Sample: *Counties that are at least 40 percent Black in Population*[a]

Black Population of District (%)	Black	Nonblack[b]	Total
0–20	0 counties	44	44
21–30	0	91	91
31–40	43	112	155
41–50	21	28	49
51–60	152	6	158
61–70	226	0	226
71–75	6	0	6
All	448	281	729

[a] These are counties or county portions that are 40% black or higher in population for all congressional districts in the 104th Congress (1995–96), the 105th Congress (1997–98), and the 106th Congress (1999–2000).

[b] Three of the counties represented by a nonblack legislator in this sample are represented by a Latino legislator (Jose Serrano, NY-16); the others are white.

Table A.1 details the incidence of black representatives in congressional districts with varying levels of black populations.[1] Although there is obviously an asymmetry between the race of the representative and the district black population, the inclusion of districts redrawn due to court order will help reduce the multicollinearity between these two variables so that estimation can at least be attempted.[2] For example,

[1] Unfortunately, data for many of the independent variables related to the 106th North Carolina and Virginia congressional districts are not available, and thus counties from districts in these two states for this Congress were excluded from the analysis. Following the 1998 elections, these states were forced to redraw their districts. In three of the districts, black representatives were redrawn into much whiter districts. The inclusion of these data could potentially reduce multicollinearity even more.

[2] In past models of roll-call voting, the multicollinearity is essentially equal to one, and thus scholars drop one of the variables. In the models estimated in Chapter 6, the correlation between the two variables is still very high, but not so high that I am unable to estimate the models with both variables. For instance, with the sample of counties (at least 40% black counties), the correlation coefficient between race of the representative and the district black population is a high, though not intractable, 0.8. These high correlations are not a problem given the large sample size (Achen 1982). Also, this multicollinearity is not a severe problem in this analysis because (1) the variance inflation factors (VIFs) on the race and district black population variables were low; and (2) in the analysis presented in this appendix, the variables are, for the most part, significant. Finally, in addition to the results presented here, I estimated each statistical model excluding each highly correlated variable, and the results were substantively similar.

in the sample of counties that are at least 40 percent black in population, seventy counties are represented by a legislator of a different racial background than the majority of the constituents in the district (these are indicated in bold). This is much better than many previous studies with almost no black legislators representing districts without black majorities in their samples. Clearly, the variation caused by the election of some African-American legislators in districts without black majorities is increased by expanding the sample size when the unit of analysis is the county.

This study is also a methodological advance in the projects literature. Most previous studies of project distribution have used ordinary-least squares (OLS) to look at the number of projects allocated. Often, this specification is inappropriate as the number of projects allocated to a particular geographic jurisdiction will be very low and will always have a lower bound of zero (it is impossible to allocate negative projects). However, a handful of counties are likely to receive large numbers of project allocations (e.g., very populated communities).

Also, some data used are counts of the number of projects allocated. Ideally, we could chart each individual project given to each recipient by race, but this is not possible. The next best alternative is the data at hand, which are the total number of projects allocated to each county in a particular year. Thus, the use of OLS is inappropriate, and a nonlinear count model is needed. For these reasons, I estimate the model with the negative binomial distribution. The negative binomial regression model relaxes the assumption of constant mean and variance across observations that is required for a Poisson distribution (see Greene 2003, 744–747; King 1989, 51–54; and Long 1997, 230–238 for more information on the negative binomial regression model). I have hypothesized and past research indicates (Stein and Bickers 1995) that projects are not distributed equally. Legislators attempt to reward supporters with projects. Additionally, the number of new projects allocated depends in part on demand in each county based on such variables as overall population, economic need, and the like (Rich 1989). Thus, the assumption of constant variance and mean required of the Poisson model will be difficult to meet and the negative binomial model is the most theoretically appropriate specification. Also, the model estimating the number of project allocations is estimated with robust standard errors.

Further, I estimate the model predicting dollar amounts allocated for new projects using tobit (see Long 1997). Tobit is similar to linear regression, though it corrects for censoring in the dependent variable.

Examining pork project allocation funding to African Americans results in censored data. Whereas legislators cannot allocate a negative dollar amount of projects to African Americans, some may want to. Those legislators who allocate zero projects to African Americans may in fact prefer more money to be sent to white constituents but are unable to due to existing grant programs (e.g., existing programs targeting HBCUs cannot be used to send more federal money to predominately white colleges, even though a legislator might prefer this). Thus, the use of tobit is more methodologically appropriate for analyzing dollar amounts allocated than OLS. Scholars studying campaign contributions have similarly used tobit to correct for censoring at zero.

The Empirical Models of Project Allocations and Dollars to Predominately Black Counties

The dependent variable in one model is the *number of new federal project grants allocated* to each county. The dependent variable in the second model is the *amount of federal dollars spent on new project grants allocated* to a particular county. As mentioned earlier, the FAADS dataset is utilized to measure these dependent variables (the FAADS data are available from the U.S. census on its Web site www.census.gov). For those portions of counties that are not whole, I translated the project-by-project data in the FAADS database to data at the level of the county portion using the decision rules specified by Stein and Bickers (1995), which is not an inconsequential task. For more details, see the appendix on the FAADS data in Stein and Bickers (1995).

Independent Variables of Interest: Racial Representation Variables

All of the independent variables are the same for both the model with the number of projects and the model with the dollar amounts allocated. Four variables are needed for they key explanations offered by the theory. The first one is the *black population of the district*, included to test the first hypothesis. This variable is simply the percentage of the congressional district population that is black according to census figures. Black voting age population data were not available for a significant number of districts (some of those redistricted after the initial 1992 redistricting). Thus, I use black population. The minimum value for this district variable is 11 percent black and the maximum value is 74 percent black.

Race of Representative. To test the second hypothesis, which addresses the effects of descriptive representation on the allocation of federal projects, I include a dummy variable. It is coded "1" for all counties that are represented by black legislators and coded "0" for all counties with nonblack legislators. In the 40 percent black sample of counties, three counties in the sample are represented by a Latino legislator (for simplicity, I refer to all legislators as white or black in the text, but this one Latino legislator is included in the group of legislators I call white in the text).

Racial Trust. This variable is the interaction of the district black population and the race of the representative and is specified in order to test the third hypothesis. I expect white representatives to be more responsive than black representatives to different levels of district black population. Higher levels of project allocation are one way that white representatives might bridge this trust divide. The actual variable is measured by multiplying the observations of the district black population variable and the race of representative variable together. Thus, for nonblack representatives, the variable is coded "0"; for black representatives, the variable is the district's black population percentage.

Party of Representative. I include this variable to test the fourth and final hypothesis on whether Republican legislators will allocate fewer projects to black constituents than will Democrats.

Congressional Variables

Political variables that capture the institutional perquisites and the electoral factors of legislators are also needed in models of project allocations. I specify three variables for House members and two for senators.

Member on House Appropriations Committee is a variable included to control for the access to projects that legislators serving on this committee have (Arnold 1979; Ferejohn 1974; Rundquist and Carsey 2002). The expectation is that counties that are in districts represented by Appropriations Committee members will receive more projects than counties without representation. The variable is coded "1" if the legislator representing the county is on the committee and is coded "0" if not. *Senator on Appropriations Committee* is a similar control variable. Lee (1998) and Rundquist and Carsey (2002) show that the Senate also plays a role in the distribution of projects. Here, too, the variable is coded "1" if a county is represented by a senator who is on the Appropriations Committee.[3]

Seniority of House Member. The number of years that a legislator has previously served in the House affects the allocation of projects, and this seniority could work in two possible directions. More junior members may have less access to the allocation of projects given their lower status in the House. On the other hand, very senior members, in the protectionist stage of their careers, may feel safe and will not need to work as hard to secure projects for constituents. This variable is measured as the number of years served by a House member at the opening of the Congress in which the project is allocated. Just like in the House, the *Seniority of senators* can affect the allocation of projects. This variable is the combined total number of years served by both senators in a state.[4]

Previous Election Margin of House Member. Stein and Bickers (1994; 1995) find that the lower the electoral margin of a House incumbent, the more likely an incumbent will allocate a greater number of projects in the subsequent Congress. Thus, I expect that the general election margin received by a legislator in the previous election will affect project allocations.

Demand-Level Variables

I also need to account for project demand by constituents. Distributive policy projects are sometimes allocated because of political concerns but also are often distributed purely out of need or demand (Stein 1981; Rich 1989). After all, even when political influence is involved, a potential grant recipient must still apply for a grant. A representative's influence is limited to the ability to advertise available grants to constituents and to work to procure specific grants once the grant has been applied for (see Ferejohn 1974 and Arnold 1979 for more details). Thus, well-specified models of project distribution need to consider that "some communities find project grants difficult to apply for and politically undesirable to accept" (Stein 1981).

In order to determine which explanatory variables predict project allocations to counties, I turn to the literature on project distribution. This

---

[3] No senators from the same state concurrently serve on the Appropriations Committee in this sample, so a dichotomous variable is sufficient.

[4] Average senator seniority was also used in an alternative estimation, and the results were substantively the same.

literature, though, has typically looked at only district or state level allocations. Because of this, the independent variables used are those found to
affect project allocations at these higher levels of aggregation. In some of
the analyses in Chapter 6, though, they are applied to the county level.

Levitt and Snyder (1995) find that the *median family income* has a
negative impact on project allocation. The rationale is that very wealthy
communities are more likely to seek market-based assistance or simply do
not need government projects as much as more middle- and low-income
communities. The *median family income* variable is the median family
income in each county from the U.S. census measured in thousands of
dollars. Another obvious demand-level variable is the *overall population
of the county*, measured in thousands of dollars as well. Largely populated counties will receive more projects than those counties with few
residents (e.g., Levitt and Snyder 1995; Lowry and Potoski 2004; Stein
1981). Also, very poor communities may not have the resources to seek
projects (Stein 1981), so the *proportion below poverty* – the number
of persons in poverty in each county divided by the number of persons
for whom poverty status is established (also from the U.S. census) – is
included as an independent variable.

Other demand-level variables deal with the occupational backgrounds
of constituents. Bickers and Stein (1996) and Levitt and Snyder (1995)
find that the higher the percentage employed in blue-collar jobs, the less
likely projects will be allocated. Bickers and Stein (1996) find a negative relationship between the percentage of employees in agriculture and
project allocations. The *proportion in farming occupations* is the proportion of all employed people in each county who are classified as working
in "farming, forestry, and fishing" occupations by the U.S. census. The
proportion of blue-collar workers is also calculated using census data: the
proportion of all employed people in each category who are classified as
working in one of four blue-collar occupation categories.[5]

Control variables for younger residents, senior residents, urban residents, and less-educated residents are also needed. Following Bickers
and Stein (1996), I include the variables *proportion over age 65* and
proportion under age 18 in each county.[6] Large senior populations are

---

[5] The four census occupational categories used to calculate the blue-collar variable are
the following: (1) machine operators, assemblers, and inspectors; (2) transportation and
material moving occupations; (3) handlers, equipment cleaners, helpers, and laborers; and
(4) precision production, craft, and repair occupations.

[6] Levitt and Snyder (1995) also find that the population over age 65 affects project allocation levels. The specific data for these variables is from the 1990 census.

more likely to receive projects, whereas younger populated areas are less likely to receive projects. The *proportion urban* and the *proportion with less than a high school diploma* are included to control for demand and are both from the census. The urban variable is the number of persons living in urban areas divided by all persons in the county, whereas the education variable is the proportion of all persons under age 25 without a high school diploma living in each county. Urban residents are much more likely to receive projects (Levitt and Snyder 1995). Less-educated populaces, on the other hand, are less likely to apply for grants, and thus will not receive as many (Bickers and Stein 1996).

Finally, I also include a variable that designates whether a state capital is located in the county. Levitt and Snyder (1995) find this to be a significant predictor of project allocations. Given the way that the FAADS data are reported, many projects are allocated to the state government to distribute throughout the state. However, the actual coding in the FAADS database codes all of these projects as allocated to the county in which the state capital is located (Stein and Bickers 1995). Thus, I include a dummy variable indicating the presence of a state capital in a county as these counties will receive many more projects than others.[7]

Results of 40 Percent Black and Higher Counties Analyses

Table A.2 displays the results of these models. Model 1 is a negative binomial regression model predicting the number of new project grants allocated to counties that are 40 percent black or higher. Model 2 is a tobit model predicting the dollars allocated (in millions of dollars) to these counties.

Immediately, two results stand out. Two of the four variables of interest were significant in both models – the race of the representative and the racial trust variable (the interaction of the legislator's race and district black population). Clearly, there is a robust impact of these two variables on project allocations as the results are consistent for both samples. The presence of a black representative had a positive and significant impact on allocations to black constituents at the 0.01 level for Model 1 and at the 0.05 level for Model 2. Interestingly, the racial trust variable is negative and

---

[7] I also estimated alternative models with a dummy variable for southern congressional districts, available from the author. This variable proved insignificant, and the results of the key variables were substantively the same.

TABLE A.2. *Project Delivery to Black Counties: The Effect of Race, Party, and District Black Population on Pork Projects Allocated to U.S. Counties with at least a 40 Percent Black Population*[a]

Independent Variables	Model 1: Dependent Variable: Number of New Project Grants Allocated from all Federal Programs	Model 2: Dependent Variable: Dollar Amount of New Project Grants Allocated from all Federal Programs (in millions)
Racial representation variables:		
Black population of district (%)	−0.001 (0.010)	0.101 (0.504)
Black representative	2.289 (0.628)***	72.805 (30.825)**
Racial trust (Black district population × race of MC)	−0.043 (0.013)***	−1.209 (0.678)*
Party of representative	−0.344 (0.187)*	−4.682 (8.812)
Legislative variables for those representing each county:		
Member on House Appropriations Committee	−0.058 (0.208)	−9.363 (9.230)
Previous election margin of House representative	0.006 (0.002)***	0.145 (0.106)
Senator on Senate Appropriations Committee	0.377 (0.123)***	3.354 (6.115)
Seniority of House member	−0.006 (0.009)	0.975 (0.461)**
Seniority of senators (combined total)	−0.003 (0.003)	−0.015 (0.165)
County-level project demand variables:		
Median family income in county (in thousands)	0.025 (0.041)	0.337 (0.500)
Overall population of county (in thousands)	0.003 (0.0006)***	0.195 (0.022)***
Proportion below poverty in county	5.198 (2.103)**	216.017 (60.441)***
Proportion blue-collar workers in county	0.849 (1.214)	−0.495 (52.986)
Proportion in farming occupations in county	−7.754 (1.986)***	−187.377 (99.248)*
Proportion over age 65 in county	11.385 (3.061)***	203.443 (101.836)**

(*continued*)

Independent Variables	Model 1: Dependent variable: Number of New Project Grants Allocated from all Federal Programs	Model 2: Dependent variable: Dollar Amount of New Project Grants Allocated from all Federal Programs (in millions)
Proportion under age 18 in county	−0.846 (2.978)	−394.766 (115.423)***
Proportion urban in county	1.850 (0.288)***	8.601 (12.626)
Proportion with less than high school diploma in county	−2.559 (1.773)	−1.224 (62.041)
State capital located in county	1.406 (0.220)***	134.501 (16.178)***
Constant	−0.179 (1.758)	1.730 (40.325)
α (alpha)	1.516 (0.087)***	–
N	729 counties/ county portions	729 counties/county portions

[a] The first model is estimated using negative binomial regression with robust standard errors. The second model is estimated using tobit, with left-censoring at zero. The sample for both models is all counties > 40% black in the 104th, 105th, and 106th Congresses (1995–2000).

***$p \leq 0.01$; **$p \leq 0.05$; *$p \leq 0.10$

significant at the 0.01 level for Model 1 and at the 0.10 level for Model 2. The substantive impact of these variables is discussed in Chapter 6.

Also, in Model 1, the party of the representative is negative and significant. This result, as noted in Chapter 6, is somewhat surprising, as it means that Republicans are statistically more likely to allocate a higher number of projects than Democrats, all else equal. The substantive gap between white Democrats and white Republicans, though, is small, as noted in Chapter 6.

Given the high multicollinearity between the race, district black population, and racial trust variables, we must be careful about conclusions related to just the district black population variable by itself (and its lack of significance). Because of this, I also conducted analyses not presented here, where I did not include the racial trust variable. In these analyses, the district black population proved significant.

However, instead of dropping the racial trust variable as its inclusion is theoretically appropriate, the results of the analyses in Table A.2 suggest that racial trust is an intervening variable and that the district black population, in isolation from other variables, has little impact of its own. Only when we consider the interaction of the presence of an African-American representative with the racial population of a district can we best understand the impact of racial representation on pork projects.

A clearer interpretation of the impact of these variables in the negative binomial regression model (Model 1) can be determined by computing the expected values of the number of federal project grants associated with each variable.[8] The tables and figures in Chapter 6 are based on calculating these expected counts of projects allocated (while holding the other variables constant at their means; see Long 1997, 224, 237).

Other variables also have an impact on the number of projects allocated and deserve a brief mention. As seen in the tables, most of the demand variables and a couple of the congressional variables affect levels of allocation. In one or both models, the overall county population, the proportion below poverty, the proportion in farming occupations, the proportion over age 65, the proportion urban, and the presence of a state capital, for instance, all have sizable effects on the number and/or dollar amounts of projects allocated. The three congressional variables that are both predictors of increased project allocations in Table A.2 are the previous general election margin of the House representative (Model 1), the presence of a senator on the Appropriations Committee (Model 1), and the seniority of the House member (Model 2). These congressional and demand-level control variables are almost always in the expected direction.

The Empirical Models of Project Allocations and Dollars to HBCUs

Having discussed the county-level models, I will now discuss the technical details of the models of allocations to congressional districts with HBCUs. The models on HBCU allocations are operationalized slightly differently than the ones examining project allocation to predominately black counties. Because I am gauging the effect of the district black population and the race of the representative on education projects only, different additional explanatory variables are needed. Also, instead of U.S. counties being the unit of analysis, I look at this question using the congressional district as the unit of analysis.

The first model focuses on the number of new federal projects allocated to black colleges in each district. I tally the total number of projects

---

[8] Note that for each sample, $p < 0.01$ for α. This indicates that overdispersion exists, and the negative binomial specification was therefore more appropriate than the Poisson distribution.

allocated to HBCUs per district using cross-sectional data over three time periods (104th–106th Congresses). The second model examines the amount of federal spending on new projects distributed to HBCUs, tallying across districts.

Like the counties analysis of the first model, the total number of projects allocated is a count variable. I again use negative binomial regression to model the distribution of projects (King 1989, 51; Long 1997, 230–238) and estimate the model with robust standard errors. For the model of federal spending to congressional districts with HBCUs, I use tobit.

I look at all the congressional districts with at least one HBCU in the 104th, 105th, and 106th Congresses. Over these three periods, 203 congressional districts contained at least one HBCU. Like the counties analyses, I only look at grants allocated in the final year of each session (1996, 1998, and 2000). The information on identifying all HBCUs and which congressional districts they are located in was garnered from *Peterson's Guide to Colleges*; the United Negro College Fund, Inc.; www. universities.com; and Roebuck and Murty (1993). The matching of each college over three time periods to its appropriate congressional district was done by first checking Preimesberger and Tarr (1993). Remaining cases that were not identifiable from this volume (those districts redistricted after 1992) were determined by consulting the zip code of the university and the appropriate volume of the *Congressional Staff Directory*, which lists zip codes in each congressional district. In the few remaining cases in which the zip codes of the HBCUs were split between multiple districts, I personally contacted the district offices of each possible representative until each HBCU-district match was determined. Like the analyses of allocations to predominately black counties, this sample of congressional districts with HBCUs provides more variation between the race of legislator and district black population variables than previous studies.

Empirical Specification of the HBCU Models

This section offers the full empirical specification and results for the two models of project allocations to congressional districts with HBCUs. These two models were estimated with the congressional district as the unit of analysis and the same time period, the 104th to 106th Congresses (1995–2000), was examined. In total there were 203 congressional districts with at least one HBCU within its borders. Specifically, the dependent variable in Model 1 is the *number of new projects allocated to historically black colleges and universities in each district*. The dependent variable in the second model is the *dollar amount of federal money for new project grants sent to historically black colleges and universities in each district*.

Again, I only look at *new project grants* to congressional districts with HBCUs in this analysis. Because I am looking at grants to educational institutions, it is important to exclude other federal grants such as student loans, Pell grants, and other formula-based government aid allocated to universities, as these are not pork projects.

Independent Variables of Interest: Racial Representation Variables

Like the previous analysis, I examine four key variables of interest, and they are measured as follows. *Black population of district*. In the sample of districts that contain HBCUs, this continuous variable ranges from 2 percent black (Ohio's tenth district) to 74 percent black (New York's eleventh district). I use black population instead of black voting-age population as black voting-age data for those districts redistricted in 1996 or 1998 were not available.

Race of Representative. The variable is coded "1" for black representatives and "0" for nonblack representatives. In the sample, all but three of the nonblack cases are white (Latino representatives from Texas' twenty-eighth district). I do not presume that white and Latino representatives are equivalent. However, because the measure of interest is allocations to black colleges, the key variance in legislator race is black and nonblack.

Racial Trust. This variable is included to test the third hypothesis. This variable is measured by multiplying the observations of the previous two variables together. Thus, for nonblack representatives, this variable is coded "0"; for black representatives, this variable is coded as the percent black in the district.

Party of Representative. The party of the representative is needed in the model to test the fourth and final hypothesis presented earlier. It is a dummy variable coded "1" for Democrats and "0" for Republicans.

Congressional Variables

Other independent variables are needed as controls. Variables controlling for committee membership, seniority, and electoral vulnerability are detailed here. I include a dummy variable for *Member on House Appropriations Committee* coded "1" if the legislator serves on the House Appropriations Committee. *Member on House Education Appropriations Subcommittee* is a similar measure. This is also a dummy variable, but coded "1" when a representative is on the Education Appropriations Subcommittee. Because I examine higher education projects, the Education Appropriations Subcommittee may also be important.

The *Previous general election margin* is included as an independent variable (Stein and Bickers 1995). Further, independent variables for *Senator on Appropriations Committee, Senator on Education Appropriations Subcommittee, Seniority of House member,* and *Seniority of senators* are also included. These variables are needed as the Senate also plays an important role in the federal distribution of programs and projects. The rationale and expected direction of impact for these specific Senate variables are the same as those specified earlier in the county-level analyses and are coded similarly.

Demand-Level Variables

Cross-sectional studies of federal project allocation generally must account for grant demand from those jurisdictions eligible to receive them. Applying the same rationale to congressional districts with black colleges suggests that schools with fewer resources will be less likely to receive grants. Thus, an analysis of federal projects to black colleges needs explanatory variables to capture the demand for federal project grants in addition to the "top-down" congressional variables.

The previous literature examining the distribution of education projects is less well developed than the literature looking at project allocations for all programs. Unlike the county-level analyses, the demand for projects will be driven by characteristics of the universities in the districts and not the population at large. I specify the following control variables to capture university demand. The data for these variables are from *Peterson's Guide to Colleges* (Zemsky 2000). In a couple of cases for which the data were not completely available from the *Peterson's Guide*, I contacted the college directly.

Two-year HBCUs. Twenty of the 115 colleges in the analysis only grant two-year degrees. These colleges will likely have less of a demand for projects than other institutions and will therefore drive down the total number of HBCU projects at the district level. Thus, because the unit of analysis is the congressional district, the proportion of HBCUs that only grant associate degrees in a district is included as a variable.

Full-time Faculty at HBCU(s). The more HBCU faculty that a district has, the more likely that these faculty will demand – and receive – project grants. HBCUs have obtained notoriously low levels of grant awards "because it has [erroneously] been determined that the black institutions lack the expertise to perform important scientific research" ("Scientific Research" 1997, 48). However, this may instead be related to the total number of faculty at many HBCUs. Those districts with the most HBCU faculty should receive more projects. Thus, a continuous variable of the total number of full-time faculty in each district (aggregating the number of faculty at each black college in the district) is used.

Students Enrolled at HBCU(s). The number of students at HBCUs in the district (in thousands) is also included as a demand-level control variable. The general expectation is that the more students enrolled at HBCUs in a district, the more the district's HBCUs will receive project grants. On the other hand, very large student populations may imply schools whose missions are focused primarily on teaching and less on research (and thus not on seeking grants). Basically, the infrastructure of a university may be better equipped to seek out and receive grants when the student population is smaller. Thus, the expected outcome could be either positive or negative for this explanatory variable, which is measured as the total number of enrolled students at HBCUs in the district.

Total HBCUs in Congressional District. The number of HBCUs in a congressional district will obviously affect the total amount of projects allocated to the schools in the district, and it is a critical control variable because the congressional district is the unit of analysis. If a district has only one HBCU, for instance, I would expect fewer project allocations than if the district contained more than one HBCU.

Results Of Districts With HBCUs Analyses

Table A.3 displays the results of these models. Model 1 is a negative binomial regression model predicting the number of new project grants allocated to HBCUs within congressional districts. Model 2 is a tobit model predicting the dollars allocated (in millions of dollars) to HBCUs in these districts.

TABLE A.3. *Project Delivery to HBCUs: the Effect of Race, Party, and District Black Population on Pork Projects Allocated to U.S. Congressional Districts with HBCUs* [a]

Independent Variables	Model 1: Dependent Variable: Number of New Project Grants Allocated from all Federal Programs	Model 2: Dependent Variable: Dollar Amount of New Project Grants Allocated from all Federal Programs (in ten thousands)
Racial representation variables:		
Black population of district (%)	0.025 (0.008)***	10.473 (5.154)**
Black representative	2.963 (0.614)***	1982.185 (472.062)***
Racial trust (Black district population × race of MC)	−0.074 (0.014)***	−48.619 (9.856)***
Party of representative	−0.235 (0.142)*	−53.825 (107.422)
Legislative variables for those representing each county:		
Member on House Appropriations Committee	0.329 (0.201)	−70.800 (146.850)
Member on House Education Appropriations Subcommittee	−0.545 (0.290)*	86.758 (209.727)
Previous election margin of House representative	−0.001 (0.002)	3.581 (1.659)**
Senator on Senate Appropriations Committee	0.108 (0.134)	−83.326 (103.567)
Senator on Senate Education Appropriations Subcommittee	−0.050 (0.155)	36.734 (115.604)
Seniority of House member	−0.012 (0.009)	6.570 (6.509)
Seniority of senators (combined total)	−0.004 (0.004)	−12.147 (3.023)***
District-level project demand variables:		
HBCU grants only two-year degrees	−1.857 (0.264)***	−538.720 (151.746)***
Full-time faculty at HBCU(s)	0.005 (0.0009)***	2.142 (0.482)***
Students enrolled at HBCU(s) (in thousands)	−0.0194 (0.034)	−0.016 (0.019)
Total HBCUs in congressional district	0.240 (0.071)***	272.020 (42.230)***
Constant	0.887 (0.230)***	−408.403 (167.028)**
α (alpha)	0.503 (0.079)***	−
N	203 districts	203 districts

[a] The first model is estimated using negative binomial regression with robust standard errors. The second model is estimated using tobit, with left-censoring at zero. The sample for both models is all congressional districts in the 104th, 105th, and 106th Congresses (1995–2000) that have HBCUs. The unit of analysis is the congressional district.
***p ≤ 0.01; **p ≤ 0.05; *p ≤ 0.10

As I have already discussed the substantive aspects of these results in Chapter 6 in regard to the key variables of interest, I will only briefly mention them here. As seen in Table A.3, all four variables of interest are significant in Model 1 predicting the number of project grants, and three variables of interest (all but political party) are significant in Model 2 predicting funding. The black population of the district and the presence of a black representative both cause increased project allocations to black colleges. However, the party of the representative variable and the racial trust variable are both negative. In terms of the other independent variables, most of the demand-level variables are significant and all are in the expected directions. The previous election variable is significant in the expected direction in Model 2, whereas the House Education Appropriations Subcommittee is weakly significant (0.10 level) in Model 1. This variable – and the combined seniority of senators variable in Model 2 (significant of 0.01) – are surprisingly negative. These results may occur because I am only examining HBCU grants instead of education grants broadly. Most other independent variables are in the expected direction.

Because Model 1 is a negative binomial regression of a count dependent variable, a clearer interpretation of the impact of these variables was determined by computing the expected values of the number of HBCU project allocations associated with each variable.[9] The expected number of projects is displayed in Tables 6.2 and 6.3 and Figures 6.1 and 6.2 in Chapter 6. Also, the predicted values for dollar amounts in Table 6.2 and Table 6.3 were computed by taking predictions in a tobit model, while holding other independent variables at their means. For more details regarding the substantive results of these HBCU models, please see Chapter 6.

---

[9] Note again that $p \leq 0.01$ for α, indicating that there is overdispersion, implying that the negative binomial distribution is more appropriate than a Poisson distribution.

References

Achen, Christopher H. 1982. *Interpreting and Using Regression*. Beverly Hills, CA: Sage Publications.

Aistrup, Joseph. 1996. *Southern Strategy Revisited: Republican Top-down Advancement in the South*. Lexington: University of Kentucky Press.

Aldrich, John H. 1995. *Why Parties? The Origin and Transformation of Party Politics in America*. Chicago: University of Chicago Press.

Anagnoson, Theodore. 1982. "Federal Grant Agencies and Congressional Election Campaigns." *American Journal of Political Science* 26:547–561.

Anderson, David J. and Jane Junn. 2010. "Deracializing Obama: White Voters and the 2004 Illinois U.S. Senate Race." *American Politics Research* 38:443–470.

Ansolabehere, Stephen, Alan Gerber, and James M. Snyder Jr. 2002. "Equal Votes, Equal Money: Court-Ordered Redistricting and Public Expenditures in the American States." *American Political Science Review* 96:767–777.

Arnold, R. Douglas. 1979. *Congress and the Bureaucracy: A Theory of Influence*. New Haven: Yale University Press.

1990. *The Logic of Congressional Action*. New Haven: Yale University Press.

Associated Press. 2001. "Clyburn Says Ruling May Strengthen Black Majority Districts." *Associated Press State and Local Wire*, 19 May.

Austin, Rory. 2002. "Seats That May Not Matter: Testing for Racial Polarization in U.S. City Councils." *Legislative Studies Quarterly* 27:481–508.

Bailey, Michael A. 2007. "Comparable Preference Estimates across Time and Institutions for the Court and Congress." *American Journal of Political Science* 51:433–448.

Barnes, Jeb. 2004. *Overruled? Legislative Overrides, Pluralism, and Contemporary Court-Congress Relations*. Stanford: Stanford University Press.

Barreto, Matt A., Gary M. Segura, and Nathan D. Woods. 2004. "The Mobilizing Effect of Majority-minority Districts on Latino Turnout." *American Political Science Review* 98:65–75.

Benson, Jocelyn. 2004. "Turning Lemons into Lemonade: Making Georgia v. Ashcroft the Mobile v. Bolden of 2007." *Harvard Civil Rights-Civil Liberties Law Review* 39:485–511.

Bertelli, Anthony M. and Christian R. Grose. 2006. "The Spatial Model and the Senate Trial of President Clinton." *American Politics Research* 34:535–559.
2009. "Secretaries of Pork? A New Theory of Distributive Public Policy." *Journal of Politics*.

Bickers, Kenneth N. and Robert M. Stein. 1996. "The Electoral Dynamics of the Federal Pork Barrel." *American Journal of Political Science* 40:1300–1326.

Binder, Sarah A. 1997. *Minority Rights, Majority Rule: Partisanship and the Development of Congress*. Cambridge: Cambridge University Press.

Bishin, Benjamin G. 2000. "Constituency Influence in Congress: Does Subconstituency Matter?" *Legislative Studies Quarterly* 25:389–415.
2009. *Tyranny of the Majority: The Subconstituency Politics Theory of Representation*. Philadelphia: Temple University Press.

Biskupic, Joan. 1993. "N.C. Case to Pose Test of Racial Redistricting; White Voters Challenge Black-Majority Map." *Washington Post*, 20 April.

Black, Earl and Merle Black. 2002. *The Rise of Southern Republicans*. Cambridge, MA: Harvard University Press.

Bobo, Lawrence and Franklin D. Gilliam Jr. 1990. "Race, Socioeconomic Status, and Black Empowerment." *American Political Science Review* 84:377–394.

Bonneau, Chris W. and Heather Marie Rice. 2009. "Impartial Judges? Race, Institutional Context, and U.S. State Supreme Courts." *State Politics and Policy Quarterly* 9:381–403.

Bositis, David A. 1998. "The Future of Majority-minority Districts and Black and Hispanic Legislative Representation." In ed. David A. Bositis, *Redistricting and Minority Representation: Learning From The Past, Preparing for the Future*. Washington, DC: Joint Center for Political and Economic Studies.

Bovitz, Gregory L. and Jamie L. Carson. 2006. "Position-taking and Electoral Accountability in the U.S. House of Representatives." *Political Research Quarterly* 59:297–312.

Brace, Kimball, Lisa Handley, Richard G. Niemi, and Harold W. Stanley. 1995. "Minority Turnout and the Creation of Majority-Minority Districts." *American Politics Quarterly* 23:190–203.

Branton, Regina. 2009. "The Importance of Race and Ethnicity in Congressional Primary Elections." *Political Research Quarterly* 62:459–473.

Bratton, Kathleen A. and Kerry L. Haynie. 1999. "Agenda Setting and Legislative Success in State Legislatures: The Effects of Gender and Race." *Journal of Politics* 61:658–679.

Bratton, Kathleen A., Kerry L. Haynie, and Beth Reingold. 2007. "Agenda Setting and African American Women in State Legislatures." *Journal of Women, Politics, and Policy* 28:71–96.

Brunell, Thomas L. 2008. *Redistricting and Representation: Why Competitive Elections are Bad for America*. Routledge.

Brunell, Thomas L., Christopher J. Anderson, and Rachel K. Cremona. 2008. "Descriptive Representation, District Demography, and Attitudes toward Congress Among African Americans." *Legislative Studies Quarterly* 33:223–244.

Buchler, Justin. 2005. "Competition, Representation and Redistricting: The Case Against Competitive Congressional Districts." *Journal of Theoretical Politics* 17:431–63.

Bullock, Charles S., III. 1981. "Congressional Voting and the Mobilisation of a Black Electorate in the South." *Journal of Politics* 39:662–682.

1984. "Racial Crossover Voting and the Election of Black Officials." *Journal of Politics* 46:238–251.

1995. "The Impact of Changing the Racial Composition of Congressional Districts on Legislators' Roll Call Behavior." *American Politics Quarterly* 23:141–158.

Bullock, Charles S., III, and Richard E. Dunn. 1999. "The Demise of Racial Redistricting and the Future of Black Representation." *Emory Law Journal* 48:1209–1253.

Bullock, Charles S., III, and Ronald Keith Gaddie. 2006. "Voting Rights Progress in Georgia." *NYU Journal of Legislation and Public Policy* 10:1–49.

Bullock, Charles S., III, Ronald Keith Gaddie, and Ben Smith. 2005. "White Voters, Black Representatives, and Candidates of Choice." *American Review of Politics* 26:267–289.

Bullock, Charles S., III, Donna R. Hoffman, and Ronald Keith Gaddie. 2005. "The Consolidation of the White Southern Congressional Vote." *Political Research Quarterly* 2:231–243.

Bullock, Charles S., III, and M.V. Hood, III. 2005. "When Southern Symbolism Meets the Pork Barrel: Opportunity for Executive Leadership." *Social Science Quarterly* 86:69–86.

Burden, Barry C. 2007. *Personal Roots of Representation*. Princeton: Princeton University Press.

Cain, Bruce, John Ferejohn, and Morris Fiorina. 1987. *The Personal Vote: Constituency Service and Electoral Independence*. Cambridge, MA: Harvard University Press.

Cameron, Charles, David Epstein, and Sharyn O'Halloran. 1996. "Do Majority-Minority Districts Maximize Substantive Black Representation in Congress?" *American Political Science Review* 90:794–812.

Canon, David T. 1999. *Race, Redistricting, and Representation: The Unintended Consequences of Black Majority Districts*. Chicago: University of Chicago Press.

2008. "Renewing the Voting Rights Act: Retrogression, Influence, and the 'Georgia v. Ashcroft' Fix." *Election Law Journal* 7:3–24.

Carter, Janelle. 2001. "Black Lawmakers Find Latinos Now Dominate Inner-City Districts." *North County Times (CA)*, August 19.

Carter, Selwyn. 1998. "The Impact of Recent Supreme Court decisions on Racial Representation." In ed. David A. Bositis, *Redistricting and Minority Representation: Learning From The Past, Preparing for the Future*. Washington, DC: Joint Center for Political and Economic Studies.

Casellas, Jason P. 2009a. "The Institutional and Demographic Determinants of Latino Representation." *Legislative Studies Quarterly* 34:399–426.

2009b. "Coalitions in the House? The Election of Minorities to State Legislatures and Congress." *Political Research Quarterly* 62:120–131.

Clark, John A. and Charles L. Prysby, eds. 2004. *Southern Political Party Activists: Patterns of Conflict and Change, 1991–2001*. Lexington: University Press of Kentucky.

Clinton, Joshua, Simon Jackman, and Douglas Rivers. 2004. "The Statistical Analysis of Roll Call Data." *American Political Science Review* 98:355–370.

Clinton, Joshua D. and Adam Meirowitz. 2004. "Testing Accounts of Legislative Strategic Voting: The Compromise of 1790." *American Journal of Political Science* 48:675–689.

Combs, Michael W., John R. Hibbing, and Susan Welch. 1984. "Black Constituents and Congressional Roll-Call Votes." *Western Political Quarterly* 37:424–434.

Conyers, James E. and Walter L. Wallace. 1976. *Black Elected Officials: A Study of Black Americans Holding Governmental Office*. New York: Russell Sage Foundation.

Cook, Rhonda. 2003. "Georgia Argues Redistrict Appeal." *Atlanta Journal-Constitution*, 30 April.

Cooper, Christopher A. and Martin Johnson. 2009. "Representative Reporters? Examining Journalists' Ideology in Context." *Social Science Quarterly* 90:387–406.

Cox, Gary W., and Mathew D. McCubbins. 1986. "Electoral Politics as a Redistributive Game." *Journal of Politics* 48:370–389.

1993. *Legislative Leviathan: Party Government in the House*. Berkeley: University of California Press.

2005. *Setting the Agenda: Responsible Party Government in the U.S. House of Representatives*. Berkeley: University of California Press.

Crayton, Kareem U. 2007. "Beat 'Em or Join 'Em? White Voters and Black Candidates in Majority-Black Districts." *Syracuse Law Review* 547–581.

Davidson, Chandler and Bernard Grofman, eds. 1994. *Quiet Revolution in the South: The Impact of the Voting Rights Act, 1965–1990*. Princeton: Princeton University Press.

Davis, Darren W. 1997. "The Direction of Race of Interviewer Effects Among African-Americans: Donning the Black Mask." *American Journal of Political Science* 41:309–322.

Dawson, Michael C. 1994. *Behind the Mule: Race and Class in African-American Politics*. Princeton: Princeton University Press.

DiLorenzo, Vincent. 1997. "Legislative Heart and Phase Transitions: An Exploratory Study of Congress and Minority Interests." *William and Mary Law Review* 38:1729–1815.

Dineen, J.K. 2001. "Ferrer Wins Rangel's Nod." *New York Daily News*, August 17.

Dovi, Suzanne. 2002. "Preferable Descriptive Representatives: Will Just Any Woman, Black, or Latino Do?" *American Political Science Review* 96:729–743.

Downs, Anthony. 1957. *An Economic Theory of Democracy*. New York: Harper Collins.

Duncan, Philip D. and Brian Nutting, eds. 1999. *CQ's Politics in America 2000: The 106th Congress*. Washington, DC: Congressional Quarterly, Inc.

Endersby, James W. and Charles E. Menifeld. 2000. "Representation, Ethnicity, and Congress: Black and Hispanic Representatives and Constituencies." In

Black and Multiracial Politics in America, ed. Yvette M. Alex-Assensoh and Lawrence J. Hanks. New York: New York University Press.

Enelow, James M. and Melvin J. Hinich. 1984. *The Spatial Theory of Voting*. New York: Cambridge University Press.

Engstrom, Richard L. 1980. "Racial Discrimination in the Electoral Process: The Voting Rights Act and the Vote Dilution Issue." In eds. Robert Steed, Laurence Moreland, and Ted Baker, *Party Politics in the South*. New York: Praeger.

    1995. "Voting Rights Districts: Debunking the Myths." *Campaigns and Elections* 24:46.

Espino, Rodolfo. 2007. "Is There a Latino Dimension to Voting in Congress?" In eds. Rodolfo Espino, David Leal, and Ken Meier. *Latino Politics: Identity, Mobilization, and Representation*. Charlottesville: University of Virginia Press.

Evans Yiannakis, Diana. 1981. "The Grateful Electorate: Casework and Congressional Elections." *American Journal of Political Science* 25:568–580.

Fenno, Richard F. 1978. *Home Style: House Members in Their Districts*. Boston: Little, Brown.

    2000. *Congress at the Grassroots*. Chapel Hill: University of North Carolina Press.

    2003. *Going Home: Black Representatives and Their Constituents*. Chicago: University of Chicago Press.

Ferejohn, John A. 1974. *Pork Barrel Politics: Rivers and Harbors Legislation, 1947–1968*. Stanford: Stanford University Press.

Fernandez, Manny. 2005. "*Black Voters, No Longer a Bloc, Are Up for Grabs in Mayor's Race*." *New York Times*, 26 September.

Fiorina, Morris P. 1974. *Representatives, Roll Calls, and Constituencies*. Lexington, MA: Lexington Books.

    1981. "Some Problems in Studying the Effects of Resource Allocation in Congressional Elections." *American Journal of Political Science* 25:543–568.

    1989. *Congress: Keystone of the Washington Establishment*, 2d ed. New Haven: Yale University Press.

Fleisher, Richard. 1993. "Explaining the Change in Roll-call Voting Behavior of Southern Democrats." *Journal of Politics* 55:2:327–341.

Fraga, Luis R., John A. Garcia, Rodney E. Hero, Michael Jones-Correa, Valerie Martinez-Ebers, and Gary M. Segura. 2006. "Su Casa Es Nuestra Casa: Latino Politics Research and the Development of American Political Science." *American Political Science Review* 4:515–21.

Fraga, Luis R., Linda Lopez, Valerie Martinez-Ebers, and Ricardo Ramirez. 2007. "Gender and Ethnicity: Patterns of Electoral Success and Legislative Activity among Latina and Latino State Officials in Four States." *Journal of Women, Politics, & Policy* 28:121–145.

Gamble, Katrina. 2007. Black Political Representation: An Examination of Legislative Activity Within U.S. House Committees." *Legislative Studies Quarterly* 32:421–447.

Garretson, Jeremiah. 2009. *Changing Media, Changing Minds: The Lesbian and Gay Movement, Television, and Public Opinion*. Ph.D. Dissertation, Vanderbilt University.

Gay, Claudine. 1997. "Taking Charge: Black Electoral Success and the Redefinition of American Politics." Ph.D. dissertation, Harvard University.

——. 2001. "The Effect of Black Congressional Representation on Political Participation." *American Political Science Review* 95:589–602.

——. 2002. "Spirals of Trust? The Effect of Descriptive Representation on the Relationship Between Citizens and Their Government." *American Journal of Political Science* 46:4:717–733.

George, Emmett. 2000. "Foes Rip Dickey's Talk to Blacks: Remarks to Farmers a Shakedown for Contributions, Democrat Says." *Arkansas Democrat-Gazette*, Jan. 11.

Gerken, Heather K. 2005. "Second-order Diversity." *Harvard Law Review* 118:1099–1196.

Gershon, Sarah Allen. 2008. "Communicating Female and Minority Interests Online: A Study of Web Site Issue Discussion among Female, Latino, and African American Members of Congress." *International Journal of Press/Politics* 13:120–140.

Glaser, James M. 1996. *Race, Campaign Politics, and the Realignment in the South*. New Haven: Yale University Press.

——. 2005. *The Hand of the Past in Contemporary Southern Politics*. New Haven: Yale University Press.

Goode, Shelton J. and Norman J. Baldwin. 2005. "Predictors of African American Representation in Municipal Government." *Review of Public Personnel Administration* 25:29–55.

Greene, William H. 2003. *Econometric Analysis*, 5th ed. Upper Saddle River, NJ: Prentice Hall.

Griffin, John D. 2006. "Electoral Competition and Democratic Responsiveness: A Defense of the Marginality Hypothesis." *Journal of Politics* 68:911–921.

Griffin, John D. and Patrick Flavin. 2007. "Racial Differences in Information, Expectations, and Accountability." *Journal of Politics* 69:220–236.

Griffin, John D. and Michael Keane. 2006. "Descriptive Representation and the Composition of African American Turnout." *American Journal of Political Science* 50:998–1012.

Griffin, John D. and Brian Newman. 2005. "Are Voters Better Represented?" *Journal of Politics* 67:1206–1227.

Grofman, Bernard and Lisa Handley. 1989. "Minority Population and Black and Hispanic Congressional Success in the 1970s and 1980s." *American Politics Quarterly* 17:436–445.

Grofman, Bernard, Lisa Handley, and Richard G. Niemi. 1992. *Minority Representation and the Quest for Voting Equality*. New York: Cambridge University Press.

Grose, Christian R. 2001. "Black Legislators and White Districts, White Legislators and Black Districts: The Effect of Court-Ordered Redistricting on Congressional Voting Records in the South, 1993–2000." *American Review of Politics* 22:195–215.

——. 2005. "Disentangling Constituency and Legislator Effects in Legislative Representation: Black Legislators or Black Districts?" *Social Science Quarterly* 86:427–443.

2006. "Bridging the Divide: Interethnic Cooperation; Minority Media Outlets; and the Coverage of Latino, African-American, and Asian-American Members of Congress." *Harvard International Journal of Press/Politics* 11: 115–130.

2007. "Cues, Endorsements, and Heresthetic in a High-profile Election: Racial Polarization in Durham, North Carolina." *PS: Political Science and Politics* 40:2:325–332.

Grose, Christian R., Jason Husser, and Antoine Yoshinaka. 2010. "Plus Ca Change: Race, Gender, and Issue Retrospections in the 2008 U.S. Presidential Election." *Journal of Elections, Public Opinion, and Parties* 20:187–211.

Grose, Christian R., Maurice Mangum, and Christopher Martin. 2007. "Race, Political Empowerment, and Constituency Service: Descriptive Representation and the Hiring of African-American Congressional Staff." *Polity* 39:449–478.

Grose, Christian R. and Keesha M. Middlemass. 2010. "Listen to What I Say, Not How I Vote." *Social Science Quarterly* 91:143–167.

Grose, Christian R. and Bruce I. Oppenheimer. 2007. "The Iraq War, Partisanship, and Candidate Attributes: Variation in Partisan Swing in the 2006 U.S. House Elections." *Legislative Studies Quarterly* 32:531–557.

Grose, Christian R. and Antoine Yoshinaka. 2003. "The Electoral Consequences of Party Switching by Incumbent Members of Congress, 1947–2000." *Legislative Studies Quarterly* 28:55–75.

n.d. "Ideological Hedging in Uncertain Times: Maverick Representation and Voter Enfranchisement." *British Journal of Political Science*, forthcoming.

Groseclose, Tim, Steven D. Levitt, and James M. Snyder Jr. 1999. "Comparing Interest Group Scores across Time and Chambers: Adjusted ADA Scores for the U.S. Congress." *American Political Science Review* 93:1:33–50.

Guinier, Lani. 1994. *The Tyranny of the Majority*. New York: Free Press.

Gulati, Girish J. 2004. "Revisiting the Link Between Electoral Competition and Policy Extremism in the U.S. Congress." *American Politics Research* 32:495–520.

Gurin, Patricia, Shirley Hatchett, and James S. Jackson. 1989. *Hope and Independence: Blacks' Response to Electoral and Party Politics*. New York: The Russell Sage Foundation.

Hajnal, Zoltan. 2007. *Changing White Attitudes Toward Black Political Leadership*. New York: Cambridge University Press.

2009. "Who Loses in American Democracy?" *American Political Science Review* 103:37–58.

Hall, Richard. 1996. *Participation in Congress*. New Haven: Yale University Press.

Hancock, Ange-Marie. 2004. *The Politics of Disgust*. New York: NYU Press.

Harris, Fredrick C., Valeria Sinclair-Chapman, and Brian D. McKenzie. 2006. *Countervailing Forces in African-American Civic Activism, 1973–1994*. Cambridge: Cambridge University Press.

Hawkesworth, Mary. 2003. "Congressional Enactments of Race-Gender: Toward a Theory of Raced-Gendered Institutions." *American Political Science Review* 97:529–550.

Hayes, Danny and Seth McKee C. 2008. "Toward a One-party South?" *American Politics Research* 36:3–32.

Haynie, Kerry. 2001. *African American Legislators in the American States.* New York: Columbia University Press.

Herring, Mary. 1990. "Legislative Responsiveness to Black Constituents in Three Deep South States." *Journal of Politics* 52:740–758.

Herron, Michael C. and Jasjeet S. Sekhon. 2005. "Black Candidates and Black Voters: Assessing the Impact of Candidate Race on Uncounted Vote Rates." *Journal of Politics* 67:154–77.

Herron, Michael C. and Kenneth W. Shotts. 2003. "Using Ecological Inference Point Estimates as Dependent Variables in Second-stage Linear Regressions." *Political Analysis* 11:1:44–64.

Highton, Benjamin. 2004. "White Voters and African American Candidates for Congress." *Political Behavior* 26:1:1–25.

Hill, Kevin A. 1995. "Does the Creation of Majority Black Districts Aid Republicans? An Analysis of the 1992 Congressional Elections in Eight Southern States." *Journal of Politics* 57:384–401.

Holmes, Robert. 1997. "Georgia's Reapportionment and Redistricting Process in 1995: Reflections of a Participant Observer." *National Political Science Review* 6:72–93.

Hood, M.V. III, Quentin Kidd, and Irvin L. Morris. 2004. "The Reintroduction of the Elephas Maximus to the Southern United States." *American Politics Research* 32:68–101.

2008. "Two Sides of the Same Coin? Employing Granger Causality Tests in a Time-series Cross-section Framework." *Political Analysis* 16:324–344.

Hood, M.V., III and Seth C. McKee. 2009. "Trying to Thread the Needle: The Effects of Redistricting in a Georgia Congressional District." *PS: Political Science and Politics* 42:679–687.

Hood, M.V., III and Irvin L. Morris. 1998. "Boll Weevils and Roll-Call Voting: A Study in Time and Space." *Legislative Studies Quarterly* 23:245–269.

Hurd, Hilary. 2000. "Democrat Clyburn Says 'Watch How They Vote.'" *Black Issues in Higher Education* October 12:30.

Hutchings, Vincent. 1998. "Issue Salience and Support for Civil Rights Legislation Among Southern Democrats." *Legislative Studies Quarterly* 23:521–544.

Hutchings, Vincent L., Harwood K. McClerking, and Guy-Uriel Charles. 2004. "Congressional Representation of Black Interests: Recognizing the Importance of Stability." *Journal of Politics* 66:450–468.

Ifill, Gwen. 2009. *The Breakthrough: Politics and Race in the Age of Obama.* New York: Doubleday.

Jackman, Simon. 2003. "IDEAL: Ideal Point Estimation and Roll Call Analysis via Bayesian Simulation." Unpublished manuscript, Stanford University.

Jackman, Simon and Lynn Vavreck. 2010. "Primary Politics: Race, Gender, and Age in the 2008 Democratic Primary." *Journal of Elections, Public Opinion, and Parties* 20:153–186.

Jacobsmeier, Matthew L. 2009. "Elections in Black and White: Race, Perceptions, and Voting Behavior in U.S. House Elections." Paper presented at the 2009 annual meeting of the American Political Science Association.

Jacobson, Gary C. 2003. *The Politics of Congressional Elections*, 6th ed. New York: Longman.

Jensen, Jennifer M. and Wendy L. Martinek. 2009. "The Effects of Race and Gender on the Judicial Ambitions of State Trial Court Judges." *Political Research Quarterly* 62:379–392.

Key, V.O. 1949. *Southern Politics in State and Nation*. New York: Knopf.

Killian, Mitchell. 2008. "Presidential Decision Making and Minority Nominations to the U.S. Courts of Appeals." *Presidential Studies Quarterly* 38:268–283.

King, Gary. 1989. *Unifying Political Methodology: The Likelihood Theory of Statistical Inference*. Cambridge: Cambridge University Press.

King, Gary, Robert O. Keohane, and Sidney Verba. 1994. *Designing Social Inquiry: Scientific Inference in Qualitative Research*. Princeton: Princeton University Press.

Kingdon, John W. 1989. *Congressmen's Voting Decisions*, 3d ed. Ann Arbor: University of Michigan Press.

Knuckey, Jonathan. 2006. "Ideological Realignment and Partisan Change in the American South, 1972–1996." *Politics & Policy* 29:337–358.

2008. "Explaining Recent Changes in the Partisan Identifications of Southern Whites." *Political Research Quarterly* 59:57–70.

Koch, Wendy. 2008. "Legislators to Push for U.S. Apology for Slavery." *USA Today*, February 28.

Kousser, J. Morgan. 1999. *Colorblind Injustice: Minority Voting Rights and the Undoing of the Second Reconstruction*. Chapel Hill: University of North Carolina Press.

Krehbiel, Keith. 1998. *Pivotal Politics*. Chicago: University of Chicago Press.

Kreps, David M. and Evan L. Porteus. 1979. "Temporal Von Neumann-Morgenstern and Induced Preferences." *Journal of Economic Theory* 20:81–109.

Lawrence, Eric D., Forrest Maltzman, and Steven S. Smith. 2006. "Who Wins? Party Effects in Legislative Voting." *Legislative Studies Quarterly* 31:33–69.

Lazarus, Jeffrey and Shauna Reilly. 2010. "The Electoral Benefits of Distributive Spending." *Political Research Quarterly* 63:343–355.

Lee, Frances E. 1998. "Representation and Public Policy: The Consequences of Senate Apportionment for the Geographic Distribution of Federal Funds." *Journal of Politics* 60:34–62.

LeVeaux, Christine and James C. Garand. 2003. "Race-based Redistricting, Core Constituencies, and Legislative Response to Constituency Change." *Social Science Quarterly* 84:1:32–51.

Levinson, Arlene. 1999. "Historically Black Colleges Straddle America's Racial Fault Line." *Associated Press State and Local Wire*, December 11.

Levitt, Steven D. and James M. Snyder Jr. 1995. "Political Parties and the Distribution of Federal Outlays." *American Journal of Political Science* 39:958–980.

Long, J. Scott. 1997. *Regression Models for Categorical and Limited Dependent Variables*. Thousand Oaks, CA: Sage Publications.

Lowry, Robert C. and Matthew Potoski. 2004. "Organized Interests and the Politics of Federal Discretionary Grants." *Journal of Politics* 66:2:513–533.

Lublin, David I. 1997. *The Paradox of Representation: Racial Gerrymandering and Minority Interests in Congress.* Princeton: Princeton University Press.

1999. "Racial Redistricting and African-American Representation: A Critique of 'Do Majority-Minority Districts Maximize Substantive Black Representation in Congress?'" *American Political Science Review* 93:183–186.

2007. *The Republican South.* Princeton: Princeton University Press.

Lublin, David I., Thomas L. Brunell, Bernard Grofman, and Lisa Handley. 2009. "Has the Voting Rights Act Outlived Its Usefulness? In a Word, 'No.'" *Legislative Studies Quarterly* 34:525–553.

Lublin, David I. and Katherine Tate. 1995. "Racial Group Competition in Urban Elections." In ed. Paul E. Peterson, *Classifying by Race.* Princeton: Princeton University Press.

Lublin, David I. and D. Stephen Voss. 2003. "The Missing Middle: Why Median-Voter Theory Can't Save Democrats from Singing the Boll-Weevil Blues." *Journal of Politics* 65:1:227–237.

Mansbridge, Jane. 1999. "Should Blacks Represent Blacks and Women Represent Women? A Contingent 'Yes.'" *Journal of Politics* 61:628–657.

Martin, Andrew D. and Kevin M. Quinn. 2002. "Dynamic Ideal Point Estimation via Markov Chain Monte Carlo for the U.S. Supreme Court, 1953–1999." *Political Analysis.* 10:134–153.

Mayhew, David R. 1974. *Congress: The Electoral Connection.* New Haven: Yale University Press.

McAdams, John C. and John R. Johannes. 1988. "Congressmen, Perquisites, and Elections." *Journal of Politics* 50:412–439.

McConagha, Alan. 1995. "Inside Politics." *Washington Times,* 30 January.

McKee, Seth. 2004. "Review Essay: The Impact of Congressional Redistricting in the 1990s on Minority Representation, Party Competition, and Legislative Responsiveness." *Journal of Political Science* 32:1–46.

Meier, Kenneth J., Eric Gonzalez Juenke, Robert D. Wrinkle, and J.L. Polinard. 2005. "Structural Choices and Representational Biases: The Post-election Color of Representation." *American Journal of Political Science* 49:758–768.

Merida, Kevin. 1999. "Did Freedom Alone Pay a Nation's Debt? Rep. John Conyers Jr. Has a Question. He's Willing to Wait a Long Time for the Right Answer." *Washington Post,* November 23.

Middlemass, Keesha M. 2001. "Voting Rights Policy: Preclearance and the Voting Rights Act of 1965." *American Review of Politics* 22:175–194.

Middlemass, Keesha M. and Christian R. Grose. 2007. "The Three Presidencies? Legislative Position-taking in Support of the President on Domestic, Foreign, and Homeland Security Policies in the 107th Congress" (with Keesha Middlemass). *Congress and the Presidency* 34:2.

Miler, Kristina. 2007. "The View from the Hill: Legislative Perceptions of Constituents." *Legislative Studies Quarterly* 33:597–628.

Miller, Warren E. and Donald E. Stokes. 1963. "Constituency Interest in Congress." *American Political Science Review* 57:45–56.

Minta, Michael D. 2009. "Legislative Oversight and the Substantive Representation of Black and Latino Interests in Congress." *Legislative Studies Quarterly* 34:193–218.

2011. *Oversight: Representing the Interests of Blacks and Latinos in Congress.* Princeton: Princeton University Press.

Myers, Jim. 2000. "GOP Forms College Task Force." *Tulsa World*, August 11.

Nokken, Timothy. 2000. "Dynamics of Congressional Loyalty: Party Defection and Roll-Call Behavior, 1947–97." *Legislative Studies Quarterly* 25:417–444.

Nutting, Brian and H. Amy Stern, eds. 2001. *CQ's Politics in America 2002: The 107th Congress.* Washington: Congressional Quarterly, Inc.

Orey, Byron D'Andra, Wendy Smooth, Kimberly S. Adams, and Kisha Harris-Clark. 2007. "Race and Gender Matter: Refining Models of Legislative Policy Making in State Legislatures." *Journal of Women, Politics & Policy* 28:97–119.

Orr, Marion. 1999. *Black Social Capital: The Politics of School Reform in Baltimore, 1986–1998.* Lawrence: University of Kansas Press.

Overby, L. Marvin and Robert D. Brown. 2002. "Race, Redistricting, and Re-election: The Fate of White Incumbent Democrats in the 1994 Congressional Elections." *American Review of Politics* 23:337–353.

Overby, L. Marvin and Kenneth M. Cosgrove. 1996. "Unintended Consequences? Racial Redistricting and the Representation of Minority Interests." *Journal of Politics* 58:540–550.

Owens, Chris T. 2005. "Black Substantive Representation in State Legislatures form 1971–2004." *Social Science Quarterly* 86:779–791.

Pantoja, Adrian D., Ricardo Ramirez, and Gary M. Segura. 2001. "Citizens by Choice, Voters by Necessity: Patterns in Political Mobilization by Naturalized Latinos." *Political Research Quarterly* 54:729–750.

Parker, Frank R. 1990. *Black Votes Count: Political Empowerment in Mississippi After 1965.* Chapel Hill: University of North Carolina Press.

Peress, Michael. n.d. "Securing the Base: Electoral Competition Under Variable Turnout." *Public Choice*, forthcoming.

Petrocik, John R. and Scott W. Desposato. 1998. "The Partisan Consequences of Majority-Minority Redistricting in the South, 1992 and 1994." *Journal of Politics* 60:613–633.

Philpot, Tasha S. 2008. *Race, Republicans, and the Return of the Party of Lincoln.* Ann Arbor: University of Michigan Press.

Philpot, Tasha S., Daron R. Shaw, and Ernest B. McGowen. 2009. "Winning the Race: Black Voter Turnout in the 2008 Presidential Election." *Public Opinion Quarterly* 73:995–1022.

Piacente, Steve. 2001. "Clyburn Not Counting on Census." *Charleston (S.C.) Post and Courier*, April 8.

Pinderhughes, Dianne. 2009. "The Challenge of Democracy: Explorations in American Racial Politics." *Perspectives on Politics* 7:3–11.

Pitkin, Hanna F. 1967. *The Concept of Representation.* Berkeley: University of California Press.

Platt, Matthew B. 2008a. "Surprisingly Normal: Recognition of Black Issues by Non-black Members of Congress." Working paper, Harvard University. Accessed at <http://www.people.fas.harvard.edu/~mplatt/Documents/Black%20Bill%20Sponsorship.pdf>.

2008b. "Participation for What? A Policy-motivated Approach to Political Activism." *Political Behavior* 30:391–413.

Poole, Keith T. 2005. *Spatial Models of Parliamentary Voting*. New York: Cambridge University Press.

Poole, Keith T. and Howard Rosenthal. 1997. *Congress: A Political-Economic History of Roll-Call Voting*. New York: Oxford University Press.

Powell, Lynda W. 1982. "Issue Representation in Congress." *Journal of Politics* 44:658–678.

Preimesberger, Jon and David Tarr, eds. 1993. *Congressional Districts in the 1990s: A Portrait of America*. Washington, DC: Congressional Quarterly, Inc.

Preuhs, Robert R. 2006. "The Conditional Effects of Minority Descriptive Representation: Black Legislators and Policy Influence in the American States." *Journal of Politics* 68:585–599.

Price, David E. 2004. *The Congressional Experience: A View from the Hill*, 3rd ed. Boulder, CO: Westview Press.

Ramirez, Ricardo. 2007. "Segmented Mobilization: Latino Nonpartisan Get-out-the-vote Efforts in the 2000 General Election." *American Politics Research* 35:155–175.

Reckhow, Sarah. 2009. "The Distinct Patterns of Organized and Elected Representation of Racial and Ethnic Groups." *Urban Affairs Review* 45:188–217.

Reeves, Keith. 1997. *Voting Hopes or Fears? White Voters, Black Candidates and Racial Politics in America*. New York: Oxford University Press.

Rich, Michael. 1989. "Distributive Politics and the Allocation of Federal Grants." *American Political Science Review* 83:193–213.

Rocca, Michael S. and Gabriel R. Sanchez. 2008. "The Effect of Race and Ethnicity on Bill Sponsorship and Cosponsorship in Congress." *American Politics Research* 1:130–152.

Rocca, Michael S., Gabriel R. Sanchez, and Ron Nikora. 2009. "The Role of Personal Attributes in African American Roll-call Voting Behavior in Congress." *Political Research Quarterly* 62:408–14.

Rodrigues, Janette. 1998. "Black Schools' Advocate: Forth Worth Attorney Serves as Howard University Trustee." *Fort Worth Star-Telegram*, May 20.

Roebuck, Julian B. and Komanduri S. Murty. 1993. *Historically Black Colleges and Universities: Their Place in American Higher Education*. Westport, CT: Praeger.

Rohde, David W. 1991. *Parties and Leaders in the Postreform House*. Chicago: University of Chicago Press.

Rosenberg, Gerald N. 1991. *The Hollow Hope: Can Courts Bring About Social Change?* Chicago: University of Chicago Press.

Rundquist, Barry S. and Thomas M. Carsey. 2002. *Congress and Defense Spending: The Distributive Politics of Military Procurement*. Norman: University of Oklahoma Press.

Rush, Mark E. 1993. *Does Redistricting Make a Difference? Partisan Representation and Electoral Behavior*. Baltimore: Johns Hopkins University Press.

Saito, Leland T. 1993. "Asian Americans and Latinos in San Gabriel Valley, California: Ethnic Political Cooperation and Redistricting 1990–92." *Amerasia Journal* 19:55–68.

Scherer, Nancy and Brett Curry. 2010. "Does Descriptive Race Representation Enhance Institutional Legitimacy? The Case of the U.S. Courts." *Journal of Politics* 72:90–104.

"Scientific Research: Black Colleges Caught in a Catch-22." 1997. *Journal of Blacks in Higher Education* 15:48–49.

Serra, George and Albert D. Cover. 1992. "The Electoral Consequences of Perquisite Use: The Casework Case." *Legislative Studies Quarterly* 17:233–246.

Shafer, Byron E., and Richard G.C. Johnston. 2001. "The Transformation of Southern Politics Revisited: The House of Representatives as a Window." *British Journal of Political Science* 31:601–625.

2006. *The End of Southern Exceptionalism: Class, Race, and Partisan Change in the Postwar South*. Cambridge: Harvard University Press.

Sharpe, Christine LeVeaux and James C. Garand. 2001. "Race, Roll Calls, and Redistricting: The Impact of Race-Based Redistricting on Congressional Roll Call." *Political Research Quarterly* 54:31–51.

Shepsle, Kenneth A. and Barry Weingast. 1981. "Political Preferences for the Pork Barrel: A Generalization." *American Journal of Political Science* 25:96–111.

Shingles, Richard D. 1981. "Black Consciousness and Political Participation: The Missing Link." *American Political Science Review* 75:76–91.

Shotts, Kenneth W. 2002. "Gerrymandering, Legislative Composition, and National Policy Outcomes." *American Journal of Political Science* 46:398–414.

2003a. "Does Racial Redistricting Cause Conservative Policy Outcomes? Policy Preferences of Southern Representatives in the 1980s and 1990s." *Journal of Politics* 65: 216–26.

2003b. "Racial Redistricting's Alleged Perverse Effects: Theory, Data, and 'Reality.'" *Journal of Politics* 65:1:238–243.

Sinclair, Barbara. 2000. *Unorthodox Lawmaking*, 2nd edition. Washington, DC: Congressional Quarterly Books.

2002. "Do Parties Matter?" In eds. David W. Brady and Mathew D. McCubbins, *Party, Process, and Political Change in Congress*. Stanford: Stanford University Press. Paper presented at the Midwest Political Science Association, Chicago, IL.

Sinclair-Chapman, Valeria. 2002. *Symbols and Substance*. Ph.D. dissertation, Ohio State University.

Sinclair-Chapman, Valeria and Melanye Price. 2008. "Black Politics, the 2008 Election, and the (Im)Possibility of Race Transcendence." *PS: Political Science and Politics* 41:739–745.

Sinclair-Chapman, Valeria, Daniel Q. Gillion, and Robert W. Walker. 2009. "Exploring the Micro-dynamics of Political Participation: Unpacking Trends in Black and White Activism Over Time." *Electoral Studies* 28:550–561.

Snyder, James M. Jr. and Timothy Groseclose. 2000. "Estimating Party Influence in Congressional Roll-Call Voting." *American Journal of Political Science* 44:193–211.

Stanley, Harold W. 1987. *Voter Mobilization and the Politics of Race: The South and Universal Suffrage, 1952–1984*. New York: Praeger.

Stanley, Harold W. and Richard G. Niemi. 1999. "Party Coalitions in Transition: Partisanship and Group Support, 1952–96." In eds. Herbert F. Weisberg and Janet M. Box-Steffensmeier, *Reelection 1996: How Americans Voted*. New York: Chatham House.

Stein, Robert. 1981. "The Allocation of Federal Aid Monies: The Synthesis of Demand-Side and Supply-Side Explanations." *American Political Science Review* 75:334–343.

Stein, Robert M. and Kenneth N. Bickers. 1994. "Congressional Elections and the Pork Barrel." *Journal of Politics* 56:377–399.

1995. *Perpetuating the Pork Barrel: Policy Subsystems and American Democracy*. Cambridge: Cambridge University Press.

2000. "The Congressional Pork Barrel in a Republican Era." *Journal of Politics* 62:1070–1086.

Stein, Robert M., Stacy G. Ulbig, and Stephanie S. Post. 2005. "Voting for Minority Candidates in Multiracial/Multiethnic Communities." *Urban Affairs Review* 41:157–181.

Stewart, Thomas J., Joseph M. Prinzinger, James K. Dia, John T. Bowden, James K. Salley, and Albert E. Smith. 1989. "The Economic Impact of a Historically Black College Upon Its Local Community." *Journal of Negro Education* 58:2:232–242.

Stimson, James. 1990. "A Macrotheory of Information Flow." In eds. John Ferejohn and James Kuklinski, *Information and Democratic Processes*. Urbana: University of Illinois Press.

Swain, Carol M. 1995. *Black Faces, Black Interests: The Representation of African-Americans in Congress*. Cambridge: Harvard University Press.

Tate, Katherine. 1993. *From Protest to Politics: The New Black Voters in American Elections*. Cambridge, MA: Harvard University Press.

2001. "The Political Representation of Blacks in Congress: Does Race Matter?" *Legislative Studies Quarterly* 26:623–638.

2003. *Black Faces in the Mirror: African Americans and Their Representatives in the U.S. Congress*. Princeton: Princeton University Press.

Terkildsen, Nayda. 1993. "When White Voters Evaluate Black Candidates: The Processing Implications of Candidate Skin Color, Prejudice, and Self-Monitoring." *American Journal of Political Science* 37:1032–1053.

Theobald, Bill. 2006. "3 Congressmen Offer Rare Look at 'Pork' Requests." *The Tennessean* (Nashville, TN), 1 May.

Theobald, Nick A. and Donald P. Haider-Markel. 2009. "Race, Bureaucracy, and Symbolic Representation: Interactions between Citizens and Police." *Journal of Public Administration and Theory* 19:409–426.

Thernstrom, Abigail M. 1987. *Whose Votes Count? Affirmative Action and Minority Voting Rights*. Cambridge, MA: Harvard University Press.

Thernstrom, Stephan and Abigail Thernstrom. 1997. *America in Black and White: One Nation, Indivisible? Race in Modern America*. New York: Simon and Schuster.

Thomas, Ken. 2005. "Congressional Panel Examines 1921 Oklahoma Race Riot." *Associated Press State and Local Wire*, 10 May.

Thomas, Sue. 1992. "The Effects of Race and Gender on Constituency Service." *Western Political Quarterly* 45:169–180.

Treier, Shawn. 2006. "Ideal Point Estimation Using Overlapping Constraints in the Senate." Manuscript, University of Minnesota. <http://www.tc.umn.edu/~satreier/southern06_Treier.pdf>.

U.S. Department of Education. 1996. *Historically Black Colleges and Universities, 1976–1994*. Washington, DC: Department of Education, Office of Educational Research and Improvement, National Center for Education Statistics.

Voss, D. Stephen and David Lublin. 2001. "Black Incumbents, White Districts: An Appraisal of the 1996 Congressional Elections." *American Politics Research* 29:141–182.

Washington, Ebonya. 2006. "How Black Candidates Affect Voter Turnout." *Quarterly Journal of Economics* 121:973–998.

Weingast, Barry. 1979. "A Rational Choice Perspective on Congressional Norms." *American Journal of Political Science* 23:245–263.

Weingast, Barry, Kenneth Shepsle, and Christopher Johnsen. 1981. "The Political Economy of Benefits and Costs: A Neoclassical Approach to Distributive Politics." *Journal of Political Economy* 89:642–664.

Whitby, Kenny J. 1985. "Effects of the Interaction Between Race and Urbanization on Votes of Southern Congressmen." *Legislative Studies Quarterly* 10:505–517.

1997. *The Color of Representation: Congressional Behavior and Black Interests*. Ann Arbor: University of Michigan Press.

2007. "The Effect of Black Descriptive Representation on Black Electoral Turnout in the 2004 Elections." *Social Science Quarterly* 88:1010–1023.

Whitby, Kenny J. and Franklin D. Gilliam Jr. 1991. "A Longitudinal Analysis of Competing Explanations for the Transformation of Southern Congressional Politics." *Journal of Politics* 53:504–518.

Whitby, Kenny J. and George A. Krause. 2001. "Race, Issue Heterogeneity and Public Policy: The Republican Revolution in the 104th U.S. Congress and the Representation of African-American Policy Interests." *British Journal of Political Science* 31:555–572.

Wielhouwer, Peter W. and Keesha M. Middlemass. 2005. "Black Representation in Georgia." In eds. Charles E. Menifeld and Stephen D. Shaffer, *Politics in the New South*. Albany: SUNY Press.

Williams, Melissa S. 1998. *Voice, Trust, and Memory: Marginalized Groups and the Failings of Liberal Representation*. Princeton: Princeton University Press.

Wilson, Walter. 2009. "Latino Representation on Congressional Websites." *Legislative Studies Quarterly* 34:427–448.

Wink, Kenneth A. and Andrew Bargen. 2008. "The Consolidation of the White Southern Congressional Vote: The Roles of Ideology and Partisan Identification." *Politics & Policy* 36:376–399.

Yoshinaka, Antoine. 2005. "House Party Switchers and Committee Assignments: Who Gets 'What, When, How?'" *Legislative Studies Quarterly* 30:391–406.

Yoshinaka, Antoine and Christian R. Grose. 2005. "Partisan Politics and Electoral Design: The Enfranchisement of Felons and Ex-felons in the U.S., 1960–1999." *State and Local Government Review* 37:49–60.

Zemsky, Robert. 1999. *Peterson's Four-year Colleges, 2000.* Princeton: Peterson's Guide.

Zilber, Jeremy and David Niven. 2000. "Stereotypes in the News: Media Coverage of African-Americans in Congress." *Harvard International Journal of Press/ Politics* 5:32–49.

Index

Abrams v. Johnson 42
Accountability 2, 21
Achen, Christopher 50, 199
Adams, Kimberly 5–6
AFL-CIO scores 52
African-American candidates 10, 22, 30–2,
    46–7, 127, 136, 174–80, 182
African-American congressional staff 4, 12,
    91, 100, 102, 110–19, 121–6, 128–31,
    133, 174
African-American consciousness. See black
    consciousness.
African-American constituents 2–14,
    16–21, 28–9, 34–7, 48, 63, 87–92,
    98–104, 110–19, 124–6, 131–3,
    135–42, 144–9, 153–6, 158–60,
    162–71, 185–6
African-American counties, analysis of
    predominately. See Black counties,
    analysis of predominately.
African-American-decisive districts.
    See black-decisive districts.
African-American district population.
    See Black district population.
African-American district staff,
    congressional 119–22, 126–7, 129–31,
    133, 185
African-American districts, historically.
    See Black districts, historically.
African-American electoral success.
    See black electoral success.
African-American influence districts.
    See Black-influence districts.

African-American interests 3, 5–6, 8–9,
    17–20, 24, 28–9, 31–2, 35–7, 47–50,
    55–6, 62, 79, 89, 135–7, 148, 170–3,
    182–4, 186
African-American legislators 2, 4–24, 27,
    30–2, 33–7, 39–40, 44, 46–9, 53–62,
    65, 70–84, 93–4, 106–8, 120, 126–7,
    131–3, 135–8, 143, 149, 151–3,
    155–65, 163–7, 169–83, 185–6,
    198–200
African-American majority districts.
    See black-majority districts.
African-American members of Congress.
    See African-American legislators.
African-American minority districts.
    See Black-minority districts.
African-American pluralities. See black
    pluralities.
African-American representation 4–5, 11,
    13–14, 17, 32, 37–8, 53, 111, 129,
    135, 144, 170, 180, 183
African-American Republicans 151, 153
African-American turnout 22, 27, 29–37,
    108, 114, 118, 159, 160, 169, 181,
    183
African-American voters 1, 3–4, 11–16,
    18–9, 21–4, 28–31, 33–8, 46, 48–9,
    56, 58, 70, 77, 85, 91, 95, 99–100,
    102, 104, 107–8, 114–5, 118, 127–8,
    132, 137, 141, 144–6, 148–9, 153–4,
    159–61, 163–5, 167–9, 171–2,
    179–82, 194
Agenda setting 25, 74, 76, 79, 166, 171

Aistrup, Joseph 64
Alabama 14, 65, 71–2, 79–80, 100–3, 112,
    133–4, 143, 148, 180
Albany, Georgia 92, 105–6
Aldrich, John 25
Alexander, Bill 67, 69
Allocation decisions by members of
    Congress 8, 9, 24–26, 48, 55, 88–90,
    95–6, 100, 104, 108, 119, 131, 134–40,
    142–4, 146–51, 153–5, 157–8, 164–6,
    168–69, 171–73, 178, 182, 184–5, 193,
    197–98, 200–5, 208–14
Amendments, legislative 51, 70
American Civil Liberties Union (ACLU) 44
Americans for Democratic Action (ADA)
    scores 51–2, 161–2
Anagnoson, Theodore 24, 198
Anderson, Christopher 21
Anderson, David 47
Ansolabehere, Stephen 24
Appropriations Committee 153, 202, 206,
    208, 210, 211, 213
Arnold, R. Douglas 24, 28, 202–3
Ashcroft "fix". See *Georgia v. Ashcroft* "fix".
Asian-American legislators 19
Asian-American voters 1, 47, 141, 177, 182
Austin, Rory 3

Bachus, Spencer 113
Bailey, Michael 65
Balancing biracial constituencies 14, 16,
    30, 35, 95, 105, 107, 117, 127–8, 160,
    164, 168, 170
Baldwin, Norman 5
Banner, Sharon 118
Bargen, Andrew 64
Barker, Billy 107
Barnes, John "Jeb" 20, 86, 162
Barreto, Matt 22
Bartlett v. Strickland 56, 60, 174
Bayesian methods 187, 189
Beneficial effects thesis, racial redistricting
    3, 54–9, 61–3
Benson, Jocelyn 86
Bertelli, Anthony 24, 27, 65
Bickers, Kenneth 24, 26, 140, 149, 197,
    200–1, 203–5, 211
Bill cosponsorship 5
Bill sponsorship 5–6, 25, 51, 146
Bills, congressional 5–6, 25–6, 51, 61, 68,
    70, 74, 134, 138, 139, 145, 162, 190
Binder, Sarah 25

Biracial coalitions 1, 14, 34–5, 47, 68, 91,
    107, 137, 160, 164, 175
Birmingham, Alabama 101–3, 106
Bishin, Benjamin 27, 108, 183
Bishop, Sanford 14–16, 40, 42, 44–7, 53,
    93–5, 104–8, 113, 115, 132, 139,
    161–4, 175
Biskupic, Joan 3
Black consciousness 19, 20
Black counties, analysis of predominately
    139–40, 142–6, 148, 150–6, 158,
    163–5, 197–9, 201, 206–9
Black-decisive districts 10, 13, 136, 167,
    170, 172–4, 178–83, 186
Black district population 16–21, 23–4,
    29–34, 42–6, 48–54, 82–4, 94–5,
    118–22, 124–6, 129–31, 140–5, 150–3,
    155–61, 168–74, 198–9, 205–10
Black districts, historically 37, 132, 169
Black, Earl 29, 36, 64
Black electoral success 3, 5, 9, 12, 15, 55,
    135, 173, 175–9
Black-influence districts 10, 13, 19–23,
    34–7, 48–9, 54, 60–1, 70–1, 91–5,
    104–5, 108, 123–5, 127, 136, 164–6,
    168–9, 173–4
Black interests. See African-American
    interests.
Black legislators. See African-American
    legislators.
Black-majority districts 2–7, 9–17, 19–21,
    36–7, 39–40, 43–4, 46–9, 53–62, 65,
    70–82, 106–8, 126–7, 131–3, 135–7,
    159–65, 168–82
Black members of Congress. See African-
    American legislators.
Black, Merle 29, 36, 64
Black-minority districts 10, 17, 33, 59, 126,
    161, 166, 168, 171, 176, 180, 182
Black pluralities 47, 182–3
Black representation. See African-American
    representation.
Black Republicans. See African-American
    Republicans.
Black turnout. See African-American
    turnout.
Black voters. See African-American voters.
Bobo, Lawrence 22
Bonneau, Chris 5
Border states 59, 71, 73, 76, 79–80
Bositis, David 17, 46
Bovitz, Gregory 28

Bowden, John 146
Boyd, Allen 93–4, 106, 116–17
Brace, Kimball 32
Brady, Bob 77
Branton, Regina 31, 180
Bratton, Kathleen 18
Breaux, John 67, 69
Browder, Glen 148–9
Brown, Corrine 42, 44–6, 48, 93–4,
    104–6, 107–8, 113, 175
Brown, Robert 64
Brunell, Thomas 21, 172
Buchler, Justin 172
Bullock, Charles 17, 22, 29–31, 46, 64,
    81, 162–3
Burden, Barry 24
Bureaucracy 5, 26, 139, 148–9
Bush, George H.W. 39
Bush, George W. 97
Bush v. Vera 43

Cain, Bruce 6, 24, 89, 135
Callahan, Sonny 143
Cameron, Charles 3, 18, 50–1, 59, 79
Canon, David 3, 5–7, 10, 15, 18, 25, 31,
    50–1, 53, 58, 62, 84, 89–90, 111–13,
    121, 127–9, 167–9, 184, 188, 191, 195
Carsey, Thomas 149, 202
Carson, Andre 179
Carson, Jamie 28
Carson, Julia 178–9
Carter, Janelle 47, 183
Carter, Jimmy 14
Carter, Selwyn 46
Carter, Tim 66–7
Case studies, methods and limitations
    91–3, 193–5
Casellas, Jason 3, 47, 177, 182–3
Casework 7, 25, 28, 89, 110
Census 39–41, 44, 97–9, 118, 120, 175,
    201, 204
Chabot, Steve 179
Chapel Hill, North Carolina 106, 114
Charlotte, North Carolina 3–4, 105–6
Chesapeake, Virginia 92, 97–100, 106
Cincinnati, Ohio 179
Civil rights 51, 55–6, 58, 60–6, 69–74, 76,
    78, 80, 82, 84, 104, 138, 153, 169,
    187–91
Civil Rights Act 68
Civil rights bills 57–8, 62–3, 68, 70, 78, 81,
    185, 191

Civil rights ideal point estimates. See Civil
    rights preferences.
Civil rights issue space 57–8, 60, 64, 66,
    71, 73, 77, 86, 187–91
Civil rights movement 33, 101, 147–8
Civil rights policy outcomes, U.S. House 9,
    12, 54–5, 63, 65, 68–70, 85–6, 169
Civil rights preferences 67, 72–3, 75, 78,
    85, 173, 184, 189–91
Civil rights roll calls 53, 56–9, 63, 67,
    69–70, 74, 77, 82–5, 191
Clark, John 64
Clay, Lacy 177
Clayton, Eva 45–6, 56
Cleaver, Emanuel 177–8
Clinton, Bill 102, 148
Clinton, Joshua 65, 187–90
Clyburn, Jim 54, 76, 118, 144–5, 154, 158
Cohen, Steve 33, 132
Colonial Heights, Virginia 97–100
Combs, Michael 20
Committees, congressional 5, 25, 26, 101,
    103, 134, 144, 145, 153, 202, 206,
    208, 210–1, 213–4
Commonality members 121, 127–30,
    168–9
Competitive elections 9, 154, 167, 169,
    171–2, 180–1
Congressional Black Caucus 39, 158
Congressional offices 4, 7, 12, 23, 25,
    87–8, 90–1, 93–113, 115–24, 128–33,
    139, 141, 185, 193–5
Congressional redistricting from mid-
    1990s as natural experiment 6, 17, 44,
    53, 65, 71, 82
Congressional staff. See District staff,
    congressional and Washington staff,
    congressional.
Constituency, legislator's 1, 3, 6–7, 11, 13,
    15–7, 20–1, 24–30, 35, 47, 87–91, 96,
    103, 111–12, 115–17, 135–9, 166,
    169, 203–4
Constituency service 8, 12–13, 16, 18,
    24–7, 29, 32, 35–6, 55, 87–133, 164,
    166, 168–72, 174, 178, 181–5, 193
Conyers, James 20
Conyers, John 17
Cook, Rhonda 54
Cooper, Christopher 5
Core supporters. See Primary constituency.
Corker, Bob 132, 175
Cosgrove, Kenneth 3, 20, 50, 52, 62

Court-ordered redistricting 6, 14, 42–5,
    48–50, 53, 65, 82, 90, 143, 159–61,
    165, 175, 199
Courts 2–6, 9–10, 13–4, 20, 36–45, 47–50,
    54, 56–7, 60, 65, 82, 85–6, 90, 107,
    113–4, 120, 143, 148, 159–61, 165,
    167, 173–5, 180, 199
Cover, Albert 89
Covered states 39, 59, 65, 69
Cox, Gary 25, 74, 79, 137
Crane, Phil 189
Crayton, Kareem 22, 31, 178
Credit claiming by legislators.
    See Legislator credit claiming.
Cremona, Rachel 21
Curry, Brett 5

Darlington, South Carolina 142
Davidson, Chandler 18, 38
Davis, Artur 103–4, 132–3
Davis, Darren 194
Davis, JoAnn 93–4, 104, 106, 116, 132
Dawson, Michael 29, 38, 106
Debate, majority-minority districting 3–4,
    8–10, 13, 15, 39, 54–64, 70, 81, 126
Democratic legislators 7–8, 19, 21, 29–30,
    37, 49, 83, 122–4, 135, 153–4
Democratic party control of House 71,
    80–1, 85
Democratic party medians 74–76
Democrats 9, 29–30, 34–5, 51, 56, 65,
    68–70, 79–81, 84, 88, 93–4, 106–7,
    121–2, 154–5, 161–2, 184–5
Department of Justice 3, 38–9, 59
Descriptive representation 3, 5–6, 8–10,
    12, 17, 21, 39, 90, 101, 110–11,
    119, 125, 127, 151, 159, 165, 167–8,
    183, 202
Desposato, Scott 64
Diaz v. Silver 43
Dickey, Jay 145–6
Difference members 121, 127–30,
    168–9
Dillon County, South Carolina 141–2
DiLorenzo, Vincent 18
Dilutive effect of racial redistricting.
    See Perverse effects thesis, racial
    redistricting.
Dimensionality of choice space on civil
    rights in Congress 57, 61, 66, 191
Dineen, J.K. 47
Disfranchisement 1, 17, 29, 38

Distributive policy.
    See Federal projects.
District congressional offices.
    See Congressional offices.
District court decisions 42–3
District staff, congressional 12, 23, 25,
    87–91, 93, 95–100, 102–05, 107,
    110–133, 138–40, 148–9, 174–5, 185,
    193–95
Districts
    bleached 59–61, 71–2, 77
    coalitional 56, 86
    cracking of 38–9
    influence 10, 13, 19–23, 26, 27, 34–8,
        44, 48–50, 54, 56, 58, 60–1, 70–1,
        86, 89, 91–5, 104–5, 108, 121,
        123–5, 127, 132, 136, 158, 164–6,
        168–9, 171, 173–4, 179
    low black population 19, 36–7, 92, 94,
        164
    majority-black 2–7, 9–17, 19–21,
        36–7, 39–40, 43–4, 46–9, 53–62,
        65, 70–82, 106–8, 126–7, 131–3,
        135–7, 159–65, 168–82
    majority-Latino 43–4, 46, 183
    majority-white 37, 43–4, 61, 77, 82,
        104, 107, 114, 149, 162–3, 175,
        182, 199
    racially and ethnically heterogeneous
        47–8, 126, 172, 182
    southern 59, 92, 122, 126, 174, 194
Dovi, Suzanne 18
Downey, Butch 116
Downs, Anthony 28
Driehaus, Steve 179
Duality dilemma 19
Duncan, Philip 94, 145
Dunn, Richard 17, 22, 29–31, 163
Durham, North Carolina 3, 106, 113–15,
    139
Durham Committee on the Affairs of Black
    People 113, 115
DW-NOMINATE scores. See NOMINATE
    estimates.

Education Appropriations subcommittee
    210–11, 213
Elections
    candidate-centered 25
    historic for selecting African American
        candidates 15–16, 37, 53, 176
    special 97–8, 179

Electoral coalitions 17–18, 20, 22, 29–30, 32–5, 49, 89, 91, 100, 102, 136–7, 146, 151, 159, 164, 169–70
Electoral institutions 13, 85, 167, 169, 178–83
Electoral safety and responsiveness 2, 12, 19, 21, 24, 100–4, 132–3, 136, 157–9, 164–6, 169–72
Electoral systems. See electoral institutions.
Endersby, James 18, 20
Enelow, James 187
Engstrom, Richard 38, 81
Epstein, David 3, 18, 50–1, 59, 79
Erdreich, Ben 102
Erlenborn, John 66–7
Espino, Rodolfo 57
Etheridge, Bob 93–4, 106
Ethics committee. See House Ethics committee.
Evans, Diana Yiannakis 89
Executive agencies 26, 139, 148–9
Extensions to the Voting Rights Act 3, 38–40, 58, 60, 65, 68, 86, 88, 144, 174

Farmers 95, 98, 103, 145–6
  black 103, 145–6
Federal Awards Assistance Data System (FAADS) 197, 201
Federal education projects 148, 152, 157, 208, 211
Federal grants. See Federal projects.
Federal projects 7–9, 12–13, 16, 18, 24–9, 32–5, 55, 86, 95, 103, 134–61, 163–6, 168–74, 181–3, 197–8, 200–14
Federal projects, public opinion on 134–5
Federal spending. See Federal projects.
Female legislators 10, 20
Fenno, Richard 6–7, 24, 64, 92–3, 100, 108, 193–4
Ferejohn, John 6, 24, 89, 135, 141, 202–3
Fernandez, Manny 47
Fields, Cleo 42, 45–6
Fiorina, Morris 7, 24, 29, 89, 135, 171–2
Flavin, Patrick 21
Fleisher, Richard 20, 50–1, 62
Floor median 54–5, 58–71, 74, 76–8, 81, 85–6, 172–3, 182
Floor of U.S. House, decision-making 9, 12, 24–6, 28, 55, 57, 59, 61, 63, 68–71, 74, 78, 82, 85, 169, 185–6
Florida 44–5, 65, 79–80, 92, 106–7, 116–17

2nd district 93–4, 116–17, 161, 163
3rd district 46, 94
Forbes, Randy 93–5, 97–100, 102, 104, 106, 133, 177
Ford, Harold Jr. 26, 33, 93–4, 106, 113, 128, 132–3, 175
Formal barriers to voting 1, 17, 38
Fourteenth Amendment 39, 43
Fraga, Luis 5, 183
Franked mail 90, 103–4
Franks, Gary 39

Gaddie, Ronald Keith 31, 46, 64
Gamble, Katrina 5, 18, 163
Garand, James 20, 50, 52, 62, 160
Garretson, Jeremiah 64
Gay, Claudine 21–2, 32, 112, 164
George, Emmett 146
Gerber, Alan 24
Gerken, Heather 86
Gerrymandering. See Redistricting maps and plans; Partisan redistricting; Racial redistricting.
Gershon, Sarah Allen 5
General elections 29, 31, 35–6, 113, 159–61, 169, 176–8, 180, 203, 208, 211
Geographic constituency 28, 115, 140, 154
Georgia 14, 20, 40, 44, 48–9, 54, 56, 58, 60, 65, 71–3, 77, 79–81, 86, 105–6, 161–2
  1st district 93–4
  2nd district 40, 46, 93–4
  11th district 40
Georgia state flag controversy 162–3
Georgia v. Ashcroft 20, 54, 56, 58, 60, 86, 173–4
Georgia v. Ashcroft "fix" 60, 86, 173–4
Gilliam, Franklin 20, 22
Gillion, Daniel 22
Gillis, Paul 100
Gilmore, Dee 97–9
Glaser, James 29, 32, 34, 92–3, 118, 149, 159, 193–4
Gomillion v. Lightfoot 148
Goode, Shelton 5
Goode, Virgil 93–4, 106
Gore, Al 97
Governors 118, 133, 140, 162
Grants. See Federal projects.
Green, Al 177
Griffin, John 21, 22, 169, 172, 183

Grofman, Bernard 18, 30, 38, 179
Grose, Christian 5, 17, 19–20, 24, 27,
    28–9, 31, 47, 58, 62–3, 65, 82–3, 89,
    93, 103, 113, 120, 141, 160, 191
Groseclose, Tim 25, 57
Growe v. Emison 42
Guinier, Lani 3, 9, 19, 111
Gulati, Girish 172
Gurin, Patricia 194

Haider-Markel, Donald 5
Hajnal, Zoltan 17, 178, 181
Hall, Richard 7
Hancock, Ange-Marie 16, 162
Handley, Lisa 30, 32, 38, 179
Harlem 47
Harris, Claude 102
Harris, Fredrick 131
Harris-Clark, Kisha 5–6
Hastert, Dennis 74
Hatchett, Shirley 194
Hawkesworth, Mary 9, 10, 20, 23, 24, 172
Hayes, Danny 64
Hayes, Robin 93–4, 106, 118–19, 133
Haynie, Kerry 3, 5–6, 9, 18–19, 24–5, 62,
    84, 184
Hays v. Louisiana 42
HBCUs. See Historically black colleges and
    universities.
Heineman, Fred 114
Herring, Mary 20
Herron, Michael 22, 32
Heterogeneous districts 47–8, 112, 164,
    166, 172
Hibbing, John 20
Highton, Benjamin 17, 30, 46
Hill, Kevin 81
Hilliard, Earl 93, 97, 100–4, 106, 108, 110,
    112–13, 132–3, 143
Hinich, Melvin 187
Hispanic legislators. See Latino legislators.
Hispanic-majority districts. See
    Latino-majority districts.
Hispanic substantive representation.
    See Latino substantive representation.
Hispanic turnout.
    See Latino turnout.
Hispanic voters. See Latino voters.
Historically black colleges and universities
    (HBCUs) 13, 102–3, 112, 136,
    139–42, 146–55, 157–8, 164–6, 197,
    201, 208–13

Historically black districts. See black
    districts, historically.
Hoffman, Donna 64
Holmes, Robert 44
Hood, M.V. III 20, 40, 50–1, 64, 162
House Appropriations Committee 153,
    202, 206, 210
House Education Appropriations
    Subcommittee 210, 214
House Ethics committee 101
House median. See Floor median.
House representatives, black. See African-
    American legislators.
House representatives, White. See White
    legislators.
Hunt v. Cromartie 43
Hurd, Hillary 154
Husser, Jason 17
Hutchings, Vincent 3, 18, 20–1, 36, 50–1,
    58, 63, 70, 188, 191

Ideal point estimates. See Ideal points, U.S.
    House members.
Ideal points, U.S. House members 28, 55,
    60–2, 64–8, 70–8, 84, 100, 170, 183,
    187–91
Ideological positions of U.S. House
    members 25, 28, 32, 53, 55, 60–78,
    84–5, 100, 138, 170, 183, 187–91
Ifill, Gwen 132, 175
Illinois 1, 47, 80
Incentives of legislators 5, 8, 11, 18, 20, 24,
    28, 89–90, 112, 136, 158, 172
Incumbents and incumbency 25, 28, 35–7,
    44, 46, 52, 89, 175–8, 203
Indiana 179
    10th district 178
Indianapolis, Indiana 179
Institutions, political and social 9, 141,
    144, 146–8, 154, 211
Interviews 4, 11, 13, 23, 91, 93, 95, 114,
    120, 149, 193–5
Item response model 188

Jackman, Simon 17, 47, 65, 187, 189–90
Jackson, James 194
Jackson-Lee, Sheila 45–6
Jacksonville, Florida 105–6
Jacobsmeier, Matthew 32
Jacobson, Gary 25
Jefferson, William 93–4, 106, 113, 176
Jensen, Jennifer 5

Johannes, John 89
Johnsen, Christopher 138
Johnson, Hank 31
Johnson, Martin 5
Johnson v. Mortham 42
Johnston, Richard 64
Juenke, Eric Gonzalez 3, 127
Junn, Jane 47

Keane, Michael 22
Kelly Ingram Park 101
Key, V.O. 8
Kidd, Quentin 64
Killian, Mitchell 5
King, Gary 193, 198, 200, 209
Kingdon, John 24
Kingston, Jack 93–4, 106–7
Kissell, Larry 119
Koch, Wendy 17
Kousser, J. Morgan 3, 38, 59, 113, 173, 181
Krause, George 6, 50, 52, 188
Krehbiel, Keith 60
Kreps, David 187

Latino legislators 19, 153, 183, 199, 202, 210
Latino-majority districts 43–4, 46, 183
Latino substantive representation 183
Latino turnout 22, 182–3
Latino voters 1, 22, 43, 45, 47, 105, 141, 160, 175, 177, 182–3
Lawrence, Eric 25
Lazarus, Jeffrey 24, 26
Leadership Conference of Civil Rights (LCCR) 51–2, 57–8, 64, 82–3, 188–91
Lee, Frances 202
Leeway between legislators and constituents 23, 27–8, 90, 133, 162, 164
Legislation. See Bills, congressional.
Legislator credit claiming 135
Legislator position-taking 11, 16, 28, 85, 100, 162–3
Legislators, race of 6, 15, 19, 26, 32, 37, 49–51, 53, 82–3, 108–9, 121, 123–4, 150–2, 155–7, 168, 209–10
Levinson, Arlene 147
Levitt, Steven 57, 204–5
Lewis, John 30, 69
Long, J. Scott 200, 208, 209
Lott, Trent 134–5, 145
Louisiana 42, 44, 46, 65, 69, 79–80

2nd district 93–4
4th district 45
Lovett, Tracy 115, 139
Lowry, Robert 149, 204
Lublin, David 3, 17–18, 20, 22, 29–31, 46–7, 50, 52–4, 62–4, 72, 77, 84–5, 160, 172, 175, 177–9, 182, 188
Lucas, Louise 97–8, 177

Majette, Denise 31
Majority-minority districts 22, 39–40, 44, 46–7, 54–6, 58–63, 65–6, 70, 79, 84–6, 172, 176–8, 182
Majority party in Congress 12, 55, 63, 74–9, 82, 85
Majority party median in U.S. House. See Party median.
Maltzman, Forrest 25
Mangum, Maurice 13, 120, 193, 195
Mansbridge, Jane 5, 19
Markov Chain Monte Carlo (MCMC) 68, 187, 191
Marlboro County, South Carolina 141–2
Martin, Andrew 65, 187
Martin, Christopher 13, 120, 193, 195
Martinek, Wendy 5
Maryland 65, 79–80, 147
Maximization of majority-minority districts 3, 54, 58, 65, 81, 85, 167, 173–4
Maximizing African-American substantive representation 178–83
Maximizing Latino substantive representation 182–3
Mayhew, David 24
McAdams, John 89
McConagha, Alan 56
McCubbins, Mathew 25, 74, 79, 137
McIntyre, Mike 93, 106–7
McKee, Seth 20, 40, 59, 64, 81
McKenzie, Brian 131
McKinney, Cynthia 14, 31, 40, 42, 45–7, 177
Meadows v. Moon 43
Median, House floor. See Floor median.
Median voter in legislator's district 28, 172
Meier, Kenneth 3, 127
Meirowitz, Adam 190
Memphis, Tennessee 33, 73, 106, 113, 128–9, 132, 134
Menifeld, Charles 18, 20
Merida, Kevin 17

Michaux, Mickey 3
Mid-1990s redistricting. See Court-ordered redistricting.
Middlemass, Keesha 19, 59, 89, 103
Miler, Kristina 27
Miller, Warren 24
Miller v. Johnson 14, 37, 40, 42, 49, 50, 56, 161, 173, 185
Minimal effects thesis, racial redistricting 12, 57–63, 77–8
Minority legislators. See African-American legislators; Asian-American legislators; Latino legislators.
Minority representation. See African-American representation.
Minta, Michael 5, 19
Mobilization. See Voter turnout and mobilization.
Montgomery, Alabama 101–2
Moore, Gwen 177–8
Morris, Irwin 20, 50–1, 64
Multicollinearity 49–50, 121, 198–9, 207
Murty, Komanduri 146, 209
Myers, Jim 153–4

NAMUDNO v. Holder 174, 180
National Civil Rights Museum 33
National Black Election Study (NBES) 135
National Election Study (NES) 135
Natural experiment 6, 17, 44, 53, 65, 71, 82
Neal, Steve 67, 69
New York 44, 46–7, 59, 65, 69, 74, 77, 210
   11th district 210
   12th district 43
Newman, Brian 183
Newsletters, congressional. See Franked mail.
Niemi, Richard 29, 32, 38
Nikora, Ron 62
Niven, David 5
Nokken, Timothy 25
NOMINATE estimates 52, 62, 64, 189, 190
North Carolina 3–4, 23, 39–41, 43–4, 55–7, 65, 69, 71–3, 77, 79–81, 105–6, 113–14, 118, 139, 149, 167, 180, 195, 199
   2nd district 93–4
   4th district 93–4
   7th district 93–4
   8th district 93–4
   12th district 3–4, 39–41, 46, 94, 114
North Carolina Central University 139

Norwood, Charlie 49
Nutting, Duncan 94, 145

Oakland, California 120
Obama, Barack 1–2, 14–15, 47, 175–8, 180
Observational equivalence 49, 84, 185
O'Connor, Sandra Day 20, 39
Office hours, mobile 25, 96
O'Halloran, Sharyn 3, 18, 50–1, 59, 79
Ohio 80, 179, 210
Oklahoma 72
Open seat elections to Congress 47, 175–8
Oppenheimer, Bruce 28
Orey, Byron 5–6
Orr, Marion 146
Overby, Marvin 3, 20, 50, 52, 62, 64
Owens, Chris 19
Oxford, Mississippi 134

Pantoja, Adrian 182
Parker, Frank 19, 30
Participatory shirking, Hilliard and newsletters 103–4
Partisan control of Congress 12, 55, 59, 63–4, 71, 74, 79–82, 89, 182, 185
Partisan gerrymandering. See Partisan redistricting.
Partisan redistricting 43, 80
Partisan seat swing, U.S. House 79–81
Party activists 114
Party control of Congress. See Partisan control of Congress.
Party effects in Congress 24–7, 74–6, 79
Party leaders and leadership 5, 25–6, 74, 128, 134, 147, 154
Party median 12, 55, 74–9, 81–2, 85
Party of legislator and party effects 12, 18–19, 22–9, 34–5, 45–6, 49–52, 82–4, 88–91, 93–6, 107–8, 120–5, 150–1, 153–5, 184–5, 205–6, 212–13
Party switchers 81, 93
Party whip 147
Pennsylvania 33, 59, 65, 77, 147
Penny, Tim 66–7
Peress, Michael 28
Personal preferences of legislators 10, 24
Perverse effects thesis, racial redistricting 3–4, 38, 54–9, 63–4, 77, 81
Petersburg, Virginia 98–9
Petrocik, John 64
Philpot, Tasha 36, 47, 153, 155

Piacente, Steve 158
Pinderhuges, Dianne 1
Pitkin, Hanna 3
Pivotal legislators 5, 7, 9, 12, 55, 58–62, 64–82, 85, 169, 185
Pivotal politics and minority representation. See Pivotal legislators.
Platt, Matthew 5, 31
Policy implications and prescriptions 5, 10, 166–7, 172–83
Policy outcomes in Congress benefitting African Americans 2, 11–12, 15, 54–5, 57, 60–2, 65, 81, 84, 86, 159
Polinard, J.L. 3, 127
Political empowerment 125, 174
Poole, Keith 52, 57, 64–5, 77, 190
Pork projects. See Federal projects.
Porteus, Evan 187
Portsmouth, Virginia 97–9
Position-taking by legislators. See Legislator position-taking.
Post, Stephanie 175
Potoski, Matthew 149, 204
Powell, Lynda 24
Preimesberger, Jon 209
Presentation of self 90, 111, 116, 127–9
Presidency 1–2, 14–5, 22, 39, 47, 97, 102, 147–9, 175–6, 178, 180
Presidents. See Presidency.
Press releases from legislators 6, 141
Preuhs, Robert 6, 19
Price, David 93–4, 96, 106–7, 113–15, 119, 131, 139
Price, Melanye 2
Primary constituency 11, 16, 26, 46, 98, 100, 102–4, 108, 114, 117, 159–60, 166
Primary elections 29, 31, 34–6, 47, 101, 104, 113, 127–8, 132–3, 160–1, 163, 178, 180
Prinzinger, Joseph 146
Project allocations. See Federal projects.
Prysby, Charles 64
Public opinion and attitudes 46, 60, 62, 85, 135

Qualitative methods and research 12, 91–3, 95, 107, 112, 119–20, 133, 174, 193–5
Quantitative methods and models 32, 49–50, 53, 63, 82–4, 120–1, 152, 187–91, 197–214

Quinn, Jack 67, 69–70
Quinn, Kevin 65, 187

Race-of-interviewer effects 195
Race of legislator effects 19, 23, 48, 53, 83, 96, 151, 167, 184, 206, 213
Race-unconsciousness 173
Racial gerrymandering. See Racial redistricting.
Racial redistricting 8–9, 12, 14, 37, 42–3, 55–63, 65, 69, 71–4, 76–82, 85, 138, 166–7, 169, 171, 181–3
Racial redistricting maximization. See Maximization of majority-minority districts.
Racial representation 12, 17–18, 25, 48–9, 51–2, 61, 86, 90, 92, 109, 135, 146, 158–9, 165, 172, 206–7
Racial trust 12, 21, 23–4, 29, 32, 37, 82–3, 90–1, 130–1, 135–7, 143–5, 148–50, 155–7, 164–5, 184–5, 205–7
Racially polarized voting 29–31, 38, 47, 97, 175, 180
Raleigh, North Carolina 106, 114
Ramirez, Ricardo 22, 182
Rangel, Charles 47–8
Rational choice and rational behavior 5, 10, 11, 15–16, 18, 20, 23–24, 28, 31, 48, 136, 158, 172
Realignment, South 56, 63–4, 73–4
Reckhow, Sarah 3
Redistricting. See Racial redistricting.
Redistricting maps and plans 4, 9, 20, 28, 39–40, 44, 54–5, 57–9, 70, 80, 84–6, 127, 136, 173, 179
Reelection constituency 11, 98, 100, 102, 104, 109, 118, 154, 162, 166
Reeves, Keith 30, 38
Reilly, Shauna 24, 26
Reingold, Beth 18
Republican legislators 4, 36, 68–9, 71, 77, 79, 83, 92–3, 118, 122–4, 133, 135–6, 145–6, 153–4, 166, 171
Republican party control of House 55, 63, 72–3, 80–1, 85
Republican party median 55, 74–6, 81
Republican takeover of Congress in 1994 55–6, 80–1, 85, 114
Responsiveness. See Electoral Safety and Responsiveness.
Retirements, congressional 39
Rice, Heather Marie 5

Rich, Michael 200, 203
Rivers, Douglas 65, 187
Rocca, Michael 6, 62
Rock Hill, South Carolina 96, 106
Rodrigues, Janette 147
Roebuck, Julian 146, 209
Rohde, David 25, 79
Roll-call voting or roll-call votes 2–9,
    11–12, 16, 18, 24–9, 34, 36–7, 48,
    50–3, 57–9, 61–86, 89–91, 108,
    135–9, 149, 154, 159–61, 164–6,
    168–72, 181–5, 187–91, 199
Rosenberg, Gerald 55, 85
Rosenthal, Howard 52, 64–5, 77, 190
Rundquist, Barry 149, 202
Rush, Mark 46

Saito, Leland 182
Salley, James 146
Sanchez, Gabriel 6, 62
Sanford, Mark 93–4, 106, 118, 140
Scherer, Nancy 5
Scott, Robert 43, 45–6
Section 2 Voting Rights Act 59–60
Section 5 Voting Rights Act 56, 59–60, 65,
    69, 174, 180–1
Segura, Gary 22, 182
Selection bias 120, 194
Selma, Alabama 101–3, 106
Senators or U.S. Senate 1, 31, 36, 47, 56,
    68, 104, 128, 132, 134, 175, 202–3,
    206, 208, 211, 213–14
Seniority, legislator 92, 203, 206, 211, 213
Serra, George 89
Shafer, Byron 64
Sharpe, Christine LeVeaux 20, 50, 52, 62,
    160
Shaw v. Hunt 43
Shaw v. Reno 39, 43, 56
Shepsle, Kenneth 138
Shingles, Richard 19
Shotts, Kenneth 3, 32, 54, 61–3, 72
Sinclair, Barbara 25, 79
Sinclair-Chapman, Valeria 2, 5–6, 22, 25,
    131, 170
Sisisky, Norman 97–9
Sixteenth Street Baptist Church 101
Smith, Albert 146
Smith, Ben 31
Smith, Steve 25
Smithwick, Jerry 116–17
Smooth, Wendy 5–6

Snyder, James 25, 57, 204–5
South, U.S. and its politics 1, 3, 8, 11,
    14–15, 29, 30, 36, 39, 44–5, 47, 51,
    55–7, 59–60, 63, 65, 68, 71, 72–4,
    76–81, 91–3, 95, 100, 105, 119–20,
    122–6, 129, 131, 144, 147, 154,
    159–60, 170, 174, 181–2, 194, 205
South Carolina 30, 36, 44–5, 54, 65, 76,
    79–80, 96, 118, 140–2, 144–5
    1st district 93–4
    5th district 93–4
Southern members of Congress 51, 63, 76,
    80, 92–3, 122, 147, 170, 205
Southwestern Athletic Conference (SWAC)
    102
Spatial model of voting 24, 59–62, 187–9
Speaker of the House 25–6, 74
Spratt, John 30, 89, 93–6, 106, 108, 141–2
Square Books 134
Staff, congressional. See African-American
    congressional staff; District staff,
    congressional; Washington staff,
    congressional; White congressional
    staff.
Stanley, Harold 29, 36, 64
State delegation median 73–4
State delegations in Congress 57, 59–61,
    63, 71–4, 76–7, 181
State legislatures and legislators 6, 39, 42,
    56, 85, 162
*Statewide Reapportionment Advisory
    Committee v. Theodore* 43
Stein, Robert 24, 26, 140, 149, 175, 197,
    200–1, 203–5, 211
Stevens, John Paul 54
Stewart, Thomas 146
Stimson, James 28
Stokes, Donald 24
Strategy of ambiguity 162
Stripling, Hobby 105, 139, 162, 164, 175
Subconstituencies 27, 108, 183
Substantive representation 2–3, 5–10,
    17–21, 23–4, 27–9, 31–2, 34–7, 48–53,
    62, 72, 79, 81, 83–6, 88–90, 110–12,
    115–16, 119, 128, 131, 135–8, 143–4,
    148, 151, 155, 159, 165–8, 170, 172,
    174, 178–9, 181–5, 198
Supreme Court 2–5, 9–10, 13–14, 20,
    37–44, 54, 56, 60, 85–6, 107, 148,
    161, 173–5, 180
Swain, Carol 2–3, 7, 18–19, 23, 37, 50, 52,
    62–3, 79, 84, 89–90, 92–3, 111, 113,

126–7, 131–2, 167, 169–72, 188, 191, 193–5
Sweeney, John 67, 69
Symbolic politics and representation 2, 57, 103, 108, 132, 154, 169–70

Tallon, Robin 76
Tarr, David
Tate, Katherine 3, 5–7, 19, 21–2, 24–5, 29, 38, 50, 52, 62, 84, 134–5, 167–70, 184, 191
Tennessee 26, 33, 72–3, 113, 128, 132, 142, 175
    9th district 93–4
Terkildsen, Nayda 30
Texas 44, 65, 79–80, 210
Theobald, Bill 5
Theobald, Nick 33
Theoretical argument 17–37
Thernstrom, Abigail 38, 46
Thernstom, Stephan 46, 68
Thomas, Ken 17
Thomas, Sue 90
Thurmond, Strom 36
Tokenism 119, 171
Treier, Shawn 57, 64–5
Trust between voters and legislators 21–2, 36, 91, 137, 145, 162, 195, 202
Tuscaloosa, Alabama 101–2, 104–6
Tuskegee, Alabama 148–9

Ulbig, Stacy 175
Unified theory of African-American representation 11, 13–15, 17–19, 24–37
United Negro College Fund (UNCF) 147, 209
Universal coalitions in Congress 26–7, 138–9
Upstate New York 69

Variance inflation factors (VIFs) 199
Vavreck, Lynn 17, 47
Virginia 44–5, 65, 69, 71–2, 79–80, 97, 99, 100, 102, 116, 199
    1st district 93–4
    4th district 93–4, 97, 99
    5th district 93–4
Voss, Steven 3, 17, 22, 29–30, 46, 54, 62–3, 72, 85, 160
Vote dilution 38, 39

Voter turnout and mobilization 22, 27, 29–37, 108, 114, 118, 149, 159–60, 163, 169, 180–3
Voters, African-American. See African-American voters.
Voters, Asian-American. See Asian-American voters.
Voters, black. See African-American voters.
Voters, Hispanic. See Latino voters.
Voters, Latino. See Latino voters.
Voters, white. See White voters.
Voters and voting behavior 6, 30, 38, 47, 59, 97, 175, 181
Voting records of members of Congress. See Roll-call voting or roll-call votes.
Voting rights 2, 9–10, 12, 28, 44, 49, 57, 69, 86, 102, 179–80
Voting Rights Act 3, 13, 20, 29, 36–40, 56, 58–60, 68–9, 86, 88, 92, 144, 174, 180–81
Voting Rights Act extensions. See Extensions to the Voting Rights Act
Voting Rights Act, Section 2. See Section 2 Voting Rights Act.
Voting Rights Act, Section 5. See Section 5 Voting Rights Act.

Wallace, Walter 20
Walker, Robert 22
Washington, Ebonya 22
Washington staff, congressional 121, 128–9
Washington state 80
Watt, Mel 4–5, 8, 43, 45–6, 56, 94, 104–7, 113–15, 132, 149, 167, 175, 191
Watts, J.C. 153–4
Weingast, Barry 138
Welch, Susan 20
Whitby, Kenny 3, 6, 18, 20, 22, 24, 50, 52–3, 58, 62–3, 81, 84, 167–8, 170, 172, 184, 188, 191
White congressional staff 12, 88, 98, 103, 110, 112–3, 115–9, 125, 128
White constituents 30, 87–8, 98, 102, 105, 119, 128, 155, 161–2, 169, 183, 195, 201
White Democratic legislators 4, 9, 13, 22–3, 27, 33–5, 39, 56, 72, 76–7, 89–90, 93–4, 96–7, 102, 106–8, 113, 116, 118–20, 130, 132–3, 136, 141, 148, 151–4, 159, 161–2, 165, 171, 179, 207